D0149271

CONDUCT UNBECOMING

CONDUCT UNBECOMING
The Rise and Ruin of Finley, Kumble

by Steven J. Kumble and Kevin J.
Lahart

Carroll & Graf Publishers, Inc.
New York

Copyright © 1990 by Steven J. Kumble and Kevin J. Lahart

All rights reserved

First Carroll & Graf edition 1990

Carroll & Graf Publishers, Inc.
260 Fifth Avenue
New York, NY 10001

Library of Congress Cataloging-in-Publication Data

Kumble, Steven.
    Conduct unbecoming : the rise and ruin of
Finley, Kumble / Steven J. Kumble, Kevin J.
Lahart. — 1st Carroll & Graf ed.
      p.   cm.
    Includes bibliographical references.
    ISBN: 0-88184-625-2
    1. Finley, Kumble—History. 2. Law firms—
United States—History. I. Lahart, Kevin J.
II. Title.
  KF300.K86 1990
  340'.06'073—dc20   90-43432
                                   CIP

Manufactured in the United States of America

For Peggy, for her courage and understanding.
—SJK

For Justin Daniel Lahart, who is on his way.—KJL

The authors would like to thank the dozens of former partners in Finley, Kumble and others associated with the firm. Their cooperation in granting lengthy interviews and their insights and recollections were invaluable in preparing this book. We would also like to thank our agent, Russell Galen, of the Scott Meredith Literary Agency, whose enthusiasm and diligence kept this project on track. We are indebted to John Walsh and Ned Rosenthal for their advice and counsel. A final, joint nod of appreciation is due to Kent Carroll of Carroll & Graf for his suggestions, deft editing and good sense.

Steven Kumble expresses his gratitude to his longtime friend Frank Wright for his patience, loyalty and support throughout this recent period of transition, and to Phil Zweig for introducing him to Kevin Lahart.

Kevin Lahart wishes to thank a small handful of close friends—most particularly James and Jeanne Vanecko, Diana Henriques, Thomas Patrick Lavin, and Maria del Rio Low—for their generosity, support and applause. Special thanks are due to Steve Kumble. One could not find a better collaborator or story teller. Frank Wright said it best: "He was always straight."

Leon Finley. A founding partner of Finley, Kumble, was in his early 60s at the time the firm was formed. Over time played a smaller and smaller role.

Steven J. Kumble. A founding partner and force behind the firm's growth.

Robert F. Wagner. Former mayor of the City of New York, former Ambassador to Spain and special envoy to the Vatican. Recruited by Kumble and joined Finley, Kumble in late 1975.

Andrew N. Heine. Recruited by Kumble to head the firm's corporate department in 1973, a post he held until he resigned under duress in mid-1987.

Neil Underberg. A founding partner and head of its real estate department.

Marshall Manley. Recruited by Kumble in 1978 after he was thrown out of the Los Angeles firm of Manatt, Phelps etc. Headed and oversaw the growth of the L.A. operation. In later years, while still a partner and major force in the firm, took on the added job of president of the Home Group.

Harvey D. Myerson. A flamboyant and free-spending litigator recruited to the firm by Kumble and Heine in 1984 over the fierce objections of the existing litigation department. He gained national celebrity representing the United States Football League against the broadcast networks and the National Football League. After Finley, Kumble went under, Myerson joined forces with former baseball commissioner Bowie Kuhn in the now-bankrupt firm of Myerson and Kuhn. Now under investigation by the United States Attorney for the Eastern District of New York.

Robert Casey. A name partner but minor player. Joined Finley, Kumble in 1979 from Shea, Gould, Casey and Klemenko.

Robert Persky. A founding partner and head of the firm's corporate department. In 1973, Persky was convicted on charges of false statements with the Securities and Exchange Commission. He was disbarred and imprisoned, serving four months of a two-year sentence.

Norman Roy Grutman. One of Finley, Kumble's most outspoken critics, Grutman, a flamboyant litigator, was a partner in the firm from 1970 to 1976.

Alan Gelb. A litigator and founding partner of the firm. Outspoken in his opposition to bringing in Harvey Myerson, he later became a staunch Myerson ally.

Hugh Carey. Former two-term governor of the State of New York recruited by Kumble, at the urging of his old friend and political ally, Robert Wagner, in 1983.

Joseph M. Tydings. Former U.S. Senator from Maryland that Kumble recruited, along with his entire firm, Danzansky, Dickey, Tydings, Quint and Gordon, at the beginning of 1981.

Robert Washington. Part of the Danzansky firm and a major mover in local District of Columbia business and politics, and later on a national scale as African-Americans became a dominant force in big city politics across the country.

Thomas Tew. Headed the Miami firm that Finley, Kumble merged with in late 1982.

John Schulte. Joined Finley, Kumble from Miami's Smathers and Thompson at same time as Tew et alia. With Tew, ran the Miami office.

Alan U. Schwartz. When Mel Brooks, in his movie "Spaceballs," a sendup of the "Star Wars" trilogy, said "May the Schwartz be with you," this is the Schwartz he was referring to. A noted entertainment lawyer, he joined Finley, Kumble's Los Angeles office in 1982.

Paul Laxalt. Former U.S. Senator from Nevada and "first friend" during the Reagan administration. Joined Finley, Kumble at the beginning of 1987.

Russell Long. Former U.S. Senator from Louisiana and head of the Senate Finance Committee. Joined Finley, Kumble at the beginning of 1987.

ONE

O ne day, a scorpion, scuttling along the bank of a flood-swollen river, got too close to the water and was swept in. The current carried him quickly away from the shore. He couldn't swim and began to drown.

"Help! Help!" the scorpion cried.

A turtle, riding downstream, heard the shouts and swam over. When he saw it was a scorpion, he turned to swim away. The desperate scorpion begged the turtle to save him, spluttering promises not to hurt him.

The turtle relented. "Climb on my back. I'll take you to the shore."

As they reached a point close to the riverbank, the scorpion crept forward, positioned himself at the edge of the turtle's shell, and, with a perfect shot, stung the turtle in the neck. The turtle felt the jab.

"Why did you do that? Now we're both going to die."

"Because, I'm a scorpion."

* * *

On a brutally cold Sunday afternoon in January 1987, I hosted a meeting in my Fifth Avenue home with Harvey D. Myerson, who had come across Central Park from his apartment in the San Remo on Central Park West, and with Robert Washington, who had come up from Washington, D.C. The three of us, co-managing partners in the law firm of Finley, Kumble, Wagner, Heine, Underberg, Manley, Myerson and Casey, the law firm I founded in 1968, gathered to discuss profit distributions for the fiscal year about to close and to work out partners' compensation levels for the upcoming year. It was basically a budgeting process that anticipated revenues and expenses and rewards each member of the firm for his or her contribution in the previous year.

We always paid well at Finley, Kumble, particularly as the firm grew by adding lateral partners and through mergers with entire law firms. By 1987, the firm, which had started with a small handful of attorneys, had grown to nearly 700 lawyers, with close to 250 partners. Revenue growth had been equally spectacular, from less than $1 million in our first fiscal year to an anticipated $200 million in 1987.

A process that had been straightforward and simple, and could be done over drinks on a couple of sheets of a yellow legal pad, had taken on the trappings of high finance and the extensive use of the firm's million-dollar computer system.

It had also taken on the air of melodrama.

My wife, Peggy, remembers that even though the door to the library, which faces Central Park on the second floor of the duplex that once belonged to David Rockefeller, was closed, it was obvious from the acrimonious tone of the conversation that it was not an amicable meeting. "I was working on some things of my own in another room on the same floor," she recalls. "There was a lot of shouting— Harvey's a big shouter—and it got very loud."

I recall that Sunday afternoon meeting very well. It was

the beginning of the end, a long and heated conversation during which I argued, unavailingly, against what Washington and Myerson were proposing. The two of them were speaking as much for Marshall Manley as for themselves, and Manley wanted his compensation for fiscal 1988 raised to $2 million and his expense account increased to $250,000. Manley had resigned as co-managing partner of the firm in favor of his designees, Myerson and Washington, the previous September. But he remained a partner in the law firm and a member of its management committee even though he was serving full time as the president of the Home Group, Inc., the $15 billion in assets insurance and financial services conglomerate that was paying him an annual compensation package of about $3 million. Although he had withdrawn from his management role in the firm, he was still responsible for bringing Finley, Kumble about $15 million a year in legal fees, and his power was undiminished.

Myerson, whose expensive tastes are legendary and whose greed is boundless, insisted that he personally should get a raise from about $900,000 to $1.5 million. Washington, Myerson opined, should go from $645,000 to $865,000. Both Myerson and Washington insisted that my own compensation should be raised from $940,000 to a million dollars. "You have to take that increase," they argued, "so it will look right."

I objected. I told them that I would not take any raise. My strong suggestion was that the people at the top of the firm should either cut back or stay where they were, not because any reduction would be meaningful in terms of controlling costs, but for its effect on everyone else. The kind of increases they were championing for themselves would give partners unattainable expectations.

Otherwise, the slipstream theory would come into play. If you shoot a bullet—really, any fast-moving object—it creates a kind of vacuum that sucks along everything behind it. Applied to the firm, if the people at the top set standards for themselves that were unconscionably high, everyone else would demand proportionate increases. Since they all saw themselves in relationship to the top people, there would be no way to control it.

I was sure that would happen. And I argued that the senior people should make available to those partners at the bottom a larger share of the profits.

What happened? Instead of taking $2 million, plus a quarter million for expenses, Manley settled for a total of $1.75 million, up from $1.2 million the year before. Myerson had wanted a total package of $1.7 million. He reluctantly agreed to a mere $1.3 million, an increase of 44 percent over the prior year. Washington went from $645,000 to $865,000 for no particular reason. I told them, "You people are crazy. You must leave something on the table or else everyone on the management committee will be sucked along in this stream of greed."

It was madness. I planned to fight this at the management committee meeting scheduled for Miami in February.

I never got the chance.

Less than a month later, I was having a cup of coffee and a large glass of fresh squeezed orange juice on the terrace of the Grand Bay Hotel in Miami. Most of the twenty-nine partners who were members of the management committee of Finley, Kumble had assembled at the hotel for our quarterly meeting. It was the first meeting of the whole group where compensation schedules could be discussed, and that was the key matter on the agenda.

As I finished the orange juice, Joe Tydings came up to me with several other partners and said, "Steve, we'd like to talk to you." I picked up my coffee and followed Joe over to a corner of the terrace. He said, "We have been thinking about running the New York office a little differently. And we have decided, in the interest of harmony and to strengthen the firm, that it would be better if one person, not two, ran the New York office. And we think that person should be Harvey Myerson."

I was stunned. I said, "What? How can you even think such a thing? That is totally unacceptable."

Joe Tydings, my friend, said to me "We have the votes."

And they did.

The next day, Harvey Myerson, the agent orange of the legal profession, was made managing partner of the New York office. I was removed from power in the firm I founded and whose growth I had shepherded from an unknown group of eight lawyers to one of the powerhouses in American law; a firm with eighteen offices, seven hundred lawyers, and a reputation that had, for weal or woe, changed the face of American legal practice.

What I did not understand then was that a network of financial connections bound Manley, Myerson, Washington, and Andrew Heine. Manley and Heine and Washington had all loaned money to the perpetually cash-starved Myerson, hundreds and hundreds of thousands of dollars, either personally or through banks they controlled, or both. Washington owed Manley for much of his national prominence. Manley had engineered Washington's rise to co-managing partner of the firm, giving him a status that could be claimed by no other black lawyer in the country. Manley had made Washington a director on at least one board that he, Manley, controlled and had arranged for Finley, Kumble to handle Ronald and Nancy Reagan's wills. Robert Washington owed Manley and delivered the Washington, D.C., office votes for Manley's schemes.

Just as important, Manley controlled a small Beverly Hills bank, the Merchant Bank of California. It had come to the brink of failure because, among other things, of questionable lending practices. When the Federal Deposit Insurance Corporation told the bank to recapitalize, Manley, Myerson, Heine, and Washington pressured partners to make capital contributions to the ailing bank. To ease the pain, Robert Washington saw to it that the National Bank of Washington, where he had a seat on the board of directors, made over $2.5 million in personal loans available to partners in Finley, Kumble. Then, Manley, Heine, Washington, and Myerson demanded that partners take the loans and invest the proceeds to recapitalize the Merchant Bank.

Later, when Finley, Kumble's New York banks started to cut the firm's credit, Robert Washington helped arrange a $10 million loan from the National Bank of Washington.

Myerson owed everyone in town. He lived well beyond his means, with several expensive homes, a collection of Ferraris, and a decorating bill that could support a half-dozen upper middle-class families. The big New York banks cut him off: Manufacturers Hanover, Bankers Trust, Citibank. The National Bank of Washington lent him $700,000. And after the firm cratered, he defaulted on the loans and had to borrow yet again to avoid financial ruin.

Heine, whom I recruited in 1973 with the promise that the two of us would run the growing firm, had long since fallen out with me over my taking credit for the firm's success and growth. By 1984, Heine was actively and vocally looking for ways to bury me. By the middle of 1985, the two of us, once close and still occupying neighboring offices, were not speaking to each other, largely because of my bitterness over Heine's practice of consistently badmouthing the firm and his partners in public. Heine had personally lent substantial sums to Myerson and was a stockholder in, a director of, and a borrower from Manley's bank.

What I did not know—at the time of the meeting at my home or at that February management committee meeting where they dumped me—was that these men were bound together financially. Had I known, I would have gone after them. I am not sure whether it would have done any good. But it would have been worth the try.

Less than one year after that Sunday meeting in January, Finley, Kumble, Wagner, Heine, Underberg, Manley, Myerson & Casey lay in shambles, leaving the partnership dissolved, 700 lawyers and cases scattered, and a staggering debt of well over $100 million.

In mid-December of 1987, the breakup of the law firm made the front pages of major American newspapers. The *New York Times* printed pictures of familiar faces leaving the offices of Finley, Kumble, over stories of the bitter fight that destroyed the firm.

Why all the fuss? After all, what was this except a divorce among petulant, overpaid, egomaniacs? Good copy for the tabloids and for the trade papers, perhaps, but what's new about lawyers fighting with each other? Hardly a day goes by that a legal partnership is not dissolved.

But this was different. It involved 250 partners, more than 450 associates, a total of nearly 2,000 employees in 18 offices in 16 cities in the United States and abroad generating nearly $200 million in annual revenues. Among the partners were men of influence whose names were well-known: Hugh Carey, Mario Cuomo's predecessor as governor of New York, Robert F. Wagner, a long-time mayor of New York City, former United States senators Joseph Tydings, Russell Long, and Paul Laxalt, along with a generous sprinkling of former government officials, congressmen, and judges.

The partners themselves were among the best-paid, best-known, and accomplished lawyers in America. Two hundred of them had six figure incomes. Six made over a million dollars a year.

The firm's client list was a who's who of corporate power and aggressiveness: Shearson Lehman Brothers, Occidental Petroleum, the State of Israel, The Home Group, Donald Trump, the Federal Deposit Insurance Corporation, the United States Football League, Citibank, Bear Stearns, Mobil Oil, Air France, Prudential-Bache.

And in achieving that size, wealth, and stature, Finley, Kumble had done something else.

By the time Finley, Kumble vaporized, the firm had changed the practice of law in the United States. Before it came on the scene, large law firms were developing, and firms with well-known names on their bronze plaques were not uncommon. But never before had anyone tried to do what we had done. No longer was it necessary to refer a matter in another city to a firm in that city. No longer was it necessary to refer a matter that the firm couldn't handle to a firm that could.

Never before had anyone created a full-service, national firm, whose top-flight practitioners could handle any legal matter: a company merger, a leveraged buyout, trade contracts, a real estate deal in Florida, a proxy fight, a lobbying effort in Washington, a highly publicized criminal trial, financing and defense contracts for small countries.

In creating such a firm, we broke the rules and changed the rules. Our aggression in seeking out new business stomped on the white-shoe traditions of lawyerly gentility, and we became the firm our competitors loved to hate. But because we were so good at what we did, we also became a legal powerhouse.

Rather than wait for generations of associates to come of age, Finley, Kumble chose to grow in a new way. We raided other firms, offering star performers top dollar. Such behavior was unheard of at the time. Gentlemanly firms did not steal experienced attorneys and their clients from other members of the club. A partner in a law firm was a partner for life.

With its size and power, and the tens of millions of dollars in fees that flowed into the firm, problems were sure to arise. But what killed Finley, Kumble? Greed, certainly. And the lust for power. But those are not sufficient causes. Management problems? Those, too.

This is the story of what happened, from the day in October 1968 the firm was formed to the confrontations among partners over chits for furs and jewelry and the rent on a mistress's apartment; and the questionable business practices of senior members of the firm who threw millions of dollars in business from companies in which they had decision-making powers to Finley, Kumble and demanding seven-figure salaries in return.

I know the story. I was there at the beginning. I was the architect of the firm's growth. I was witness to its destruction.

On January 4, 1988, the firm of Finley, Kumble, Wagner, Heine, Underberg, Manley, Myerson & Casey officially closed.

A dozen firms have since been built from its parts. The defunct firm left behind over $100 million in debts and hundreds of people out of work.

The partners in Finley, Kumble did not set out to alter the legal profession. We wanted power and wealth. We got them. But in the process we changed forever the way lawyers operate and the way law is practiced in America. And, in the end, we destroyed our own creation.

This is the story of a failed vision; of close-knit ties turned to hatred; of trust and civility turned to warfare. It is the story of men for whom competition meant not only the desire to win, but the compulsion to try to destroy opponents. It is the chronicle of friendships built on little more than the convergence of pecuniary interests, and of the destruction of those friendships. It is the story of a law firm that in the words of Roy Grutman, a former partner who became the most savage of its critics, "revolutionized the practice of law in the United States."

It is the story of the greed and the power-lust of a group of men who did not quite fit into the organizations where they first began to taste the success that would later become unbridled self-enrichment. They are bright and educated far beyond the ordinary, and came, in many cases, from ordinary upbringings in The Bronx and Brooklyn and Camden and Philadelphia. Men who came to feel, or at least to look, as if they belonged on Park Avenue, in the backseats of cars driven by beefy men in dark jackets, who sailed half-million dollar yachts on Long Island Sound, rode to the hounds in upper Westchester County, hung Picassos and Mirós on the walls of their homes.

Along the way, they shucked wives and children. Women,

if not children, are fungible in the world they created for themselves. They can be and are traded in for newer, sleeker, firmer, less cranky models. They abused their junior partners. They lied to the world and to each other. They betrayed one another. They let their envy and rage run without check.

They destroyed what they built.

But first they built it.

TWO

W hat ended in contention was born in acrimony. When Finley, Kumble imploded in late December 1987 and early January 1988, it did so in a cloud of highly publicized name-calling, litigation, and financial disarray that would take years to sort out.

But the firm's beginnings were no less steeped in an incivility that found its way to court and in financial confusion that took a court-appointed referee half a year to unravel and adjudicate. Indeed, the name of the firm that was born in early October 1968 reflected the order in which the principals' names appeared as defendants in a suit that our former partners brought against us to keep us from leaving their firm.

Toward the end of July 1968, Leon Finley and I met with Herman Weisman and his son, Robert (Bobby) Weisman, our then-partners in Amen, Weisman, Finley and Butler. We had been trying for several weeks to schedule a meeting with the Weismans, but the elder Weisman had been spending a good deal of time out of the office on business or in Palm Beach. Finley, who had undergone surgery in early July, was also not available.

Finley wanted the meeting because he felt doubly aggrieved. He had, only months before, merged his prospering practice with Amen, Weisman and Butler to form Amen, Weisman, Finley and Butler. It had not taken him long to figure out that he was bringing in by far the greater proportion of the firm's business and that he and I were, in fact, carrying the Weismans. In addition, the outspoken Finley had had several run-ins with Robert Weisman, who, Finley said, had addressed him in "abusive language so vile that the exigencies of good taste preclude setting forth the exact words."

The exact word was "cocksucker."

Leon Finley was not a man who was above using such words in the course of conversation, heated or not. Colleagues from that era refer to him in terms ranging from colorful to oafish to "one of the crudest men I've ever met." Nevertheless, he was a generation older than young Weisman and took great offense. The afternoon of the argument and name-calling incident, he stopped by my office to tell me that he would never again speak to Bobby Weisman and that he was going to leave the firm. I tried to calm Leon down.

I tried to persuade him not to leave. The idea of disrupting our little firm was irksome. But Leon's unhappiness continued, and after a while I was convinced that if there was to be a future, it would have to be without the Weismans.

More to the point than the name-calling, Finley felt that Herman Weisman had sold him a bill of goods. He had played a round of golf with the elder Weisman in February of the previous year in Palm Beach and the two hit it off. A couple of months later, Leon made a courtesy call on Weisman at Weisman's townhouse office at 17 East 63rd Street, just off Fifth Avenue. They talked for a while and then, with

Robert Weisman, walked the two blocks to the Pierre Hotel for a drink. There, they discussed the possibility of a merger between Amen, Weisman and Finley's firm, Finley and Gore. Finley ran his own firm more like a candy store than a law firm. There were other people, but it was essentially the office of Leon Finley. Everyone else was working for him.

By the end of June, accountants for each firm had met. Details were worked out, and two and one-half months later, via a partnership agreement backdated to September 1, 1967, the merged firm came into being. Finley said that he entered the agreement on the basis of assurances from Herman Weisman that his son, Robert, was a "brilliant" lawyer, that the firm had a large and growing practice and was in a strong financial position, and that the Weismans had an unsullied professional reputation.

Within months of the merger, Finley was complaining that things were not as they had been represented. In December, 1967, Robert Weisman came to him to ask him to speed up the collection of fees because the expense of moving the firm's offices was causing a cash crunch. Finley told Bobby that it would not be wise to depart from the ordinary collection routine and suggested that if there were a cash problem resulting from the move to new quarters, then the partners should establish a fund of $200,000 to handle it.

The Weismans said no.

As for the unsullied reputation, Finley discovered, long after the red flags of financial difficulties had begun to snap in the breeze, that a federal district court judge had criticized Herman Weisman for abusing the trust of his clients a dozen years before.

In addition, Finley was also coming to the realization that Robert Weisman, despite his father's description, was proving to be something less than brilliant. Finley said that not only was the younger Weisman incapable of performing the basic legal services required of members of the partnership, but that Bobby was devoting most of his time to his personal affairs.

There were other burrs. Lester Renard, Herman Weisman's brother-in-law, was serving as "counsel" to the firm and being paid $30,000 annually. Nettie Kramer, Herman's sister, was earning $22,000 for secretarial and office management services—a good deal more than most of the attorneys in the firm. The firm's non-CPA accountants—listed on the firm's annual expense sheet to the tune of $17,000—were Weisman and Weisman, Herman's brother and nephew (that nephew was later indicted, convicted and jailed for Mafia-related bankruptcy fraud).

Finally, it became clear that the practice, if it was growing, had been doing so on my shoulders and those of other, younger lawyers who were not equity partners. Finley contributed significantly to further growth. Within a very short time of his arrival, he was bringing in twice as much in revenues as both of the Weismans.

Between February 1, the beginning of the firm's fiscal year, and May 24, 1968, Leon had counted things up. What he found was that he had brought in $168,000 and that I had brought in $113,000. Alan Gelb, who had the title of partner, but was not in fact an equity partner, had generated revenues of well over $50,000. During the same period, Bobby Weisman's contribution to revenues was $12,500 and Herman's $82,200, including $75,000 from an extremely slow-paying client whose balance was over $375,000. Finley, Neil Underberg, Robert Persky, Herbert Roth, and I were responsible for ninety percent of the firm's business, and all the associates were working on matters that originated with us.

The major source of Amen, Weisman's cash flow problems stemmed from work the firm was doing for the Schine Hotel chain, the owner of hotels in places such as Boca Raton, Florida, and Saratoga Springs, New York. Our work for them centered on the sale of the chain, but completion of the deal was being delayed and delayed, and we were not being paid. We had been in negotiations with Harry Helmsley, and his lawyers, Wien, Lane and Klein, were giving us a very difficult time on the contract. Finally, Schine called off the sale. He said the deal was never going to get done and that he was going to find another buyer. The new buyers put up a $6 million deposit and were then unable to close. They attempted to get the deposit back, and we defended Schine in the litigation. It was a time-consuming defense and Schine, who was strapped for cash, was not paying the legal bills. We were suffering.

In addition, I had a different grievance. I wanted to build the firm. The only way to do that was to recruit, and keep, skilled and experienced lawyers. Without the enticement of partnership, it could not be done. I was a partner, but several of the other younger men—Donald Zimmerman, who would later become a judge, Alan Gelb, Roth, Underberg, Persky, Theodore Greene—were either associates or partners in name only.

A partner in a law firm has a share in the firm's profits (or losses) and has at least a modicum of power via a vote in partnership matters. When a partner acts, moreover, he acts on behalf of the firm. If he makes a mistake, the firm is liable. If the firm comes under attack, he is liable. That's the way partnership is generally understood to operate.

Not so in the never-never land of Amen, Weisman, Finley and Butler. Some partners were more equal than others. When I joined the firm, Herman Weisman told me to feel free to call myself a partner, even though I was simply working on commission, taking a percentage of the business that I originated. After a couple of years, I became a bona fide partner in the firm.

I had joined Amen, Weisman and Butler in 1964. John Harlan Amen, the son-in-law of Grover Cleveland, and Butler had long since died and the firm's two partners were the Weismans. By 1967, the year they admitted me to partnership with a one-third share, fees paid by clients that I had brought to the firm had increased from $30,000 to

$480,000 a year. My deal with the Weismans was changed, largely without my knowledge, when their conversations with Finley began. I had been vacationing in Europe and returned to discover that a merger was about to take place. Herman had decided that symmetry was important and had promised Finley a thirty percent share. Herman would keep thirty percent and the two younger partners, Robert Weisman and I, would keep 20 percent each.

I had always thought that one of the things partners got to do was approve new partners. They were changing the name of the firm. They were reducing my percentage share of the firm in relation to that of the Weismans after I had made what I thought was a pretty substantial contribution. My name was evidently not going to appear on the letterhead of the newly-structured firm. I had not met Leon Finley, and when I did I took an instantaneous dislike to him. During my first encounter with him, I found him bombastic and loud and offensive.

I have always been good at getting along with people, even those I find distasteful. And after my initial reaction, I found Leon to be quite a charming guy. He and I were able not only to get along, but to forge a relationship that would endure through the years the firm we would found was growing. Finley, at the time of the dissolution of Amen, Weisman, Finley and Butler was approaching sixty. He had been in practice for thirty-five years. He had been a minor power broker in the Democratic Party's Tammany organization and was well-plugged in to the judicial network.

I was twenty-five years younger than Leon. I had begun practicing law nine years earlier, in 1959, following graduation from Harvard Law School and two years in the Army. I was not part of any power structure, and like so many lawyers of my generation, I had bootstrapped myself to the threshold of success. Before Harvard Law, graduating in the top ten percent of my class, I had gone to Yale where I was elected to Phi Beta Kappa and graduated magna cum laude.

In today's market, I would have had a large handful of offers from the top firms. But in 1959, things were different. I was a good student and had worked hard. I had been an officer in the Army and had gone to the best schools. But it was difficult in those days to find a job just out of law school. The going rate paid by the best firms to the best graduating students was $6,000. Today, it's close to $90,000. The cost of living has not gone up fifteen times since 1959.

The difference is that today there is far more competition among the big firms for the best students. Under the current system, top firms take a lot of lawyers out of law school, work them unmercifully and, over time, weed out those who are not going to make it.

But when I finished law school I had two offers, one in Washington from the Department of Justice and the other from a well-respected law firm of seventeen in New York— Goldstein, Judd and Gurfein. I had clerked there the summer before and liked the place. Nathaniel Goldstein was the former Attorney General of the State of New York during the Dewey administration. Orrin Judd was a well-known legal scholar. Murray Gurfein had been a brilliant prosecutor and an assistant district attorney when Thomas Dewey was New York County District Attorney. Gurfein was later appointed a Federal district judge and was subsequently elevated to the Court of Appeals for the Second Circuit.

I was toying with the Washington offer and had visions of becoming a great trial lawyer, but in June, following my graduation from Harvard Law School, my father died, leaving my widowed mother alone and living in the New York area. That made up my mind to stay in New York.

I joined Goldstein, Judd and Gurfein in 1959. While I was there, the partner I spent most time working for was Burton M. Abrams, a brilliant lawyer in his early forties who was doing a good deal of securities work.

One day Abrams announced he was leaving Goldstein to start his own firm. He asked me if I'd like to come with him.

Bob Haft was leaving as well, and we were going to join forces with Howard Stamer, Ted Sternklar, and Barry Cohen. They were forming a firm called Cohen, Abrams, Stamer and Haft. Abrams formally announced that he was leaving. I walked into Attorney General Goldstein's office to tell him I was leaving with him. Goldstein was unhappy with me. He said I was making a big mistake. But I told him I had decided to go.

Over the weekend, the firm broke up. Not the old firm, the new firm. Abrams had a fight with Stamer and Haft, and everything came apart. I didn't know anything about it until I showed up for work on Monday morning at the new office. There was no firm. It looked like Goldstein was right.

The members of the stillborn new firm split in two directions and formed two new firms, Stamer and Haft and Cohen and Abrams. I went with Cohen and Abrams.

Abrams, as I well knew, was a tough taskmaster with a ferocious temper. Over time, Abrams became increasingly abusive, and I was threatening to leave. At about the same time, I met Bud Maytag, a member of the appliance family, in a bar and struck up a conversation. As a result, I served as a go-between and put Maytag in touch with the Goldfield Corporation for the possible sale of Frontier Airlines, which Maytag controlled. For that, I received a substantial six-figure finder's fee. I was then earning $8,000 a year as a lawyer. The fee was about $225,000—the equivalent of nearly thirty years' salary.

That fee became the focus of a serious disagreement between Abrams and me. I refused to turn over the finder's fee to the firm. Not only was there was no legal work involved, but there was no partnership agreement stipulating that I should. In addition, Abrams had already made it clear that he wanted me to leave, and I was in the process of looking around for another job.

We wound up in a fight over it, a physical fight, during which Abrams attempted to throw me out the window of the 44th floor of the Chanin Building. The window was open. In his rage, he picked me up bodily and was propelling me toward the window. I didn't want to wind up on the sidewalk below. Luckily, Abrams stopped short of that.

We wound up in a lawsuit.

I kept the finder's fee and retired.

I had that incident in mind several years later when we drafted the partnership agreement that would govern the partners of Finley, Kumble. There is an issue in all firms about what outside income is included as part of the firm income, income that a partner must turn over to the firm. Different law firms have different views. Some require that a partner who serves as a corporate director turn over director's fees to the firm. Others do not because the firm could become liable for a partner's activities as a corporate director. Some firms take the position that fees earned as a trustee or as the executor of an estate be turned over to the firm. Others do not. From time to time partners who are named executors of big estates will leave a firm and change their status to "of counsel" so they can keep the millions of dollars that can come from their duties as executor.

As a matter of course, though, law firms require that compensation of any kind that comes to a partner for personal services goes to the firm. That includes such things as trustee's fees, brokerage commissions, finder's fees, and executor's fees. When I drafted the partnership agreements for Finley, Kumble, I made sure the compensation issue was clear. If a partner's focus is on anything other than the firm, some of his value is lost. So, our agreement said that any earned income belonged to the firm.

But that was all after I came out of retirement. Having done the Frontier Airlines transaction, I thought I was quite a dealmaker and prided myself on being a hot investor as well. I put most of the finder's fee into the stock market and sat back to watch it grow into a fortune. Before it could, the stock market suffered a sharp reversal, and I found myself broke and in need of work.

I went to see Kenneth Everett, an attorney in New York

who also ran Harvard Placement, a job clearinghouse for
Harvard Law School graduates. Everett told me about
Amen, Weisman and Butler. Herman Weisman ran the firm,
and I went to see him. They were ensconced in the most
beautiful townhouse I had ever seen, on 63rd Street, between Fifth and Madison. There were eight people in the
office, but what I did not understand at the time was that
most of them were related, directly or indirectly, to Herman. There was Herman's son, Robert, who wore a Salva-
dor Dali moustache. There was Herman's sister, Nettie
Kramer, who was a kind of bookkeeper and office manager.
There was Herman's brother-in-law, Lester Renard, who
was associated with the firm. The other lawyers were Her-
bert Roth and Alan Gelb. And a couple of secretaries.

Herman was in his sixties at the time, a fatherly fellow
who was essentially a litigator. His wife was from a rich
family, and while Herman was a good lawyer, the law was
not the main focus of his life. He spent a lot of time down in
Palm Beach, and when he was in New York, he played a lot
of golf at the Fairview Country Club in Westchester.

For me, practicing law was the only way to recover. I was
broke, totally without funds. I needed a job. Herman invited me to join them and told me I could call myself a
partner. My deal was for $1,000 a month against fifty per-
cent of the business I could bring in. For a young man not
long out of law school, it was a gutsy thing to do. My list of
retainer clients was flimsy. I was just out there swinging
away and really didn't know what I was doing. It was just
balls.

E.B. White said that to make it in New York, you have to
be willing to be lucky. I think that I was both willing and
lucky. Shortly after joining Amen, Weisman and Butler, I
ran into a law school classmate, Leonard Levine, who had
been doing legal work for a real estate developer named
Richard Cohen. Richard was building post office buildings
and shopping centers. Len was about to join Cohen in that
business. After several meetings with Len and one meeting

with Cohen, they proposed hiring me as house counsel to their new company. I refused because I did not want to leave the private practice of law, such as it was for me. But I did agree to be their attorney at twenty dollars an hour. That was substantially less than the going hourly rate, but I was prepared to work twice as many hours to make a decent living.

It was an important piece of business. They had a considerable amount of legal work, all of it involving highly complicated real estate law, in which I had no experience. To learn it, I read and reviewed every document that I could find on deals that they had previously negotiated using good real estate lawyers. It was on-the-job training with no tutors. After a short while, the work became too much for me to handle myself, so we recruited Neil Underberg, a real estate lawyer who was with Eastern Shopping Centers. He was making $18,000 at the time, and he came with us for a $2,000 raise.

Cohen and his Goodrich Group, as it was known, became one of the major clients of Amen, Weisman and Butler. By the time of the merger with Finley and Gore, the Goodrich business, along with the related legal work generated by the Goodrich connection, accounted for almost $400,000 in annual revenues, the bulk of the small firm's gross income.

I was by then a true equity partner in the firm, and I wanted, along with Underberg and the other younger lawyers, to restructure things so that partnership equity was distributed more broadly. But Herman Weisman wasn't having any of it. It took the arrival of Leon Finley, and his subsequent disenchantment with the Weismans, to bring things to a crisis.

I felt I was not in a position to object strenuously to the proposed merger with Finley and Gore. But after I got over the idea that a merger was to take place, without my having been consulted, I did protest that the division of the new partnership equity was unfair. I calculated that the three

existing partners, the two Weismans and I, each owned
33–1/3 percent of the firm's equity. Finley wanted 30 percent of the restructured firm's equity. To accomplish that,
the Weismans and I would each toss 10 percent into the pot
for Finley. That meant that I would be entitled to 23–1/3
percent of the restructured equity, not the 20 percent that
Herman put forward.

I didn't care what Herman did with Bobby. I just wanted
to make sure that I wasn't getting screwed. Herman agreed
that they'd take care of me for the other 3–1/3 percent. They
would simply transfer it to me from their share of the profits at the end of the year. A year and a half later, that
transfer proved to be crucial to a judge's decision about
who would get what in carving up the firm.

Trouble continued to ferment through the late winter of
1968. At a meeting with the Weismans in March 1968, Leon
and I complained to the Weismans about their relatively
paltry contributions to firm revenues. They were concilia-
tory. But when I told Herman that Finley and I backed the
idea that Underberg, Roth, and Persky should be real partners, Herman pounded on the table and said, "That's not
what I want. If that's what you want, you can take your
clients and get the hell out."

I was really interested in the idea of expansion from the
outset. It was clear that we could not provide full service to
clients, or be competitive with other firms, or have real
stature unless we were much bigger and had within our firm
a group of lawyers with diverse legal specialties. That
would enable us to provide a full complement of legal
services without going outside the firm. And the only way
to attract really talented, dynamic lawyers was to allow
them to earn, or to give them up front, a partnership interest.

The Weismans were opposed. Herman said that he and
Bob together held fifty percent, and if they diluted that
position, they would lose control. My position was that
control was illusory. What could he control? Lawyers can't

be controlled and neither can clients. As a consequence, the idea of getting control of something in a law firm was really a joke. That was demonstrated time and time again in other firms and proved forcefully in the Finley, Kumble debacle.

Partnership is everything to lawyers. When young attorneys come to a firm, the first thing they want to know is how long it takes to make partner and what are the criteria. It used to be that once a partner always a partner. Partners did not leave, and it was difficult to force a partner to exit a firm involuntarily. That's less true today, in part because of the revolution that Finley, Kumble worked in the profession. Still, partnership remains very important; something all lawyers strive for. It takes them out of the realm of being employees. It gives them a status among their peers. It sets the mantle of maturity on them. It admits them to the world of responsibility and the riches lawyers can accumulate. They share in the profits and losses of the firm. What they say binds the firm. It ties them to the destiny of the firm. They are taken more seriously by clients. ("I don't want to deal with some damned associate; I want to deal with a partner," goes the client's demand.) And they can charge more for their time.

The problem is that unless the firm rewards people with partnership after a period of time, they move on. And a little firm like Amen, Weisman, Finley and Butler could not attract the kind of people the firm needed desperately—unless we brought talented lawyers in as partners, particularly some who had legal specialties.

By late spring 1968, Finley had decided the end had come. He insisted on a formal meeting with the Weismans, during which he planned to announce he was going to leave the firm. At first, I tried to discourage him, but later agreed I would join him at the meeting and we would leave together.

I had discussed that decision with several contract partners—Persky, Roth, Underberg—and it was generally understood that wherever I went, they would follow or if Leon and I were to form a new firm, they would join us. I planned to make one last effort to get the Weismans to change their policy on admitting new partners. If I succeeded, and if Finley was agreeable, then we would stay.

The meeting did not go well. Finley was the senior partner. He was the big-business producer. He had thirty-five years of experience as a lawyer. This was a crucial meeting. I expected him to do the talking. One minute before the meeting was to start, Finley turned to me and whispered, "I have laryngitis." So, it was left to me. I made our points about the money situation. I talked about the importance of the firm growing and said it could not grow unless we permitted some of the younger men to become partners. It was important for their futures. It was important for the firm.

Herman replied that he was doing everything possible to turn the case he was spending so much time on into cash. He said that he very much regretted the problems between Bob and Leon, and asked his son to apologize to Finley for calling him a cocksucker.

Then, he said he would not dilute his and Bob's position by admitting other people to partnership. I repeated my say about control. It went on and on like that.

At the end of the meeting, I said, "Look, I have a great idea. And I think I can speak for Leon when I say that you and Bob can have one-hundred percent of the firm. Because we withdraw. We quit."

Weisman was not happy. He told Finley and me that we could not leave, that the partnership agreement forbade it. The strains in the office continued until mid-August. On August 14, Finley, Underberg, Persky, Roth, and I were served with restraining orders, forbidding us to leave the firm. Finley was in Palm Beach and flew back for a meeting with those of us who had decided to leave.

Normally, when law partnerships break up, and they do so with some frequency, the procedure is accomplished without resorting to the courts. Often enough, the division of accounts receivable, work in process, leases, assets, and the like needs arbitration, but it's unusual for the dispute to get to court. At best, it's time-consuming and, at worst, it costs a great deal.

But Herman Weisman was enraged about what was happening. He also knew very well that if the firm's big producers left, most of the firm's business would leave with them. In his action, Weisman claimed that Finley, myself, and the others were breaking a contract and that if we withdrew, we would do so with no rights to any of the firm's assets. We counterclaimed, asserting that we were not withdrawing but that the partnership was being dissolved for cause.

Charges and papers flew back and forth for several days. In a city where a civil matter might, with extraordinary luck, come to trial within two years of the initial filing, justice proved something more than speedy. The case came to trial before New York State Supreme Court Justice Samuel M. Gold on September 25, exactly six weeks after the complaint was served. I've never seen anything like it. There was no pretrial discovery. Nothing. The other side wanted a delay. The judge denied it. The plaintiffs, Herman and Bobby Weisman, were represented by Skadden, Arps, Slate, Meagher and Flom. They took almost three days to present their side of the case.

On the 27th of September when John Logan O'Donnell, the lawyer for Finley, Kumble, Underberg, Persky and Roth, rose to present his case, Judge Gold told him it would not be necessary. O'Donnell, somewhat surprised, promptly rested his case and sat down.

Then, with no real break, the judge launched into his opinion. From the bench. It was amazing. The interlocutory judgment, given orally but reduced to writing on October 3 and then restated on October 17, dismissed the Weisman's complaint and basically gave us the firm. We got the lease on the firm's new premises at 477 Madison Avenue and the firm's January 31 fiscal year. [A firm starting *de novo* could not have had a non-calendar fiscal year, but as the continuation of the pre-existing firm, Finley, Kumble was grandfathered in.] The odd configuration of the fiscal year allowed partners a significant tax deferral because all the money they earned as their partnership distribution was taxable in the calendar year in which the fiscal year ended. Thus, partners' income for the last eleven months of 1972, for example, was considered 1973 income for tax purposes. It is a wrinkle that proved a potent selling point as the firm was expanding, and one that was the source of considerable anxiety as the firm fell apart years later.

In addition, Finley, Kumble got the larger share of all other firm assets because Gold found that the de facto partnership shares were 30 percent to Finley, 23–1/3 percent to me and 46–2/3 percent to the Weismans. Gold appointed Richard Cooper, a New York attorney, to serve as arbitrator.

O'Donnell now recalls that "There was a lot of tension around among those guys. Judge Gold decided quickly and then appointed Cooper to whack up the firm's assets. They were in dispute about virtually everything."

Charles McCaghey, then a young associate at Olwine, Connolly, Chase, O'Donnell and Weyher, worked with O'Donnell on the case and did a good deal of work on the arbitration. "They fought about everything," says McCaghey, who not long after the matter was settled became a partner at Olwine, Connolly.

Settlement of the accounts took from the middle of October until the end of March and included 31 days of hearings before the referee. Each side submitted evidence about accounts receivable, for example, understating the value of the receivables from their clients and then arguing that their own understatement was as reasonable as the other side's was despicably dishonest.

"It was like a matrimonial. A civil war," says O'Donnell.

McCaghey laughs about it now, but remembers the pain, "It was gruesome. It was unbelievable. It was horrible.

After it was over, when people would come to me to litigate partnership disputes, I would show them the transcripts, just the volume of them, from the Amen, Weisman, Finley and Butler hearings. That would be enough to cause them to go back and to settle their disputes. Because no one could make any money. You just can't spend that amount of time litigating."

After the lawsuit was over, the remaining issue was how we would adjust the accounts receivable and work in process that each side kept. We decided they would take the accounts they had originated and we'd take those we had. And a court-appointed referee would determine the value of each, and the extent to which one exceeded the other.

In the end, this financial squabbling turned out to be of such little consequence that I don't even remember how it came out. But it took forever. There we were, running this fledgling law firm, and spending every other day in a session with the court-appointed referee. But the important thing was we had the firm. And we were on our way.

THREE

It's often the little oddities that divert attention. Among the minutiae in Judge Gold's finding was an order to remove the plaque bearing the old firm's name from outside the office's reception area and another to answer the telephone not with a firm name, but with the last four digits of the phone number: 5900.

The old firm was dissolved, and Finley, Kumble, Underberg, Persky and Roth entered the races. It was not a clean start. The beginning of the race was being run in the very same offices we had been sharing with our former colleagues. And although in winning the case, Finley, Kumble had won the lease on the premises at 477 Madison, the Weismans had until January 31, 1969, to vacate. The two groups of lawyers were like a couple who'd been granted a divorce sharing the same house while they were fighting over the division of property.

For the first several months, not only was the new firm scrambling for business, but its partners were also trucking back and forth to hearings on the division of the former firm's assets, instead of looking for new business and practicing law.

That handful of lawyers had no idea then that the firm would become a giant legal powerhouse in the years ahead. We had neither the intention nor the grand design to do so. And even though detractors later acknowledged that the firm "fundamentally changed the practice of law in the United States," I can state without hesitation that there was no comprehensive strategy or desire to be a mammoth law partnership.

But I did have some ideas about the law and its practice.

Those were different times in American law. No megafirms existed. Firms with 75-100 lawyers, then considered almost unwieldy, seem lightweight today in an age defining a 400-lawyer firm as medium sized.

The large, old-line firms—some dating back to the 1800s —were run like elite private clubs. There was great loyalty, not only among partners, but between firm and client. Beyond loyalty, there was an intertwining that went on from generation to generation. For example, White and Case represented the United States Steel Corporation, and many of the presidents of U.S. Steel came from White and Case. A young associate there had contact with people in high-level positions at that company far more frequently and on a different plane than a person his age who worked for the company as a low-level executive. So, he'd be noticed, and perhaps be wooed by U.S. Steel. Or, if an associate were not going to make it as a partner at White and Case, he could be moved over to a position at U.S. Steel. No one ever had to tell him he was a failure. They just moved him into the corporation. There were generations of relationships between firm and corporation. No one was going to displace that firm.

Within the system of the firms themselves, partners did not leave one law firm for another. Short of a felony indictment, a member of the firm was a member for life. And the firms guarded their privacy. Finances, strategies, and other business aspects of the legal business were crucial to survival and prosperity, but it was the image of comity, probity, and pursuit of the public weal that lawyers wanted to project. The pursuit of money, strains among partners, the scramble for business were kept well out of public view. No one discussed such things. It would be another ten years before Steven Brill altered the journalistic portrayal of the law by starting the *American Lawyer* with its gossipy, business-oriented coverage of firms.

Like Brill, his publication, the *American Lawyer,* was and is mean-spirited. It titillated its readers with stories about the law as a business—the movement of partners from firm to firm, compensation issues, and the financial, not the substantive, aspects of the practice of law. It never had much of a paid circulation, but its readership was such that a critical piece would make recruiting young lawyers more difficult, and a favorable article could be helpful.

While the *American Lawyer* was the new wave of legal journalism in the 1980s, the profession is now regularly the subject of reportage by the *Wall Street Journal,* the *New York Times,* the news magazines, business publications, and other media with far wider circulation and influence. At this point, it is unclear what will become of Brill and his enterprise, although there has been talk of him getting into the television broadcasting of sensational trials.

But in the early 1970s, legal publications contented themselves with publishing court calendars and learned pieces. And the general press paid little or no attention to the legal profession. No one wrote about the internal workings of law firms or about how much money we made. The articles were scholarly; lawyers writing about some aspect of the law. But no one wrote about who socked who in the men's room.

The complexion of the firms was different, too. The downtown New York partnerships—as prestigious firms elsewhere in the country—had begun to admit Irishmen,

Jews, and Italians, but women were as rare as Hispanics and
Blacks are today. A further segregation had to do with the
kind of business that the old-line, establishment, "white-
shoe" firms would engage in. For example, they found
bankruptcy law distasteful and avoided it. At the time Finley, Kumble was created, small, specialized firms handled
bankruptcy cases, and those firms were Jewish. Bankers
Trust was represented by White and Case, and the firm
handled most of their business. But when a loan went sour,
the matter did not go to White and Case. They did not sully
themselves with such stuff. It went to Moses and Singer.
Today, most of those boutiques have been absorbed, and
firms like Milbank Tweed or Skadden Arps have serious
bankruptcy practices.

White-shoe firms sniffed at real estate law. They had no
labor law capability. They do now. But to this day, they
won't go near personal injury and medical malpractice law.
Granted, it is an area of the law that numbers among its
practitioners the scummiest of ambulance chasers. But it is
also an area of the law that can boast the likes of Joseph
Jamail, the personal injury lawyer who led Pennzoil's winning fight against Texaco, a fight that resulted in Texaco
agreeing to pay Jamail's client $3 billion. With the fees
from that case, Jamail wound up on *Forbes* magazine's list of
the four hundred richest Americans.

One man's snobbery becomes another man's opportunity. The securities traders and deal makers portrayed as
crass, if not downright unsavory, in books as diverse as
Wharton's *The House of Mirth* or Fitzgerald's *The Great Gatsby*
or even Ken Auletta's *Greed and Glory on Wall Street* now share
the spotlight with corporate finance people with two last
names followed by numerals and are masters of the uni-
verse of Wall Street. They play squash in the morning, dine
with senators and, on weekends, helicopter to the country
to clomp around in their own stables mucking up their
boots with manure from their own horses, or retreat to the
Sound where they wear red trousers, breathe the salt air,

and feel the pressure of water upon rudder as they stand at the wheels of their own boats. And maybe best of all, they, too, can grouse to their perfect wives about having to dress for dinner yet again.

Lawyers followed the same path. The white-shoe firms sneered at Finley, Kumble. The young firm had no history, no tradition. Its lawyers would take on almost any kind of case. They raided other firms for talent at a time when no self-respecting firm would dream of taking on a partner laterally.

The white-shoe firms sneered. Then they emulated the upstarts.

The change was due to many factors. Grabbing opportunity where opportunity existed, finding a niche, doing the work others didn't want was crucial. So, too, was looking at the broader frame to see where clients were heading, discerning their current and prospective needs. Finally, and this was the case with Finley, Kumble, the angle of vision, the fresh look that allowed one to see clear through the miasma of the day-to-day made the great leap possible.

I had no detailed, specific plan of action. On reflection, I could look back and say, "What have I done? What was in our minds when we did those things?" And what we did mirrored what was happening in the business and financial communities. At the time, our clients were growing and diversifying. And we were growing and diversifying in a collateral way to fill clients' needs and, at least for public consumption, that became our game plan. Reporters would ask, how big do you want to become. We had no answer. You don't manufacture law like you produce widgets. You cannot create a market for your legal services in the same way that you can create a market for a new toothpaste, so we grew in response to clients' needs. If we accumulated a great number of clients and their needs grew dramatically, we would expand dramatically. And if a client developed a need for services in a particular area, we would develop a specialty in that area of the law.

From 1968, the profession began on a path of rapid change. Finley, Kumble was on the cutting edge of many of the changes, incorporating into its practice specialties that had been on the outskirts of the legal establishment, enticing partners away from other firms, swallowing up entire firms via mergers, looking across the country for opportunity. Those changes paralleled other segments of the economy, in advertising, on Wall Street, in banking, and in the accounting profession.

The law may be a highly disciplined profession, but it lives or dies as a service business. And like other specialized services, it involves well-trained, highly-skilled people who produce a custom-tailored product for specific clients.

Changes in the legal profession lagged behind other service businesses, but were prompted by the same forces. First, more and more American companies, which only a few years before had concentrated on local and regional markets, were viewing themselves as national concerns. Advertising, investment banking, commercial banking, accounting, and the law had to follow their clients' lead and deliver their professional services on a national basis, or risk losing the clients' business. So, they either opened offices in other parts of the country or merged their way into the new markets. And while law firms could always refer matters to other firms, that meant losing control of the quality of the work. It also meant giving up fees.

Second, clients started to demand more efficient delivery of legal services. The well-heeled, larger firms, though they had to economize, came up with the significant new capital needed to improve efficiency. They bought the word processors and computers that sped the preparation of documents. They subscribed to the services that put entire law libraries on line. They made other capital expenditures that helped them gain efficiency and keep competitive. But it was far easier for a firm of seventy-five lawyers to bear the cost of such improvements than for a firm of twelve. As a result, smaller firms found it progressively more difficult to remain competitive; they did not have the funds to invest. For the first time, economies of scale became a factor in the practice of law.

Third, the legal profession as a whole was seeing a pronounced trend toward specialization. As clients' businesses expanded, they needed more and more specialized services. A law firm could farm out matters it could not handle itself, but again, that risked losing control and fees. It also risked losing the client. The alternative was to bring on someone who could handle the client's needs. And that became a strong impetus to the growth of the firm.

When advertising agencies, accounting firms, and investment banks adapted to the needs of the changing environment, there was no great public outcry. Who complained, for example, as Carter, Berlind, Weill and Levitt—which was a tiny securities firm at the start—began its surge toward growth? In the early 1970s, no one had heard of them. Now, what started out as Carter, Berlind, Weill and Levitt is called Shearson Lehman Brothers, a huge powerhouse of a firm with hundreds of offices here and abroad. The same thing happened in accounting. What business of any consequence thinks it would be better served by a sole practitioner, or even by a small local shop, instead of one of the Big Six firms? In advertising, look at Maurice and Charles Saatchi. They started their business in 1972 with modest resources and grew—mostly by merger—to the point that they became a dominant global force.

No one made much of a fuss when it happened in advertising or in accounting or in investment banking, but when lawyers did the same thing—even though it was a concomitant of doing business in the United States—the legal profession expressed great shock.

The lawyerly environment where the Finley, Kumble upstarts found themselves may have been primed for change, but that was not what I had in mind. Twenty years later I can look back and understand what evolved, but then we had no grand scheme. We did not plan or foresee that the firm would grow as it did. We were just scrambling, trying to survive.

I was in my mid-thirties, and was, after a series of false starts, ready for success. I had already been with three law firms and retired once. Finley, who was in his early sixties and had little to do with what "those boys" would be up to in the years to come, was content to do what he had been doing for years: bringing in business. None of the others, despite respectable school credentials, had exactly been burning up the professional track. Moreover, at the beginning—even with a handful of lawyers—as at the end, there was something out of balance with the firm: intense rivalries festered even before they came together. It was not an enterprise anyone would have voted most likely to succeed.

Neil Underberg was a real estate lawyer. A few years older than me, he had graduated from Syracuse and Cornell Law and had been recruited by Amen, Weisman and Butler from a position as counsel for Eastern Shopping Centers. He is a short man and very dapper. At one point, he took to wearing a pince-nez. He was and is a skilled lawyer, a much more conservative individual than I, a team player with a high degree of integrity. He is basically loyal, but I would not characterize his actions as the firm was crumbling with the word courageous.

Underberg, like the rest of the small group of lawyers at the outset, was not on his way to being a partner at a major downtown firm. He was forty years old and less than a screaming success. His starting compensation at Amen Weisman of $20,000 fell short of that of the overpaid office manager. Two years into the existence of Finley, Kumble, he was earning nearly five times that, and at the end he was one of the best-paid lawyers in the country, taking close to $1 million a year out of the firm. Every now and then I remember the enthusiasm Neil and I had in those early days about building the firm. I used to tell him, "This is going to be great. We're going to be a great success." And his wife didn't know what to make of it. She thought I was the Wizard leading her husband off to Oz.

As small as Neil was, Herb Roth was big. He's 6'4" or 6'5" and weighs maybe 250 pounds. In those days, he had a crew cut and looked like a concentration camp warden. His credentials were terrific. He was Dartmouth and Harvard Law. He had clerked for a federal district court judge and had been an assistant U.S. Attorney. He was a conservative guy, especially financially. He lived in Peter Cooper Village, a complex of middle-income apartments, and later, even when he was making $200,000 or $300,000 a year, he was still living there.

Herb was the firm's litigator, but he seemed either unable or unwilling to make the kinds of personal and social sacrifices necessary to develop new business. In order to promote Roth, I began, at my own expense, a golf tournament, "The Herb Roth Cup." I'd invite Herb and a crowd of potential clients for a day of golf followed by dinner and the presentation of trophies.

Herb did not seem to pick up on it. He never caught on to the necessity of mixing his social life with his business life. The most striking sign of that was that after years of putting on the golf tournament and on many, many occasions inviting him and his wife to my home for dinner, I told him one day that I was surprised that he had never asked me to his home.

His answer summed up the problem. "My home is my castle," he said. "I never mix business with pleasure."

Bob Persky was a West Side liberal; his wife espoused liberal causes. She never liked me because I stood for everything she didn't. She wore hippie dresses and sandals and had that whole modified Sherwood Forest look. Persky liked that. It turned me off. I liked women looking just so. To me, the country club types were more understandable; what Tom Wolfe calls social X-rays. I felt more comfortable with that sort of woman. I found them easier to comprehend.

I never got along with Bob. He felt he was a better lawyer than me, but he wasn't making as much money, and he resented me. A few years later he reached out to do a favor for a client and got himself into serious trouble. In 1969, while serving as general counsel and secretary of a small Miami company, Microthermal, Persky drafted the prospectus when the company went public. The prospectus stated that the proceeds of the stock issue were to be in certificates of deposit. Instead, Microthermal's founder and head, Morton Kaplan had put a portion of the money into a highly questionable investment fund called Takara Partners.

In 1970, as secretary of Microthermal, Persky filed a report with the Securities and Exchange Commission that misstated the disposition of the cash. He knew it, but signed off on the report anyway. The Takara investment proved worthless, and the money was lost. A series of coverup transactions were attempted, but word got out and several large holders of Microthermal stock complained to the SEC, and Persky was indicted. He went on trial in May 1973 for filing false statements with the SEC and was found guilty. He was disbarred and imprisoned, serving four months of a two-year sentence.

Alan Gelb had gone to Columbia and Columbia Law. He had married young, while still in college, and then he and his wife divorced. She eventually committed suicide. Alan was a bachelor who liked strong-willed women and was always on the verge of getting married. Alan and I were close. He was someone whose company I enjoyed, a man I turned to when I had problems. He advised me during my divorce from my first wife and he was one of the few people I invited to the wedding when Peggy and I got married. He had an interesting circle of friends. Parties at his home were likely to include people like Joseph Heller or Peter Jennings or Arthur Gelb, who was no relation, of *The New York Times*. He was a good lawyer, but he was a follower. For one reason or another, he did not have the star quality to de-

velop a substantial litigation practice on his own. And over
time, that became a matter of great concern to the firm.

Finally, there was Leon Finley. Leon had an interesting
past. When you talk to these old fellows, they all have
stories. They all grew up poor. All of them played the violin
in bars for pennies as children—that kind of thing. His real
name was Finkelstein. One evening years later, we were at a
charity dinner at the Plaza or the Waldorf, and Charley
Finley, then the owner of the Oakland A's baseball team
was there. Charley Finley, a proud Irishman was sitting a
few tables away, and Leon stood up and shouted to him,
"Hey, Charley, did your name used to be Finkelstein, too?"

Another time, Leon was drinking and I had to help him
into the men's room. He stood there, holding onto the pipe
above the urinal, and he looked down at himself and said,
"You, too. I've outlived you, too, you little bastard."

Leon was not a man who always adhered to social convention. Some people found him a lovable and charming
old character, but others found him extremely offensive.
Not long after his first wife died, he married a woman,
much younger than him, a former airline stewardess. The
wedding was at his apartment, and at the end of the ceremony he turned to Ted Green, who was the head of our
trusts and estates department, and said to him, "Teddy,
have you got the will?" It was so crude, just unbelievable.
"Teddy, have you got the will?"

The bride was mortified. She was shushing him and saying, "Not now, later."

And Leon, who's got a loud voice, said, "No, I said I was
going to do it and I'm going to do it right now." Then he
said, "This is the part where I give you all the money." And
he signed the will right there at the wedding. We were all
witnesses.

Former partners and others also disagree about just how
good a lawyer he was. But they all agree he had a real ability
to bring in business. Leon was amazing. He'd get on an

airplane, sit down next to a stranger, and by the time the plane landed he'd have a signed retainer agreement.

Norman Roy Grutman, who came to the firm early on and left extremely bitter after several years, recalls Finley as "an oaf and a blowhard. He didn't know anything, and yet he managed to convince people. Leon Finley was a joke. The man had the ability to get clients and the ability to deceive people, but he was some excuse for a lawyer."

Andrew N. Heine, who never resisted the temptation to snipe at his partners and was thrown out of the firm in part because of that, said Finley's reputation was such that the firm suffered and "There were a lot of people who considered him terribly déclassé."

That was the core group that benefited from the great legal victory over the Weismans. Having done that, however, we had to make the business work. With the exception of Finley, who was a big business producer, and myself—I was originating maybe $450,000 a year, which is not exactly a home run—there was no one who was a major rainmaker. And the idea of these men forming a firm and going out to practice law together, with no visible means of support, was kind of crazy. But we did it, and we succeeded.

I had a pleasant life. I had a beautiful home in the suburbs, a wife and two kids, and I thought I was doing very well. I liked the excitement and the freedom of being an entrepreneur. I found the lack of security exhilarating. I never stayed awake at night worrying about where the next piece of business was coming from. I still feel that way. I've had a lot of disappointments, and I have been depressed, but when I was down to my last *sou* and had no one to turn to, that, to me, was exciting. And I always came up with a solution. Because I had to.

In 1968, we had eight lawyers. The firm had been formed the week before. There was no tradition, no rules, no culture. We were scrambling to make a living. We had no farreaching strategy for the growth of the law firm. Our hiring reflected the growth of our client roster and our clients' needs. If we had a lot of work in a particular area, we recruited people capable of doing that kind of legal work and enough staff to service the business.

How we evolved over the years paralleled and was fed by changes in business and finance and in the society itself. With the benefit of more than twenty years of hindsight, many of those changes are clear.

The year we started, 1968, saw the assassinations of Martin Luther King and Robert F. Kennedy. Lyndon Johnson announced that he would not seek another term. Almost coincidental with our secession from Amen, Weisman, Finley and Butler, the violence surrounding the Democratic National Convention was erupting. The anti-war movement was gathering strength, as was the reaction to it. The Vietnam War would drag on for seven more years. George Wallace was becoming a force in national politics. The moon had no footprints. Earth Day and the burgeoning of the environmental movement were two years off. The National Organization for Women and the entire women's movement were still gestating. Datsuns were dumb-looking little cars almost no one bought. No one had even heard of Honda or Mazda or Mitsubishi. "Made in Japan" was a pejorative. If you bought a television, it was an RCA or Motorola or General Electric. What was good for General Motors was good for the country. A gallon of gasoline cost thirty cents. A thirteen-room apartment on Park Avenue in the nineties sold for $105,000.

Jogging was generally undiscovered. People who were thirtysomething were not to be trusted. Men worked. Women stayed home with the kids. The starting salary for the cream of law school graduates at the very best firms was less than a tenth of what it is now.

Michael Milken had graduated from Berkeley in June and started at the Wharton School that fall. Donald Trump's family owned real estate in Queens. Carl Icahn, T. Boone Pickens, Ivan Boesky were unknown. Ronald Perelman had gotten an MBA from Wharton two years before and was working in his father's metal fabricating business. Saul Steinberg was running Leasco, a computer leasing company he had founded seven years before, had taken over the Reliance Insurance Company, and was a year away from making his failed bid—some say it failed because of the Establishment's anti-Semitism—for New York's Chemical Bank.

It is clear that the changes in our society have been enormous: from the way we do business, to the tools people use to work, to the way we see the world. The firm's existence spanned two decades of social, political, and economic upheaval and saw business transformed by a telecommunications and computer revolution.

What happened in business and the law reflected and fed back into those changes. Changes in the law, particularly in the areas of consumer protection, the environment, and equal rights meant companies had even more need for the services of lawyers than in the past. Corporations needed advice about what they could and could not do, and about what they had to do. Virtually entire litigation departments eventually became involved in defending huge corporations against suits by governments and consumers over issues such as pollution, asbestos-related cancers, the health hazards of cigarette smoking, the side effects of drugs like DES.

Complex law breeds the need for more and more lawyers. And that is what we got. In addition, there was a further breakdown in civility. What people like Walter Lippmann began to notice after the end of World War II— that there had been a serious erosion of what he called the Public Philosophy, the sense of common beliefs that tied the society together—continued. Riots in the streets, assassinations, terrorist acts in the name of peace, students shot and killed for demonstrating, a president driven from office by the threat of impeachment and criminal charges were not things that reflect or engender civil harmony.

Drugs and sex and rock 'n' roll became the rallying cry

for the younger generation. For many of their elders, the ethos was the same, although they may have skipped the rock 'n' roll. It was a short trip from "Do your own thing" to "Gimme, gimme, gimme."

The technological revolution transformed business with astonishing advances in telecommunications and computing. Access to information became instantaneous. And information itself changed. Analyses that previously took weeks or months to complete without a computer were done in a matter of hours, then minutes.

No longer could business be conducted at a leisurely pace. You moved fast, you changed, or you got killed. For years, family connections, where you had prepped and gone to college were enough for success. The 1970s and 1980s saw a huge change. Power and influence in many areas, particularly in advertising, in investment banking, and the law, shifted to those with the skills, talent, training, creativity, and above all, the aggressiveness to cope with change and work it to their own and their client's advantage.

We founded Finley, Kumble as that era began. We were neither so clever nor so prescient to recognize that it was the start of an era or to plan to exploit it. We were just hungry young men who wanted ours.

FOUR

Like hundreds of other lawyers in New York, the partners of Finley, Kumble, none of them household
names in the legal community, were working their
eyes bleary, hustling for business. We had brought work
and clients with us from Amen, Weisman and while the
biggest client was the Goodrich group, the bread and butter of the business was fairly routine stuff.

We were growing nicely; working nights and weekends,
and business, after a relatively short time, far exceeded our
meager resources. We were developing specialties that clients required so that we could provide them a full range of
legal services. We would do anything of a commercial nature. We took on personal matters; we did a lot of matrimonial work at the beginning. We did house closings and,
because of Neil Underberg's sophistication and creativity
in the field, we also did the most complicated real estate law
possible.

It was an exciting time, but nobody had visions of a great

national law firm. We simply needed to shore up our professional resources to handle the volume and diversity of work. That took different forms, but the first area where I thought we needed help was litigation. It was my view that Herb Roth, who then headed the litigation department, was never going to be the star attraction that we had hoped.

So, I began to look outside the firm for someone to lead the litigation effort. It marked the first time that we trampled a member of the firm in the quest for the bigger, the better, the more. And, as happened in other cases where a member of the firm got stepped on in favor of someone from the outside, it would pay bitter dividends.

The search led me to a man whose contempt for me today seems boundless, Norman Roy Grutman. Grutman hates me. He refers to the firm as "Finley, Swine," blithely calls me "a crook" and has, over the years, said that we were a cancer on the legal profession. Anyone who wanted a derogatory slant for a story could get a great quote about us from Roy. He would say anything. He'd make the most vile comments.

But at the time, the spring of 1970, joining forces more than suited both of us. It seemed a good choice. Roy Grutman had the skills and the magnetism to make a star litigator. He was an interesting man. He was fat, balding, and eccentric as hell. He drove a Rolls Royce. He carried a walking stick. He had a collection of weird hats, all in black, and would show up in a homburg one day, a bowler the next, and a plantation-owner's hat the next. He always wore a black tie; he had an assortment of black ties and said with no trace of irony that when you're trying a case you don't want to draw attention to your dress, so he always wore a dark suit and a black tie.

Grutman, who in recent years has gained fame and, by most accounts, great fortune, has represented such diverse clients as the Reverend Jerry Falwell in the Jim and Tammy Bakker case and *Penthouse* magazine publisher Bob Guccione.

When I first contacted Grutman, he was thriving as a personal injury/medical malpractice lawyer. Roy had previously been in a partnership with Burton Pugach, a lawyer who achieved notoriety when he threw lye in his girlfriend's face, blinding her and scarring her for life. He went to jail for it, and, ultimately, after he got out, married her.

I reasoned that Grutman's substantial skills in the area of medical malpractice litigation could be transplanted to general commercial litigation, that Grutman could be transformed into a great corporate trial lawyer. A good litigator is a good litigator. He was a known entity, had a certain reputation, and was something of a character. He was articulate. Besides, I remembered him from my Yale days when he had debated Bill Buckley.

While at Yale, Grutman's greatest fame came from a column he wrote for the school paper called "Slings and Arrows." Roy has always exhibited a lack of sensitivity toward other human beings. When he was a senior, he did a column on the Columbus Day parade. Because much of New Haven's population is Italian-American, Columbus Day was a big holiday. The mayor was of Italian descent, as were the police chief and a large number of other city officials.

In addition, there was always a great deal of friction between the townspeople and the students at the university, regarded by many of the citizens of New Haven as overfed, overdone, overrich, spoiled, and uncaring. The relationship was strained at best.

In this context Grutman wrote his column on the parade, comparing it to the Roman Legions entering the capital after one of their conquests. And, if I recall correctly, he characterized the parade's participants as pimple-faced, pizza-eating legions.

Of course, someone in town got hold of the column. The city fathers called the university's president, Whitney Griswold, and told him that they could not guarantee the safety of one of the students, namely, Norman Roy Grutman.

Norman Roy had to leave town and he spent most of the

remainder of his senior year hiding out at Columbia University. When he returned to New Haven in the spring just before graduation, he wrote a public apology for the column.

These days, Grutman is again working in his own small firm. He still wears the uniform of dark suit and black tie. He explained his reference to Finley, Kumble as "Finley, Swine" in a lengthy discourse: "That is what I have always called him. They were swine led by Kumble. I thought I was a man of the world and had seen a lot of life, but I had not seen anything until I got to Finley, Kumble."

Grutman, whose wonderfully theatrical voice almost distracts from his formidable ability to construct rather complex English sentences, recalled our early connection: "I was class of '52. Kumble was class of '54. I was a big man on campus, and Kumble knew me. He was not a person of any great consequence or notoriety, but I did know him.

"By the spring of 1970, I had been practicing law for fifteen years and had achieved a level of importance and recognition as a personal injury specialist for a very small firm of which I was the sole proprietor. It was a very lucrative practice and if I had not joined Finley, Kumble, I could have gone on for many, many years trying the same sorts of cases, just getting bigger and bigger verdicts. I craved something else. I wanted the variety and diversification of matters outside of personal injury, and that desire on my part coincided with Steven J. Kumble's interest in looking for someone to head the litigation department of the firm he was then building. So, in the spring of 1970, at the instance of a Horace Mann and Yale classmate, I had dinner at the home of Dr. Roger Rose where Steven J. Kumble dazzled me with the notion that I could become the head of the litigation department of the firm that he was building, that I could achieve the things that I wanted and he could get a world-class litigation lawyer.

"Within no time at all, I was invited by Kumble to come and visit with him, and we almost instantaneously con-

cluded an agreement. Looking back now, with the benefit
of hindsight, I cannot believe that I was as stupid to be
taken in as I was.

"But, he was a Yale man. I trusted him. And the law firm,
when I visited it at 477 Madison, looked like it was filled
with intelligent, ambitious, driving lawyers who might
achieve the realization of what Kumble was planning to
build, and which I thought coincided with my plans. So, I
took all of my assets, all of my work in process, and $75,000
in cash as capital, and I made a deal with Kumble that gave
me only thirty-six percent of what I brought in. And the
alleged difference between that and one hundred percent
was my alleged overhead. Kumble got the rest of it for a
period of about six months, until I became a partner. Kumble claimed that the overhead was sixty-four percent. I
failed to recognize that he had no costs. That was totally
illusory."

Also illusory, Grutman claims, was my vision of what
would happen. "I discovered that what the firm was going
to do for me by providing opportunities and other clients
and so forth just did not happen. And what happened was
that I created the larger practice, the diversification and
whatnot that I wanted, and I became a name partner. I was
the first of the people that Kumble engrafted. I was the first
of the substantial practices that were drawn in under false
pretenses."

Steven Kumble as the great seducer is a theme that re-
curs again and again. I have been described by friends as a
"man who could charm the birds out of the trees" and in
similar terms by those who hate me. Grutman qualifies as
one of the latter. "He was very smart, very terrific at numbers, and he could have a kind of boyish charm that he used
to ingratiate himself."

I disagree with Roy about a lot of things concerning the
firm. He has been an outspoken critic of Finley, Kumble for
well over a decade. Grutman recalls that when he arrived,
"There were several cultures there. It began as a mix be-

tween Kumble and Finley. Finley was an oaf and a blowhard and Kumble was a sharpie and a hustler.

"And then," says Roy, puffing himself up to his full width, "I came. And I brought the idea of the English barrister."

Grutman discounts the notion that a grudge of more than a dozen years is at the heart of his comments on the firm. "I am not carrying on a burning contempt and hate for the people at Finley, Kumble who tried to ruin me. I have long since purged myself of that antipathy and have risen above it. That does not mean that I don't recognize what they did to me personally and what I think they have done to sully the profession."

In 1974, Grutman prevailed on me to hire Jewel Bjork. Bjork had been a classmate of Grutman's at Columbia Law School and, as Grutman recalled, she was ". . . the smartest person in the class. And that was the class that produced the president of the university and the dean of the law school. She came to Finley, Kumble, joined the litigation department, and very rapidly advanced, being the outstanding lawyer that she is. She became a partner. It was a mistake that Kumble made that he greatly regretted. He hated [her] partly because she was as independent and moral as she is." And partly, said Grutman, because Bjork, whom he subsequently married (I represented Grutman in his divorce from his previous wife), ". . . had such an influence over me."

By this time, Grutman had been with Finley, Kumble going on five years, a period during which, he now says, I cheated him and failed him in various promises. Grutman says the firm was a "scuzz pile." I disagree with that assessment, of course, but I can't understand why he stayed as long as he did, or why he brought a woman he thought so highly of, into such a terrible place.

Grutman claims that only after he had been with Finley, Kumble for several years did he recognize it as a cesspool. "I had indications, of course. Kumble spoke only in numbers and the language of Finley, Kumble was bucks. They did not care too much about anything except about bill collecting, no matter how you did it." Later, after it had become apparent, at least to him, that the firm was corrupt, Grutman says, "I tried very hard to reform that firm, and I could not get other people in that firm, including some very able lawyers, to take the corrective action to correct Kumble's approach, his immorality."

My only response is that Roy has his own agenda and distorted view. Like most litigators, he's enthralled by the sound of his own voice, and he puts on a great show. But Grutman just could not function in a corporate environment. He really is not a team player, in the sense that a firm needs a team approach to conduct major corporate litigation. His inability to sustain any long-term partnership relationships is borne out by a series of law firm breakups involving Grutman after he left Finley, Kumble.

And my recollection of Jewel Bjork does not dovetail exactly with Grutman's. Grutman recruited a classmate from Columbia, Jewel Bjork, and brought her into the firm. She was very bright and had worked at Debevoise Plimpton, considered one of the whitest of white-shoe firms. She had been married to a fellow named Bob Bjork. They were divorced, and she had been out of law practice for a period of time raising her child.

She was very WASPy, very white-shoe. She was a Christian Scientist and eventually Grutman became a Christian Scientist, too. That is ironic since he had spent most of his professional life in medical malpractice law and his office was crammed with medical books.

He brought Jewel in, and they had what, for Roy, passed for a love affair. He insisted that she be made a partner. And immediately on becoming a partner, Jewel began making her feelings known. Her first complaint, as I recall, was that the firm was too Jewish. At one point she told Alan Gelb, "All of you people should be named Cohen." Alan took it as a slight. She had disparaging comments on a number of other things as well.

One of Grutman's big clients was Guccione's *Penthouse* magazine, which was forever getting into libel trouble with its investigative reporting, among other things. One of the biggest suits brought against the magazine was filed in 1975 by La Costa Rancho, the California resort, after *Penthouse* suggested that La Costa had some unsavory connections with organized crime.

The case was underway and Gelb was dispatched to California to handle depositions. While he was out there, he stayed at the Beverly Hills Hotel. The hotel has a series of small, detached buildings on the grounds that it calls bungalows. Gelb was staying in one of the bungalows. They are a little bigger, a little more expensive, and a little more private than the rooms in the hotel. Although, if you leave your windows open, they are not so private.

And that is what Gelb managed to do while he was entertaining some model or starlet in his bungalow. And the people on the other side of the case apparently saw to it that photographs of Gelb and the young woman in various stages of undress and activity were taken. Later, he was confronted with the pictures. Apparently, it was some kind of attempt to intimidate him or get him to ease off on the case. Gelb has a terrific sense of humor and when he saw the pictures of himself with this beautiful, voluptuous, young woman, he asked for two hundred copies so he could hand them out to his friends.

It was the last matter that Gelb and Grutman worked on amicably.

Gelb had a curious relationship with Grutman. He was more like a disciple than a colleague or subordinate. And it got carried too far.

Gelb did not have the respect for Roth that he developed for Grutman. Grutman was extremely well-read. He was extremely articulate. He knew literature and the theater.

And he was an experienced trial lawyer with a great flair for the theatrical in the courtroom.

Gelb was starstruck and tried to emulate Grutman, trailing after him like Sancho Panza following Don Quixote. As Grutman took on various windmills, there would be Gelb behind him, carrying his bag. He even started using Grutman's tailor.

It went beyond style and hero worship, though, and led to a great falling out between them. The talk was that Gelb had developed a real attachment to Jewel, and further, that Jewel had an attachment to Gelb. Grutman was older. He was kind of paunchy and not a particularly attractive man. Gelb was younger and good looking.

No one is exactly sure what happened, but Grutman, who had announced to the world that Jewel (he called her "Bij," short for *bijou,* French for jewel) was his "intended," stopped speaking to Gelb.

Grutman, who represented several former junior partners of Finley, Kumble in post-break-up litigation, has many grievances against the firm. Among them, the way partners financed their capital contributions. He puts the worst face possible on a practice, invented by our then-banker, Frank Wright and me, that has since become a standard mode of financing partnerships of all kinds. Grutman's version is that the partners ". . . were all over-compensated, and Kumble kept them all in economic chains. He made them borrow money on promissory notes from the banks that he controlled so that everyone was his financial vassal."

Grutman may have gone to Horace Mann and Yale and Columbia. And he may be articulate enough to debate William F. Buckley. He may have made $3 million–$5 million a year defending *Penthouse* magazine (until Guccione brought in a seasoned publishing executive who largely solved the magazine's huge problem with libel litigation by insisting that the magazine follow the rather simple practice of having pieces read for libelous material *before* they were published). But, to this day, he seems not to understand the simple, but innovative, mechanics of financing partnership capital that the firm began to use. It is a strategy now employed broadly in all kinds of partnerships.

Unlike Grutman, most of the lateral partners that Finley, Kumble recruited over the years of its staggering growth came from firms where they were not the sole proprietor. And in the course of coming to Finley, Kumble they could not simply plunk down $75,000, as did the subsequently disgruntled litigator. But they had to come up with the cash somehow. And while they may have had tens of thousands or hundreds of thousands of dollars tied up in capital with the firms they were leaving, it is a rare partnership that will pay out immediately and in full the partnership capital of a departing member of the firm. Much more likely, whether the partner withdrawing is defecting or retiring, the firm will pay out his or her capital over a period of time.

And that creates problems. Law firms are not capital intensive operations: property or leases, office improvements, office equipment, furniture, fixtures, and the like pretty much make up the list of expenditures that can be classified as capital. But still, those things are significant expenditures that must be covered. In addition, if a lawyer moves, it generally takes anywhere from three to six months before the work he does for the new firm begins to generate revenue. In the meantime, expenses have to be covered: the electric bill and the telephone bill have to be paid; the secretary's salary and benefits; the salaries of the associates and other staff that work on the matters he has brought with him; the postage and Xeroxing and official filing fees.

Growth in a law firm creates short-term cash-flow problems. For a firm expanding as fast as Finley, Kumble, such costs were gargantuan. With eighteen offices around the country in its final year, the firm was providing working space for nearly two thousand people.

But even without costs on such a large scale, the need

was there. And it was a problem. For a firm to grow, it needs a certain capital base. A law firm can't go public. It's against the law. So, the only way it has of raising the money necessary to operate is to force partners to contribute capital outright, or simply to leave a portion of their total compensation in the firm each year. At Finley, Kumble that would not have worked because we were growing so quickly. If you expand very slowly, you can require people to put the money in at a leisurely pace, but our expansion required a much bigger capital base. The only way to do that was to have partners make immediate contributions.

We could have said to a potential recruit, "Look, if you want to come to Finley, Kumble at this level, you should have a capital position in the firm that is commensurate with the kind of compensation you are taking out. So, if you want to join us, bring cash."

There was little chance that such a recruiting approach would work, even as the firm grew and gained a certain notoriety. At the beginning, at a time when the lateral recruitment of partners was a rarity in the profession, it would have worked even less well. Facilitating the payment of partners' capital as they became partners, and later as they increased their capital positions, became a challenge. The method developed at Finley, Kumble became a key ingredient in recruiting because it removed the payment of capital contributions as an obstacle.

The origin of the strategy Finley, Kumble used illustrates not only the way Frank Wright, our banker (more recently my partner in an investment banking business), and I developed the financing plan, but also the manner in which the young law firm enlarged its business. It was a long way from the tasteful, star-studded dinner parties my wife and I would host for clients and friends and potential clients in our Fifth Avenue home years later. It was a long way from the pressure for law business that someone like partner Marshall Manley could put on investment banks that wanted to do business with his Home Insurance Co. And it was a long way from the influence that Finley, Kumble could exercise by having partner and former New York Governor Hugh Carey host a meeting on tax legislation, featuring partner and former Senate Finance Committee Chairman Russell Long on the subject of attempting to reinstate the special capital gains tax.

When I was in high school in Teaneck, New Jersey, I played piano in a small ensemble, Binky Boyle's Band. Frank Wright played trumpet. Frank says now, "Steve was a good piano player. We played pretty much every weekend and the band got a lot of local notoriety. It broke up at the end of the summer after our senior year in high school. Then Steve went off to Yale. I went to Dartmouth, and we lost touch."

Years later, we reconnected. Frank had become a banker. He recalls, "I was working for Manufacturers Hanover and doing business with a fellow named David Mandelbaum. He was a CPA, and his father owned a small factoring business that I had started banking. David's wife, Rosemary, had been a classmate of mine and Steve's from Teaneck High School. Dave and Rosemary were neighbors of Steve's up in Westchester and they used to pal around socially with Steve and his first wife, Barbara. David mentioned it one day, and Steve and I got together.

"At that time, he was still with Amen, Weisman, trying to build a practice there. Herman was doing some business with big clients, but others in the firm weren't doing much. Steve was the only one out hustling business. This was before Underberg and Roth and the others joined the firm. I was out hustling banking business myself, and one of the things that Steve did was to introduce me to a client of theirs named Toby Ritter. The Ritter family was somehow connected with the Weisman family and had large real estate holdings. Toby was about my age. He was running around collecting the rents and things. We hit it off. The family needed a bank credit facility, and I was able to arrange it. When they borrowed, they borrowed in substantial amounts, and it was a good piece of business for me.

"From pretty much that point on, Steve and I would talk regularly about situations that he saw that needed financing. I'd pick his brain a bit and he'd pick mine to see how to finance things. Sometimes they were bankable, and that would mean business for me. We saw each other more and more, both on a business level and socially."

After I left Amen, Weisman to form Finley, Kumble, Frank Wright and I did more and more business with mutual clients. Meetings became frequent. I'd talk about my clients' financial needs, without naming them, and try to figure out how those needs could be met. Frank would explain the financing possibilities to me so I could structure a solution. The quid pro quo was that if the problem could be solved by a bank, I would send the client around to see Frank at Manufacturers Hanover. My clients became bigger and bigger. Frank Wright, who eventually became an executive vice-president at Manny Hanny, became a more and more important executive at the bank.

Parenthetically, Wright remarks, "We kind of grew up together in our business life. He was very good with numbers. It was unusual for a lawyer, and it was a pleasure to talk business with him because he had such a good grasp of the way things worked. And I did not know anybody I could trust more than Steve. He was always straight. Sometimes he would take a guarantor role with a client. I'd always advise against it, but sometimes he would do it, and occasionally he would get stuck. And when that happened he would always make it good. His word was always good."

One of the problems we talked about was my concern about growth and the capital needs it required. I wanted to expand the firm, wanted it to grow. We met at the Four Seasons, and as we talked about it, it appeared that the real reason professional organizations such as law firms did not grow was that capital requirements could not be met easily. Rapid growth required more capital to support the added receivables and work in process, but usually it was not there. And if a firm wanted to expand and was forced to wait for a new partner's capital, it would always be in a deficit position.

We puzzled over how to solve the capital problem. I credit Frank with coming up with the idea, and he gives me credit, but whoever puts his name on it, we came up with the idea that enabled me to expand the law firm. And, not insignificantly, it added to Wright's product line a financial tool that could be sold to all kinds of partnerships: other law firms, accounting practices, advertising agencies, and investment banking and securities firms.

We devised a solution whereby, when a new lawyer came to the firm, the bank would lend him whatever was required as a capital contribution. The loan was guaranteed by the firm itself. That way, if the lawyer left the firm, he would leave his capital and, instead of being paid back to him, it would be paid back to the bank. As we expanded, our capital needs increased, and these loans kept pace with our expansion. Started in the early 1970s, it was the financial engine that allowed Finley, Kumble to grow.

The mechanics are somewhat more complex than a simple loan. The bank set up an arrangement for a partner to submit a financial statement, sign a personal note for the required amount, and have the firm guarantee the obligation. The loan was a direct obligation of the partner and a contingent obligation of the firm. We set up a system under which the firm would deduct principal repayments from the partner's profit distribution each year. It was a flat fifteen percent of the profit distribution. Then, the firm would pay the partner a percentage return on his capital investment equivalent to the interest payment due on the loan. We would pay it directly to the bank in his name, so the partner was never bothered with making the interest payments.

The strategy was a key ingredient in our recruiting efforts. It was simple. And paying back the money was relatively painless.

Such payment became painful, however, after the firm's collapse. Nearly $23 million of the $83 million that the firm owed to its creditor banks represented its guarantee of individual partners' capital loans. But it was not partners' capital borrowings that sank the firm. More than any other single financial factor, the firm's rapid deterioration can be laid to the suspension of a practice that made me something of an ogre in my own firm: an almost brutal emphasis on the collection of fees. It was also the practice that made high levels of compensation possible; that was part of the lure that attracted individuals, and later, entire firms, to Finley, Kumble; and that served, along with partner capital loans, as the mechanism of growth for the law firm.

A widespread view among lawyers, many of them partners in Finley, Kumble, was that for me the business of the law overshadowed the practice of law; that collecting fees was pre-eminent. As Grutman put it, "They did not care much about anything except bill collecting; profit was the sole motive."

Another view of what I was doing comes from a former partner who otherwise has less than flattering things to say about me. "Steve had the knack of showing people that they were not billing correctly; that their collection practices and policies were not right; that they were not keeping time properly; that they were not paying attention to the basics of the business."

I didn't go to Harvard Law School to become a bill collector, but it dawned on me that the old firm of Amen, Weisman, Finley and Butler blew up because people were doing a lot of work and not being paid for it. Hundreds of thousands of dollars in fees from one client went uncollected and still the firm continued to work for the client, incurring greater and greater unreimbursed expenses and costs. As a result, one set of partners carried the whole firm. I was determined that it would not happen at Finley, Kumble. It is impossible to run a big firm without a system to insure that all your work is productive.

But implementing such a system requires overcoming significant obstacles. It may be obvious, but a law firm is a service business. Lawyers spend time for which they bill a client. As those time charges are billed, they become accounts receivable, and as they are collected they become the firm's revenues. Each lawyer in a firm, from the rawest associate to the most senior partner, must account for all his time. He or she is assigned an hourly billing rate, depending on seniority, experience and, to a certain degree, what clients are willing to pay.

Lawyers are not particularly good at business, yet they must account for each day's work. It is something they must do while facing a great deal of pressure to accomplish the work itself. Then, they have to do the billing and after that make sure that collections are made. They find it unseemly. A lawyer has a special relationship with a client, and dunning for payment strains the cordiality of that relationship. In addition, lawyers often become enamored of working for certain clients, or become fascinated with working on certain matters. As a result, they sometimes spend time and effort on matters that bear no reasonable relationship to what those matters are worth.

The biggest business problem for law firms is the willingness or ability to turn time into money. For the most part, law firms bill clients on the basis of time spent, but most firms do an inadequate job of turning that time into cash. That is particularly true in small- and medium-sized firms because their clients do not have the same financial wherewithal and sense of financial responsibility that the clients of larger, more established firms have. In the old days, if you represented General Motors and you sent them a bill, it would be paid promptly and without question. That has changed at big corporations with the rise of in-house counsel who have learned to question bills. But even today, large clients tend to be timely in their payments. For example, Finley, Kumble represented the State of Israel in certain ongoing matters. The firm sent bills monthly. They were paid ten days later.

But that was the exception, not the rule. And even though Finley, Kumble, as it grew larger, more prosperous, and more important, represented a long list of blue-chip clients, it still served a great number of small and mid-size companies. At the end, the firm had on its roster nearly 14,000 active matters. On each one, time had to be logged, monthly bills sent, tracked, followed up on, and collected.

From the outset, I developed a rigorous system to insure timely financial flows. The plan's execution was tinged with a certain harshness, but I was adamant about the issue. Why should a lawyer work very hard and not get paid for it? Most of the lawyers I know are better educated, brighter, and work harder than the people they represent in the business world. But they make less money. Why? Because the business people focus eight or ten hours a day, five or six days a week on their own money. And lawyers focus eight or ten hours a day, five or six days a week on their clients' money. They work feverishly for the clients, and the clients make all the money. There is something wrong with that, and I was determined from the beginning to change it.

We adopted a system that in substance said that if a lawyer did not put in his time charges on a regular basis, he did not get his check or his draw. If he did not send out his bills on a timely basis, he had to answer questions about why he had not sent them. And if, after a certain time, a bill had not been paid, we would institute vigorous collection efforts to recover the money, up to and including selective law suits. This last is abhorrent to most law firms.

No system works unless someone is willing and able to make it work. I made it work, although it was not something I enjoyed doing. I concluded that there was no one else who could or would do it.

I made myself unpopular by focusing a lot of attention on bill collecting. As a result, we were able to pay very well, to recruit, and to grow all at the same time. People saw that as nothing short of miraculous. Unlike Shearman and Sterling, or Simpson, Thacher and Bartlett and other firms where a handful of clients account for a huge chunk of revenue, we had 2,000 or 3,000 clients and a million little bills. There were thousands of checks coming in. And in order to keep those checks coming in, we had to send out thousands of little bills.

From the firm's earliest days, our lawyers came to dread finding me at the doors of their offices or on the other end of the phone, playing the role of the enforcer. I would say to a lawyer, "Why didn't you bill this?" And he'd begin to make an excuse and I would say, "I want it billed today. And if you don't, you won't get paid." Or I would say, "Hey. Look, friend, if you don't send this bill out, I'm going to send it out." Or worse, I would say, "Stop working for this client. The guy hasn't paid his bills. Stop working on his problems until he pays his bill." If the lawyer protested, I would cut him off saying, "You want me to make the call telling him we're stopping work on this matter?"

Because of my toughness, I acquired a reputation as kind of an ogre. There was one incident that involved one of the partners, E. Howard Rappaport, that solidified the image.

Rappaport was a real estate lawyer. He was a terribly overweight, balding fellow who was concerned that he was the only Rappaport on earth who was Episcopalian. His father was Jewish and his mother was not, and Howard had been raised as an Episcopalian. The fact that no one else knew it kind of bothered him.

At the time, he was under a lot of pressure. He had marital problems and apparently various physical disorders, reflected in the variety of pills he took. Because of his ailments, Howard was spending more and more time out of the office.

One day, I walked into his office and discovered him lying on the floor writhing in pain, holding his hand on his back near his left kidney. I am never good in those situations. I never know what to say or do. So, I said the first thing that came into my mind: "Howard, are your time sheets in?" I didn't really mean it, but that story got around very quickly.

I was equally tough about billing with partners at every level. It was one thing to get on Harry Jones, a young partner at the bottom of the totem pole. It was another thing to say to Bob Washington, who ran the Washington, D.C., office, "Hey, Bob, I know you like working for the government of Antigua. And I know how much you like to go down there. But they don't pay their bills. So stop working for them. And stop taking trips down there." I was very rough on him and on everybody else. It did not make me popular, but at the end of the year, we put a lot of money in these people's pockets, and they understood the connection.

The system had more wide-ranging strategic effects as well. Because cash flow was dramatically improved, we were able to finance our growth, particularly in the first dozen years. We could take any firm that was less well-managed and by applying our system improve its cash flow and financial health. We could justify holding out to partners in a firm with whom we wanted to merge, the likelihood that they could make a lot more money with Finley, Kumble. And we could do that without putting our hand in our own pockets; simply on the strength of better management of their existing business.

It was a potent management tool. Firms that employed the more customary slapdash time keeping and billing and collection practices had no way of knowing until long after the fact which lawyers or clients were unproductive, which lawyers were overworked, and which had not enough work. Nor was there a way of keeping a close watch on which clients were paying bills and which were not. By vigorously insisting on a system of control, we would know such things very quickly, and we could weed out unproductive lawyers and clients.

As the firm expanded across the country, the system, and

my hands-on administration of it, proved invaluable as a management tool and as a means of gathering intelligence. I went to every office and visited with every lawyer to review the matters he was working on and the billing and collection for those matters. Doing that provided important insights into what was going on in the firm. I could begin to see the possibilities of certain connections within the firm. There is no substitute for that in a big organization. I got to know what people were working on and was able to plug them in to people in other offices who could be helpful to them, or put two geographically separated clients together on a deal. It strengthened the synergy we were trying to develop.

Nobody else in the firm had this kind of insight. Nobody else saw the connections because nobody else spent the time it took to find them. A further advantage was that since most people eventually adhered to the system, it was not always a matter of beating them up. I could establish a relationship with a lawyer, get to know him, and recognize attributes that would be useful on other matters. I became knowledgeable about the most important asset of the firm —the people.

In the end, the breakdown of that system contributed mightily to the failure of the firm. If the system is policed, it works. And as long as I was doing it, and as long as I was getting the general support of the people in the firm, the system performed. As long as people were afraid that their failure to comply with the system would result in my extreme displeasure, it was effective. Toward the end, when my authority was challenged and ultimately eliminated, things got out of hand. And the minute that people realized they were insulated from my wrath, we began to have serious cash flow problems.

Those cash flow problems were largely responsible for the firm's failure. The whole edifice of Finley, Kumble was built on money pouring in. Other, very serious problems had developed—spending was going unchecked, expansion got out of hand, the top partners' greed had gotten the better of them, bank borrowing took off on a vertical trajectory, and the firm's banks began to cap credit facilities at levels well below their previously negotiated maximums. But the serious slowdown in cash flow was not only a cause of some of those problems, it also foreshortened the horizons for solving them.

FIVE

Lawyers work strange hours. Wander into a law office at 9:30 in the morning, and you'll see people just arriving, putzing around, getting coffee. The day starts late.

But it ends late. If you want to get hold of a lawyer, call him at six in the evening. Chances are he'll be in his office. It is unclear whether any real work is being accomplished, but dishonor and an aura of wimpiness are attached to leaving a law office much before 7:00 p.m.

On a pleasant spring evening in 1973, Robert Persky came back from a meeting with his lawyer, John Logan O'Donnell, at Olwine, Connolly, Chase, O'Donnell and Weyher; the same Jack O'Donnell who had represented us against the Weismans five years before. Persky, the head of Finley, Kumble's corporate department, was facing trial on criminal charges of violating securities regulations.

On his way to his desk, Persky poked his head into my office and asked me if I knew anything about a lawyer named Andrew Heine. "He's over at Marshall Bratter. What about him?"

Persky said he had heard Heine was looking for a job and that Olwine, Connolly was considering him. I said, "Tell them he's a piece of shit."

Persky left, closing the door behind him. The latch clicked into place, and I was on the phone. The firm needed someone to head its corporate law department, and Andrew N. Heine seemed a likely prospect.

It was about 6:00 in the evening when I called. Heine was still in his office and picked up the phone himself. He and I had met briefly before on a number of different transactions. One of two senior corporate partners at Marshall Bratter, he had decided to leave. He was talking to several firms. When I called and said I understood he was thinking about leaving Marshall Bratter, Andy said he wasn't thinking about it, he had already decided to leave. I asked if I could come right over and talk to him.

Heine, like so many partners at Finley, Kumble, had been around the legal block. He was from Camden, New Jersey, the son of a successful businessman, a rabbinical scholar, and an erstwhile lawyer. After attending Amherst, where he was Phi Beta Kappa and captain of the tennis team, Heine had gone on to law school at Yale. He was a law clerk to federal Judge Samuel Kauffman and later worked at Sullivan and Cromwell, headed the real estate department at Rosenman Colin, and wound up at Marshall Bratter, a firm that would eventually be destroyed by dissension among the partners.

Andy told me he had people in his office, but he would be free later that evening. I met him in his office at 7:30 p.m. and said, "Look, this is the deal. I'd like you to come on board, and you and I can build the law firm. Fifty-fifty." I didn't know him, but I knew about him, and he was kind of a hot guy. We needed a corporate lawyer. Persky was going. And we needed somebody with a little panache since our 15- or 20-man firm was going to be embarrassed by Per-

sky's indictment and possible conviction. We needed someone with a good reputation to replace him. After several
meetings, I convinced Heine to join us. And for that, God
has punished me.

For the last eighteen months that Heine was with Finley,
Kumble, though our offices were just yards apart, Andy and
I did not speak to one another. He holds me responsible
now for the destruction of the firm. But for several years,
we were, if not the closest of friends, at least on cordial
terms. We had a lot of good times, laughing and working
and plotting the development of the firm. We were partners
at the bar of justice and mixing drinks several evenings
each week at the bar in Heine's office.

Later we became what Roy Grutman describes as two
scorpions in a bottle.

I respected Andy and admired many things about him.
He was smart. He was forceful. He was a capable lawyer. He
was a superior athlete—a tennis player, a good skier, a
baseball player. His first wife, Barbara—she's now Barbara
Costykian—was a writer and the daughter of Arthur Fatt,
the founder of Grey Advertising. Andy had acquired some
money and developed expensive tastes. He had his shirts
sent from Turnbull and Asser in London. His suits and
shoes were custom made. He belonged to a foxhunting
club in northern Westchester County and was a member of
the Century Club in Purchase, New York. The club is an
"Our Crowd" sort of place whose members are old-line
German-Jewish families that have been in the United States
for generations. Andy was admitted to the club after he
married his first wife, Barbara Fatt Heine, because her father was a member. After he and Barbara were divorced,
Andy kept the membership because it was in his name.

And he had funny ideas about what was proper. When
Andy first came with the firm, he told me he thought it
would be a good idea if we served tea at 3:30 or 4:00 each
afternoon. I figured what the hell, so I acceded to this
stupidity because I thought it would make Andy happy.

I went out and bought a tea cart and a silver tea service—
not sterling but silver plate because that is what we could
afford. And someone who was on our kitchen staff wheeled
this cart around every afternoon and stopped at each office
and asked if they wanted tea, just like in a British barrister's
office.

Of course, the first thing that happened was that the
associates started complaining because the tea cart stopped
only at partners' offices. They would stick their heads out of
their offices and the tea cart would go right by them.

So, I changed the rules. Associates would be served, too.
It got kind of expensive, supplying all those cookies.

The people we had pushing the cart around were not
from England. Most of them were Spanish-speaking and I
guess they hadn't had classes in tea cart driving. One afternoon, a wheel fell off the cart and the whole thing toppled
over, staining the carpeting. They managed to get the
wheel back on the cart, but the repair wasn't quite right and
the wheel wouldn't turn.

It was getting out of hand anyway, so I decided the tea
cart should be set up in one of the conference rooms.
Anyone who wanted to break for a cup could go get it
himself. It was not a tradition fated to survive.

One day, I walked into the conference room and noticed
that the silver tea service was tarnished. No one had bothered to keep it polished. I was upset that it was in such a
state and got into a harangue with one of the young people
from the kitchen, telling him in my broken Spanish that
they had to get the tarnish off.

The next day, this young fellow proudly took me into the
conference room to show me the tea service and the great
job he had done removing the tarnish. He had cleaned it
with steel wool. The tarnish was gone. So was the silver
plate. It had been buffed down to the copper. So much for
British tradition.

Despite such nutty ideas, Andy had a lot to recommend
him. He was tough, cool, a man who did not get rattled

under pressure. He was an interesting character and, for whatever reason, a contrarian. If I said black, he'd say white; if I said day, he'd say night. He always wanted to make it clear that he was his own man. He was also contrarian in his thinking, and that was sometimes quite useful because he approached problems from what seemed to be an off-the-wall point of view. Because he was so forceful, it would, at the very least, lead to a full airing of the possibilities. For example, we were representing a client who was about to be sued, and I raised the question of how we could resolve the issue without a lot of trouble.

Heine said, "No. Let's sue the other side on behalf of our client." Everyone else rolled their eyes, and I told him it was not a good idea. But Andy insisted that his idea was the best because it would show we were not patsies. And even if we did not follow the course of action that he suggested, his idea changed the way people tackled problems.

That kind of aggressive, fuck-em-all approach colored everything he did. If there was a guy ten feet tall, and he drew a line and dared anyone to cross it, the first guy over would be Heine. He might be certain that he would get his face beaten in, but he would step across the line. He was that competitive. And it was not just his winning that was important, but you had to lose. He seemed not to care about whether he would destroy himself in the process.

I recall being out in Sun Valley skiing together about twelve years ago. I rode up to the top of a mountain with him early in the day. We got off the lift. Andy adjusted his boots, fixed his goggles, and said, "Let's race to the bottom." He was in his early fifties at the time. It was the very first run of the day. And he wanted to race. He beat me, but not by much.

My wife, Peggy, has ridden with him and says that he takes crazy chances on horseback, going over obstacles that could easily cause injury to both him and the horse. Peggy is an accomplished horsewoman and has been riding since she was a small girl, so she's no stranger to what horses can and can't do. But she says that watching Heine was frightening because the chances he took were so reckless.

He was a legend in the romance department. It seemed there was always a stream of great-looking women coming to visit him in his office.

Subtlety and discretion are not Andy's long suits. At one point, he was carrying on with the secretary of one of the young partners in the corporate department, which he ran. People would blanch seeing them walking down the hall in the office holding hands or having intimate little lunches at restaurants near our offices.

He has many admirable qualities, too, but for all that, he is strange when it comes to relationships with other people. He is a tough guy, unbending and unyielding. He is not generous, not a giving kind of person, and in the final analysis, he was not a man I should have gotten involved with.

When Andy came on board at Finley, Kumble, toward the middle of 1973, we had a young lawyer in the corporate department named David Hershberg to whom we had promised a partnership as of the following February. Andy didn't like him, and said he didn't care that we had made a commitment to Hershberg, he was no good and he was not going to be made a partner.

So, David Hershberg left and joined Shearson. Eleven years later when Harvey Myerson joined Finley, Kumble, he had been representing Shearson while he was at Webster and Sheffield, and we assumed that he would bring that business with him. By this time, Hershberg was the number two man in Shearson's legal department, and he said that as much as he wanted to continue doing business with Harvey, there was no way he would follow him to Finley, Kumble. Myerson was somehow able to overcome that, but it took a lot of work.

Heine was thoroughly arrogant and stunningly impolitic. I think he believed that he was a better, finer, brighter, more deserving person than his fellow mortals. He was insensitive to the need to make others feel like worthwhile human beings. And he behaved that way to underlings, partners, clients. It made no difference. For example, we absorbed a small firm that was headed by a fellow named Dick Russell. For public consumption I tried to characterize the transaction as a merger. When we closed the deal, we had a celebration with welcoming speeches and self-congratulations all around. Heine got up to say a few words and began his remarks: "Now that we've bought you . . ."

His arrogance was equally out of control with clients. After years of struggling, when we'd gotten to the point where the law firm was really humming and the only problem was the image of being brash, we went gunning for really big, important clients. Andy couldn't reign in his overblown sense of his own importance. I was doing a great deal of real estate work, and I had brought a client, who is now a household name, into the corporate department to meet Heine. And Andy told the client in the course of conversation, "You don't know what the fuck you're doing." He'd talk that way to clients he'd never met before.

Heine is less than complimentary about our relationship and about much of the time we spent as partners. "We did extremely well for five, six, seven, ten years. Extremely well. We were very close. Steve is extremely bright. He is very attractive as a person. He has tremendous qualities in certain ways. But Steve has a lot of problems in being able to distinguish fact and fiction. He is one of the greatest liars I have ever met. He could look at you straight in the face and say that it's nighttime. And you'd go to the window and say no, Steve, it's daytime."

One of our former colleagues, a man who knows us both well and is still on friendly terms with each of us, says, "Andy is charming. He is smart. He is a good lawyer, probably the best lawyer in the firm, but I suppose the charitable thing to say about Andy is that he had a total blind spot toward Steve. They had gone from being close friends and confidants to not talking to one another."

Another way of looking at the relationship comes from a woman who knows us both: "I don't know exactly what happened between them, but they both express a sense of betrayal. They were fighting over something that was as important to them as food or water. It was the second time around for both of them. Steve had been broke or close to it at some point. Andy had been thrown out of Marshall Bratter. They were both in their middle years. And this firm was the goal they wanted. I'm not sure that Steve really wanted to share that much with Andy. And I know that Andy saw that as a deception or a betrayal. They were fighting over the thing that meant the most to them. It wasn't a law firm; it wasn't money; it wasn't principle they were fighting over. You have to understand that. The nature of what they were fighting over was their guts. They were fighting for their balls."

It may or may not have been quite so primitive. But it was a serious fight. As early as 1984, while we were still on putatively cordial terms, Heine was talking about "getting Kumble."

"Andy was plotting ways to get rid of Steve," says one of our former partners, who Heine had brought into the firm. "I was new to the firm and he talked about it to me. I was just amazed at the indiscretion of it, and the intensity. He absolutely hated Kumble. I always had the feeling that he would do anything to get revenge on Steve, even if it meant destroying the law firm. He hated Kumble that much."

I am not totally clear on the well-springs of Heine's hatred. No one has ever mistaken me for St. Francis of Assisi, with or without stigmata. People tell me that I have charm. Maybe that's true, but I'm no pushover. And like the people I brought into the firm over the years, I like to win. I like to see things done my way.

By the late 1970s and early 1980s, the firm began to seek and to get a significant amount of publicity. And in the same way that I was a lightning rod for animosity because I enforced the financial flows, I also attracted a good deal of envy. In an effort to make the firm better known, I began to court the press. And as the legal press expanded to new journals given to looking at the personalities and the business side of the law, Finley, Kumble got reams of coverage, most of it beneficial. More than any other member of the firm, I was the point man with the journalists. And for a long time, it was helpful. I wasn't trying to manipulate the press, but I worked at making a good impression on the people who wrote about the firm.

Our coverage was a public relations dream. But the dream had a shadowed side as well. Several of my partners —Heine in particular—felt I was taking far too much public credit for the firm's accomplishments. He was envious and he felt I had betrayed my early commitment that he and I would run the firm together.

Heine still remembers that initial meeting and the promise it held: "Steve came up that evening and we talked. I was very taken with the way he said to me, 'Andy, come on in. You and I will be absolutely equal from here on out. You can have your name anyplace you want, and we will run the firm together.' "

Heine thought about it for several weeks before deciding to come to Finley, Kumble. Andy says it was a decision he made over the strong protestations of a number of his partners at Marshall Bratter who wanted to leave with him. They told him they'd set up a new firm with him; that they'd go anywhere with him. Anywhere but Finley, Kumble.

Heine now says, "The Finley, Kumble people were very difficult to deal with. And even at that time, I think it would be fair to say that Finley, Kumble had a very controversial reputation." Part of that was due to the notoriety arising from the Persky debacle, but Heine says that it was more than that.

"Steve and Neil Underberg had a theory that people said negative things about the firm because they were jealous. I always told them that was a lot of baloney. I always told them that it was because people in the firm were not conducting themselves professionally in all instances. That remained a bone of contention between us."

Despite his harping about how bad the firm's reputation was, he seemed happy to join Finley, Kumble, coming on to head up the corporate law department. And as he says, those were times of great excitement, challenge, and fun.

Even before the issue of public coverage and who got credit for the firm's success began to pull us apart, something else happened that should have tipped me off to the deep-seated acrimony that seemed to be looking for an excuse to surface.

There was hardly a partner at Finley, Kumble whose marriage had survived the firm's early years. The single-mindedness required to succeed at the law, along with ten-hour days followed by dinners with clients or partners or other business associates, takes a toll. It happened to a lot of us, including me. After my marriage fell apart, I had a fairly serious love affair with a woman who was tangentially connected with the firm.

But in the course of doing business in Florida, I'd had a blind date with Peggy Vandervoort, a former professional singer, who had become a highly successful thoroughbred bloodstock agent, breeder, and consultant and was socially prominent in South Florida. I was quite taken by her striking good looks, intelligence, bearing, and wit. On our first date in May 1978—I guess it wasn't so romantic of me—I took her to a business dinner with Victor Posner, the Miami-based financier and corporate raider.

She lived way out in Golden Isles, an exclusive section north of Miami. I got a ride to her home and when I arrived, I sent the car on its way. Peggy says I was forty-five minutes early. She wasn't ready, so I had to wait while she changed. Finally, she came out. We had a drink. We talked. I was impressed.

She says now that she was charmed. "Steve had a very, very strong effect on me, and I said to myself, 'Whoa, girl. Be careful.' Then, as we were about to leave, he asked me if

I had a car. I was used to having beaux come to pick me up.
One man I dated came by in his Ferrari. Another sent a limo
stocked with cold Champagne. I didn't believe in love at
first sight, but there I was, captivated by this man after an
hour. So, I drove."

We had a great time at Posner's. Peggy had always
wanted to meet him. He was a powerhouse in business and
was very well known in Miami. She and I hit it off, and all
through the evening, I'd catch her eye and wink. We were a
team that quickly. At the end of the evening, Peggy
dropped me at my hotel and drove the twenty-eight miles
back to Golden Isles.

I've told Peggy, and it's true, that I decided to marry her
that first evening.

There was an incident with Heine that upset Peggy quite
a bit, and I suppose that it should have been a tipoff to me.
Not long after our wedding in 1979, Heine invited us to an
elegant gala. It began with drinks at the Heine's home, a
beautiful townhouse on East 57th Street, just off Sutton
Place. After drinks, the men in black tie and the women
gowned and jeweled were transported in horse-drawn car-
riages across town to Lincoln Center for the New York City
Ballet's opening night performance.

Peggy remembers it better than I do: "It was a super treat
and really a lot of fun. Everybody was gawking as we went
by. At dinner following the performance, I found myself
seated across from Steve's former live-in lover. I asked
Steve if the woman was indeed who I thought she was. He
said yes. I told him to make excuses for us. We got up from
the table—we hadn't touched the first course—and left. It
was a vicious little number. It was extremely offensive. That
was the beginning of a time when we did not see much of
the Heines."

The next day I confronted Andy over the tastelessness of
his guest selection and seating. He told me that he'd invite
whomever he damn well pleased.

There is a point at which competitiveness sloshes over

into destructiveness, but Heine's social behavior was not
what destroyed our business relationship.

By the late 1970s, I had been spending a great deal of
time building the firm and was getting a lot of credit in the
legal press for its success. That drove Heine, in particular,
crazy. So, when Andy was interviewed, instead of saying the
firm is terrific or we're doing great or whatever, he'd say,
"This firm had a shit reputation until I came along."

I'd tell him, "Andy, you can't say that, even if it's true.
Our image and reputation are sacrosant. If you, a name
partner, say negative things often enough, it gets to be true
in people's minds. Your comments are stupid and self-destructive."

My concern was that that sort of thing could hurt business. When a major piece of work is about to begin, or
when a big piece of litigation is imminent, and people are
looking for firms to represent them, they talk to several. It
is something like what happens when a company hires an
advertising agency. The legal business is handed out by the
company's general counsel. He notifies several law firms
that his company is considering them for a piece of business. In response to that, a firm usually writes to the general counsel describing its expertise in an area. It is not a
short letter. It is a whole book describing the firm's ability
to get results. You know you are competing with the best.
And in some areas, you literally bid for the work.

A very specialized way of marketing prevails at the highest levels of the law. And the higher you go, the more
institutionalized it is. But lawyers don't want to talk about it
much because they think there is something wrong with it.
We did it all the time in a lot of different areas, and other
firms do it, too. The stakes are high. The competition is
fierce. It is hardball. So, you could be absolutely sure the
competing firms would bring up anything derogatory that
was written about another firm.

I could never figure out Heine badmouthing his own law
firm in the press. It was crazy. Other firms would say to the

prospective client, "Hey, look, we're not saying negative things about Finley, Kumble, but look at what this name partner is saying about his own firm. Do you want them to represent you?"

Andy was my second big recruiting regret. But he was not my last. I thought I could oversee these men. I was wrong. I can be faulted for my naive belief that I could bring in people like Heine—and later Manley and Myerson—and control them.

Heine and Grutman think they added class to the firm. That's questionable. To my mind, in the quest for respectability and panache, one addition to the firm still stands out as a great success.

To anyone even obliquely conscious of politics in New York, the name Wagner has for the last seventy years been one with a considerable luster. In the first generation, Robert Wagner came as a child from Germany to New York where his family settled in the Yorkville section of Manhattan, a neighborhood now overrun with rich young men and women willing to pay the outlandish prices gouged for everything from housing to corn flakes. It is still a neighborhood, though, where until recently, the "Horst Wessel" song could be found on the jukebox at the Heidelberg on Second Avenue, where elderly men and women can be heard on the streets conversing in German, and where streetwise adolescents still can be found sitting on the stoops of rent-controlled tenement buildings drinking beer on a steamy evening.

The elder Wagner was elected to the New York State Assembly, became Democratic leader of the New York State Senate, and was a justice of the Appellate Division of New York State Supreme Court. Along with Alfred E. Smith, who later became Governor of New York and the Democratic nominee for the presidency of the United States in 1928, the elder Wagner pushed through radical social and labor legislation that in many ways presaged the New Deal. He was elected to the United States Senate for the first of four terms in 1928 and, following Franklin D. Roosevelt's landslide victory in 1932, became one of the leading architects of the New Deal.

In 1937, his son and namesake, Robert F. Wagner, Jr., two weeks after his graduation from Yale's law school, began his first successful race for the New York State Assembly from his father's old district. Eight years later, after service in the Army Air Corps in Europe, the younger Wagner returned to New York and the practice of law. Newly-elected New York City Mayor William O'Dwyer appointed the young Wagner to the city's tax commission. A year later, when Wagner went to see the mayor about resigning the post, O'Dwyer and Franklin Roosevelt, Jr., persuaded him to take over and clean up the city's scandal-ridden Housing and Buildings Department. The next year, he was appointed chairman of the City Planning Commission and in 1949 was elected Borough President of Manhattan. In 1953, he was elected to the first of three terms as mayor of New York.

Having returned to private life and the practice of law at the end of 1965, Wagner accepted the call from Lyndon Johnson to be United States Ambassador to Spain in 1967.

I came to know Wagner in the mid-1970s when we both sat on the board of the old Chelsea National Bank. He was a man of stature and distinction. And in many ways, his joining the gunslinging upstarts at Finley, Kumble was as unlikely as this son of one of the major forces in the New Deal chatting amiably with the grizzled Spanish Fascist Francisco Franco. He did both.

Bob Wagner was a great statesman. He was a beloved man in the city. He had been mayor of New York for twelve years. He had been ambassador to Spain. He was an adviser to governors and presidents. He was married to Phyllis Cerf Wagner, a woman of influence in her own right and the widow of Bennett Cerf, the founder of Random House. Bob was really quite a guy. I thought he could attract business, be a great rainmaker for the firm. Bringing him into the firm would be a coup.

He and I sat together at meetings of the bank's board and occasionally we would walk uptown together afterwards. I was very taken with him. He had common sense and experience, and I grew to respect his judgment about most things. A lot of lawyers can give mechanical answers to questions. But when you find a really good lawyer, what you really pay for is good judgment. Bob Wagner had that.

This young, growing firm, moreover, was suffering from a serious image problem. In addition to the stain of the Persky indictment and conviction, the firm was regarded as too young, too brash, too pushy, too Jewish. I felt that bringing in someone the caliber of Bob Wagner and having him as a name partner, and merging with his firm, which included Frank Quillinan, who was Al Smith's son-in-law, would give us a cachet markedly different from what we had in the past. It was clear at that stage of our development that aligning ourselves with a man of the former mayor's reputation would give us stature on a national level.

We were looking for business from bigger corporations, major clients that would rank in the Fortune 500. And in that league, law firm selection depends on more than simple legal competence. Stature counts for a great deal as well. I felt that Wagner could provide that. But most of all, his integrity and good judgment, and the fact that he was truly one of the nicest men I'd ever met, were the key factors. And it was my decision to try to bring him into the firm.

Wagner was not unaware of the firm's reputation, and it took considerable romancing to persuade him to join the firm. It was a long time between our initial meeting and my raising the subject with Bob. And it was a considerable time from then until he finally said yes.

For Wagner's part, his partners at his own firm, Francis Quillinan and Edwin Tennant, were getting on in years. They had a small firm, and because of the changes in the practice of law, they were also finding it more difficult to operate than in the past. Many clients wanted a firm that could provide a wide variety of services without referring work outside. "We thought it might be interesting to merge with a larger firm," Wagner recalled. "Steve approached me about merging with them. We had several talks, and all of those fellows over at Finley, Kumble looked like comers. We finally agreed to join them."

In the course of the negotiations, Wagner met for lunch with me, Finley, Heine, Underberg, and Grutman. Over lunch, the issue of whether and where Wagner's name should appear in the firm name came up. Initially, I had talked of putting Wagner's name first. Not everyone present thought that was a great idea. Grutman, who was not particularly pleased about the prospect of having Wagner in the firm at all, was adamantly opposed to adding Wagner's name to the firm name.

"I had gone to Yale," Wagner recalled. "And I think Roy had something to do with Yale, and, of course, Steve had gone to Yale. So, we met at the Yale Club. We were getting down to the nitty gritty. I thought it would be beneficial to me and to Frank Quillinan and Ed Tennant. They were going into Finley, Kumble as of counsel and would be helpful to the firm." It is common in law firms that partners who reach retirement age or want to slow down, attorneys who have spent many years in other fields or politics, or have stepped down from the bench and want to be associated with a law firm join as "counsel." They have neither the responsibilities nor the rights of partners.

Wagner says of his former firm, "We had a lot of will and estate work, and Frank and Ed had some live ones, so to speak, since a lot of their clients were quite advanced in age. These young guys at Finley, Kumble might do a will for someone and have to wait twenty-five or fifty years for them to make anything of it." The clients Quillinan and Tennant could bring in, on the other hand, provided a much shorter horizon of opportunity. They might die at any moment, and thus reward their attorneys by providing significant estate work.

It was certainly crucial to my plan, and the addition of Wagner's name to the firm's logo and letterhead would add considerable respectability and the aura of influence. That was the whole point.

"The firm did not have a great reputation," Heine says in recalling the time, "and we were not very mature. And all of a sudden we had gotten a well-known figure, a three-time mayor of New York, the son of a famous senator, a man who had entree to almost anyplace."

Roy Grutman puts as negative a slant on it as possible. "What Steve wanted was the appearance to the gullible that we had political swat. He got a whole graveyard of the corpses of dead politicians so that people would think we had political connections, power, muscle, fix. That's what it was."

Wagner, whose office walls are covered with photographs of him with presidents, popes, heads of state, and governors—the mementos of a life of distinguished public service—is a man whose public life was never touched with even a whiff of impropriety or scandal. Grutman's rantings are unfair and unworthy. In recalling the incident at the Yale Club, the septuagenarian Wagner was reluctant to say who among the partners at the meeting opposed his name being added to the firm.

"What was Wagner? What was Wagner?" Roy Grutman protests. "The name Wagner dazzled Kumble. He came up to me one day and said Bob Wagner would like to join our firm as counsel. I asked him why we would want him, and he said that Wagner's name was magic. A couple of days later, Kumble came up to me again. He said Bob was very interested and would like to be a partner. I said, 'He's not even a lawyer.'

"Another few days went by and Kumble came up to me again to tell me that Bob's wife felt that he should be a name partner. I said, 'No way. Name partner? Bob Wagner?

Bullshit.' We fought and fought and fought about it. And after ten days in which we fought day and night, Wagner came to a meeting. We showed him the proposed agreement and he said, 'What about my name?' "

At that point in the conversation, Grutman outdid himself in insulting Wagner, telling him that he might have his name in the firm after a period of time during which he proved himself worthy.

"I was sitting across the table from him," says Grutman, "and I said, 'You know, Bob, unlike my fellow management committee members, I have given this matter some thought. I appreciate that you are a non-pareil. No one has been three times mayor of the City of New York and ambassador to the Court of St. James of Compostello. But there is somebody close. John Lindsay. He was twice mayor of the City of New York. And when he joined Webster and Sheffield, his name was not put in the firm. I understand that he is making a very important contribution up there, as I hope that you could make an important contribution here. But really, name partners are either founding partners, or partners who on the basis of their qualities as lawyers and what they achieve at the bar as lawyers, have a name that everyone in the firm feels they would want on the escutcheon or the banner under which we live and fight.' "

Everybody except Norman Roy wanted to slide right under the table. But Bob handled it beautifully.

"Webster and Sheffield was an old established firm and most of the Finley, Kumble group felt that it was a benefit for them to have my name in the firm," Wagner says. "So I said, 'Look, if that is the way you feel about it, I'm leaving. We're wasting our time here.' But that was the end of it, and they compromised and the name of the firm became Finley, Kumble, Wagner." As time went by, Wagner and Grutman made their peace. Grutman and his wife, Jewel Bjork, invited Wagner to lunch at the River Club, and not long after that luncheon, they invited Wagner and his wife to their apartment on Fifth Avenue for dinner.

Following the meeting at the Yale Club, I drafted a letter of agreement with Wagner and the merger was agreed to. A day or two later, I was sitting in my office when the door was almost taken off the hinges by a wild-eyed, irate woman who walked in and said, "Who the hell do you think you are?" It was Jewel Bjork, Mrs. Norman Roy Grutman. "Who the hell do you think you are to bring in some political hack over my husband's objections?"

And I said, "Wait a minute. You're off base. You don't know what you're talking about."

Then she said to me, "This firm is not your law firm. It is our law firm, my husband's and mine, just as much as it is yours." Then she told me to go fuck myself. I was stunned. I said, "What did you say?"

"Don't tell me you've never heard the word before," she replied.

I said, "Not from a lady, but then, you're no lady."

At that, she walked out, slamming the door behind her.

A couple of minutes later, Heine and Underberg came running in asking what I had done to poor Jewel and saying she and Roy were leaving the firm. I told them the woman came in screaming at me and telling me to go fuck myself because of Wagner. They told me I had to go in and apologize to Roy and Jewel.

I said, "For what?"

I'm not sure I've ever apologized to anyone. I find it hard to do. But Heine and Underberg persisted, saying that if the couple left it would be bad for the firm and that an apology would keep them from leaving. A meeting was hastily convened in Heine's office. Heine sat at his desk. Jewel and Roy came in and sat on the couch. I faced them and apologized for my unseemly behavior and said I regretted anything I might have done to offend either of them and that I hoped my behavior would not affect our friendship and our working relationship. I promised never to behave in that manner again.

I had no idea what I was talking about, but they seemed mollified. After Roy and Jewel left, I turned to Heine and Underberg and said to them, "Don't you ever, ever, ever ask me to do that again."

SIX

Before I founded Finley, Kumble, I did more moving around than most of my contemporaries. In those days, a lawyer went to a firm, stayed seven or eight years, and either became a partner or didn't; either stayed or moved on.

If I were advising a young lawyer today, I would caution against taking the route that I chose. Succeeding on that kind of career path requires you to be too much of an entrepreneur, too much of a business person. It worked for me, but things are different now. I would advise anyone to go to a big firm, get good training, and then maybe go out on their own.

Even with the base of first-rate training in a large firm, going off on your own and starting a firm is far more difficult now. One important change is that the competition is killing. Fifteen or twenty years ago a small client would have difficulty finding a big firm willing to represent him. They didn't want to bother. Today, that same client can get a good-sized firm to handle his case or matter. They may not take landlord-tenant cases or personal injury cases, but they welcome setting up a corporation, drawing up a will, working on a real estate closing. It's not that those matters will generate large fees. Handling an incorporation is a $500–$1000 proposition. A will at a decent firm costs $250–$1000. And while the legal work involved in closing on a $500,000 home may seem hefty to the buyer, it's not significant to the law firm.

They do the work because they see it as a way to establish a long-term professional relationship. If the client's corporation becomes a business success, it can provide work for the lawyer. Every time the client changes that initial will over the course of his life, when he establishes trusts for his children, when he dies leaving estate work, it will mean business for the lawyer. And every time he buys a new home or a piece of investment property, the lawyer will have a chance to do that work as well.

Today, the best firms handle that business in a first-class way and not charge any more than a small firm. Fifteen or twenty years ago, the major firms were not terribly interested in such work, and small clients were intimidated by their white-shoe image.

They were not intimidated by Finley, Kumble. In the firm's early days, there was hardly a white shoe to be found in the place. Obviously, simple incorporations, wills, and house or apartment closings are hardly the stuff of big-time law. But Finley, Kumble would do them. And we would take on matters from small enterprises that a banker like Frank Wright, who wanted to develop his own book of business, would deem unbankable.

The law firm was hustling. There was little business that we would turn away. We didn't do much in the way of personal injury law. We did no admiralty law or customs work or patent and trademark law. We didn't practice immigration law. But anything else was fair game, to be pursued in an unrelenting way. Years later, with the firm well-established and gaining in reputation, we had lost none of our early aggressiveness.

Jerome Kowalski, a litigator who became a partner at Finley, Kumble only five years out of law school, tells a story about an incident in the early 1980s while he was still an associate at the firm. "Some computer company had called Kumble and needed some litigation done, and Steve had apparently told them that he had a partner who had made his whole career in litigating on behalf of computer companies.

"It was the luncheon hour, and everyone else in the litigation department was out. I was in my office and Kumble comes running in saying, 'Quick, come down to my office with me. It's an emergency. I'll explain as we walk.' So, he told me about this company calling. He told me to talk with them, but to say as little as possible; just to sweet-talk them.

"And I said to him, 'But, Steve, the fact of the matter is that I have had a lot of experience in these kinds of cases and I know a lot about the computer business.'

"And he said, 'Great. Great. That will convince them.' So, I said to him, 'You don't understand. I really do know a lot about this stuff.' And he said, 'Terrific. You're convincing even me.' He was a brazen guy. He had a huge set of balls."

It was that brazen quality, along with the conceptual framework we were developing, that made the growth of the firm possible. Lawyers who joined the firm after having been recruited describe the kind of persistence and outright romancing that went on as a combination of Peter Pan, the Pied Piper of Hamlin, and Don Vito Corleone.

One former partner of the firm who came on in the mid-seventies recalls, "At the time that I came to Finley, Kumble, they had no capability in the area of my specialty. They had retained my firm on a matter. Steve, it seemed to me, was the leading force in the firm and was looking to do the best job for their clients. I handled the matter, which we

won. And when it was finished I presented him with a very
sizable bill. "Steven said to me, 'Have you ever thought of
joining a larger firm?' I told him no. Then he asked, 'Would
you?' "I said, 'Yes, but only after you've paid the bill.' "

Finley, Kumble paid the bill and the lawyer, after several
conversations with me, agreed to accept our offer. He says
what he found was a young, vibrant group of lawyers with a
different slant, a different point of view. "Their view was,
'We can do it all. And if we can't, then we'll find and bring
aboard people who can help us.' Steve said even then that
he wanted to build the first and finest national law firm. I
thought that was a novel idea. And it appealed to me since
my area of specialization was one that was really national in
its scope. My practice took me all over the country even
though I was with a New York firm, and the idea of a national firm made a lot of sense."

But this particular lawyer had to think about the offer. He
was a partner in his firm, a firm that had been around for
forty years. Most of their work was referral business that
came to them from other law firms and from the accounting
community. He knew very well that if he joined Finley,
Kumble, he would be competing with the other firms that
were the source of his business and that he would lose all
his forwarding work. He says now, "I joined Finley, Kumble and my fears were realized. I lost those sources of
referral. My book of business shrank considerably and I had
to go searching for matters. But a dozen years later the firm
had grown, and I had built an origination practice, with 650
lawyers—all of them in my own firm—feeding me business.
It was good for me. It was good for the firm, and it was good
for my practice."

Many lawyers were on the receiving end of cold phone
calls from me asking whether they would be interested in
joining Finley, Kumble. I did a lot of that. I would just sit in
my office in the late afternoon and evening with the Martindale-Hubbell directory open on my desk, running a finger
down the pages, using it as a telephone directory.

In later years, when we were having a terrible time finding the right mix for our Florida operation, I was forced to recruit new people, and to do so quickly. I remember calling in Kowalski. He had done a lot of work in Florida, so I asked him who was good in Miami. He still tells the story of my sitting with Martindale-Hubbell on my desk and calling the people he mentioned. Kowalski's version is that I'd say, "Hi. I'm Steve Kumble. How would you like to merge your firm with ours?" And that after I ran out of the names he had given me, I just started cold calling out of Martindale-Hubbell. I don't recall it all that exactly, but it's probably true.

That was not the usual method of operation. But recruitment tended to be as much a matter of intuition and hunch as it was of cold logic. Background, training, and academic credentials were important. The niche where the firm wanted to develop a practice and the need we had to fill were important. So was chemistry. And so, too, were other intangibles like style and social grace. And a certain hunger.

For many many years the firm grew on the belief that we wanted to provide a platform and environment in which lawyers could achieve all their aims and aspirations from a personal, professional, and financial point of view. If we could provide such an environment, there would be no place else that anyone would want to go.

But Finley, Kumble was a firm built largely on dissatisfaction. As often as not, the lawyers I recruited were wriggling away from firms where their partners wanted them out. Many of the people we recruited were known troublemakers that other firms had either let go or had been happy to see leave. And nowhere was that more apparent than at the top of our hierarchy. Heine's partners at Marshall Bratter wanted him gone. Marshall Manley's partners at Manatt Phelps had told him to take a hike. Webster Sheffield breathed a collective sigh of relief when Harvey Myerson grabbed a limo to Finley, Kumble.

In my misguided wisdom, I thought that at Finley, Kumble they could work as a team. I foolishly thought we could mold those prima donnas into a chorus. At the same time, I worked hard to promote the star quality of the prima donnas in the press as a way of promoting business.

If they were perceived as stars, then they would be bigger rainmakers and bring in even more business.

The crucial mistake I made at Finley, Kumble was going after some of these stars. There was nothing wrong with the concept in theory. What was wrong was that some of the professional superstars, who were adept at and capable of providing the most terrific legal services, got the crazy idea they should run the firm. Just because you're a great lawyer, doesn't mean that you're a good businessman.

On the whole, though, our recruiting practices worked to the firm's advantage. At Finley, Kumble history was something that happened last week and ancient history was something that happened the week before. There was no such concept as couldn't or shouldn't. The words were not in our vocabulary. Every day was a new day. There was little structure, few rules.

The things we did were a response to the demands in the marketplace. For example, it became evident that we needed a capability in the bankruptcy field. We did not have it, so we had to go outside. I had met Gary Blum. He's a great guy and a great bankruptcy lawyer. But he's not white-shoe. He likes to take on the banks and the establishment. He is a street fighter. Since we represented small companies and not banks, Gary was perfect to fill our need. We never even thought of the possibility that taking on Gary Blum was somehow inconsistent with our image or culture. We had no rulebook, no sense of tradition. We were unfettered. We did what made sense.

The firm created other departments from scratch as well. In the mid-1970s we saw that we needed a labor law capability. The old firms would not do labor work. They had some rule against it. We didn't. So, we developed a labor practice. The practice of law was changing, and we were part of that change. Bankruptcy became a big deal. Labor law became respectable. The old firms who sneered at certain kinds of practice soon found firms like Finley, Kumble making inroads, just taking the ball away from them.

They also found Finley, Kumble chipping away at tradition. Before I started going after big names, I began to woo partners away from other firms, something other firms just did not do. We did what was appropriate for us. When we decided to develop a new capability, we didn't take some kid out of law school and ask him to develop the practice over a period of years. That would have been dangerous and unfair to clients. We went out and found the best people we could, people of skill and stature, and built from the top down, not the bottom up.

So, I went looking.

In the mid-1970s, growing, but far from the big leagues of American law, the firm's search for needed talent concentrated on medium to small firms. A partner at a big firm, who was making a great deal of money, would not have had much interest in moving to a smaller firm where the backup was not as deep. So, we tended to recruit from small or medium-sized firms, not from the big downtown powerhouses.

The experience, quality, and skill of the lawyers we recruited varied, but by and large most were highly competent lawyers. Equally important, and almost without exception, they had an entrepreneurial spirit and an ability to deal effectively with clients. Because of the size of their firms, the young lawyers we brought in had been dealing day-to-day with clients, gaining invaluable experience.

Although in later years Finley, Kumble became sufficiently well-known that recruiting was not a problem, in the early days it was hard. No one had heard of us. People were worried about their futures. So, it was a selling job, and unless a poor fellow was desperate, it was difficult.

We had a former partner who had gone to jail. We had the

reputation, to the extent that we had any reputation at all, of being too pushy, too aggressive. People accused us, unfairly, of cutting corners. We were competing with firms that would say anything to make us look less attractive. Lawyers are very competitive animals. They are very quick to criticize and miserly in giving compliments. And here we were competing with them for business at every level.

I had felt that bringing on Bob Wagner would help both internally, by having someone with his character and experience and judgment, and externally in terms of modifying our image of being too young and too brash. And in fact, I think his arrival helped on both counts.

Shortly after he joined us in late 1975, I mentioned to Mayor Wagner that I was still concerned that Finley, Kumble, Wagner was not a household name. He suggested that we hire Howard Rubenstein, the public relations consultant, to help us to broaden our celebrity and get some of the burrs off our reputation. At the time, Howard had not gained the kind of fame and influence he now has, although he had been working with several politicians.

It had never occurred to me to hire a public relations firm, and I had never dealt with one. As far as I knew, it was not something that law firms did. But what Bob suggested made sense. So, in early 1976, we arranged with Rubenstein to pay him a retainer of $3,000 a month and somehow he would make us famous. Rubenstein's suggestion was that we get several people in our firm to write scholarly articles that would appear in the trade journals, or in the general press, and it would build from there. That was the way we embarked on this great publicity effort.

The first month, we paid the $3,000, and I spent the month scanning all the newspapers. Nothing.

Then, we paid the next month's fee, and I spent that month scanning the papers and magazines. Still nothing.

In the third month, we finally got our name mentioned in the paper. Rubenstein was interviewed by a *New York Times* writer, who was doing an article on public relations firms, and Howard owned up to the fact that he had developed a whole new public relations career polishing up the images of tarnished law firms. Among the tarnished law firms whose image he was improving were Shea and Gould and Finley, Kumble.

We had finally gotten our name in the paper, described as tarnished by the guy we were paying $3,000 a month to make us look good.

After I read the story, I called Rubenstein and said, "Hey, Howie, that was brilliant. What possessed you to talk about your relationship with us? I'm concerned that we even have a p.r. firm, and then we see our name in print described as a firm whose reputation is tarnished."

He hesitated and then told me, well, he had to be honest with the reporter.

So I said, "Well, that's great. But you can take this month's bill for your retainer, roll it into a cylinder, and shove it up your ass."

From then on, we did our own public relations.

Because we were still young and small and brash, and with our "tarnished reputation," it was a tough sell, but we did an effective job of recruiting. It was my forte. I believed in what we were doing. I believed in the concept of what we were creating and that we had established a very exciting environment. It was different from Davis Polk or Sullivan and Cromwell. Still, to recruit someone away from a larger firm, we had to offer partnership almost from the outset. Unlike most other firms, we admitted partners without a long period of observation. We had to do that because we needed people at the partnership level to service our clients.

We sold growth and excitement, direct client contact, rapid advancement to partnership, more interesting work, greater responsibility and autonomy, more money. It was a very heady inducement. And it was all true.

Many people who observed it firsthand over the years say I would romance lawyers as though I were seducing them;

painting a picture of a brilliant and unlimited future; telling them what they wanted to hear and pumping them up.

I think that overstates it, but it was like being the Pied Piper.

But where the Pied Piper was indiscriminate—first in leading the rats out of Hamlin and later leading the towns-folk's young off to the Children's Crusade—I knew what I wanted and relied heavily on my hunches and intuition in going after potential recruits.

When you are interviewing someone, you make some pretty quick decisions on the basis of some pretty short conversations. If a fellow gives you a whole packet of refer-ences, you can bet your life that those are people who will say nice things about him. It's almost not worth calling them because you're only going to hear that he is brave, reverent, loyal, trustworthy, and the rest. You don't typi-cally give a lawyer a writing test, or some legal examination, or give him some legal problem to solve as a little quiz. He'd just get up and walk out.

So, I would sit and talk with a prospective recruit. You can make a lot of judgments about someone and about their personality just from a conversation. What were his academic and professional credentials? Was he articulate and alert and bright? Did he have a winning personality? After all, he would be representing the firm and its clients. We did not want anyone who had his foot in his mouth, who looked slovenly, or did not know how to dress.

Within a short time of meeting someone, I can tell, with-out looking, what color shoes they are wearing, what kind of watch they are wearing, whether their hands and nails are clean, because the minute they walk in I just notice those things. You can tell a lot about someone from that because when a person gets up in the morning, and if he has more than one shirt, one suit, one tie, he makes a selection. And the selection process he makes, however unconsciously, defines the impression he wants to make on the world. He may not know it, but he is in fact saying to himself, "Who shall I be today?" Everyone tries to convey something, out of a conscious or unconscious desire to communicate. So, if you just look, you learn a great deal.

Beyond that initial observation, I would not ask a lawyer questions about the obscure rule in Shelley's case or fee-subordinated ground leases. I would ask him about himself, where he was from, what he'd been doing, why he was thinking about leaving where he worked. I would just let the fellow talk. And while he was talking, I did more looking than listening. And all the while, I was forming a judgment. Was this the kind of person we were going to be happy to have representing the firm and the clients of the firm? I was not looking for a type. We had a lot of different kinds of people. But they were all people who could sell themselves and the firm.

Before a potential recruit could show off the shine on his shoes, he'd have to find his way to us. Word of mouth was one way Finley, Kumble heard about people, as in the case of Andrew Heine. In later years, personal introductions or third-party connections were the lead-ins to the larger mergers. But for the most part, new relationships were developed through headhunters. A headhunter would call pitching an outstanding lawyer, with eight or ten years of experience, who had gone to all the best schools, who was an associate or a partner at another firm, who brought in a great deal of business, who wanted to talk to Finley, Kumble. I almost always said yes to such conversations. Today, most firms do this. But at the time we started, it was generally frowned on by the established firms. We did it because there was no rule against it and because there was no other way we could grow in response to our clients needs.

At the highest levels of corporate executive recruiting, as headhunting is more politely known, a bank, a manufacturing company, a nationwide service business looking to fill a high-level position will contact one of a large handful of recruiting firms. The standard agreement in such transactions calls for the search firm to come up with several appropriate candidates within ninety days. It further calls for a hefty fee, thirty to thirty-five percent of the first year's cash compensation for the position, to be paid in three equal monthly installments, with the first installment paid up front. And they get paid whether or not the corporation hires the candidates they present. At that level, headhunters pay little attention to the resumes that come in over the transom. Instead, they rely on vast networks of contacts and maintain extensive computerized dossiers on a wide range of potential candidates.

At less lofty levels of executive recruiting, a more hit-or-miss mode prevails, and the business is something of a hustle. The headhunters serve much more as brokers, calling around to see which lawyers are dissatisfied and which firms are looking for people, and then making matches. They operate on a contingency basis and are paid a fee only if they succeed in filling a position. Headhunting in the legal profession tends to be more contingency-based and lawyers who want to move contact headhunters more often than the other way around. When headhunters called, I knew we would have to pay a fee only if we hired the candidate. So, I took their calls. Over the years, we paid hundreds of thousands of dollars to headhunters. I also knew that I would probably be interviewing someone who was unhappy where he was.

That happened frequently. The use of headhunters and the practice of bringing partners in laterally added to the smudge on our reputation. It is understandable, but not particularly fair. In most instances, we were approached first either by individuals directly or by a headhunter. Nevertheless, firms that lost people to Finley, Kumble were often angry. Suppose you are a senior partner at Ecks, Why and Zee, and one day your top corporate partner comes walking into your office and announces that he is leaving. You ask where he is going and he says, Finley, Kumble. So you say, "Those SOBs. They are the worst firm imaginable. They're terrible. Why are you going there?" And the fellow would say, "Well, I made a deal, and I'm going." And the senior partner would spread the word that we had just stolen his best lawyer and never even talked to him. Since we did that with some regularity, it did not make us particularly popular with our brethren at the bar. As time went by, we were doing it in cities across the country, so our reputation spread. People saw us as being raiders of talent. They saw us as a firm that would do anything to get ahead, as a firm who would take their best lawyers and their business, as people who were not nice folks. We were seen as not genteel, and at the beginning, that was translated as gentile.

New partners generally shared the Finley, Kumble ethos of not caring much about white-shoe gentility. We recruited and developed a group of lawyers whose principal interest was building their practice. Twenty years ago, the typical Wall Street or establishment law firm was structured as a hierarchy with a great deal of tradition. Those firms and their lawyers did not aggressively pursue new business. The most important thing to them was to hold on to the business they had. They were, in addition, reluctant to expand into non-traditional, non-establishment areas of practice.

In the environment of such firms, lawyers did not seek out clients. It was just the opposite. Clients sought out the firms, and it was very difficult to become a client of one of those firms. It was like qualifying for a checking account at Morgan Guaranty Trust Co. where they won't even consider you unless you are willing to place $10 million or more with the bank or its investment arms.

To be accepted as a client at a white-shoe firm, you had to be a company of some size. You had to be financially responsible and provide proof of ability to pay the fees. You had to come up with a hefty retainer. There was a prestige factor in having them represent you. Taking on a new piece of business was carefully considered. It was not likely that a younger lawyer would bring in a new client.

At Finley, Kumble, by contrast, we encouraged everyone to develop new business. And our standards for accepting new business were, perforce, not as high as at some of these other firms.

Part of the appeal of being a lawyer is having someone choose you to represent them. It's a great ego trip. If someone you know and hold in high regard is confronted with a serious problem, and they ask you to help them, it is deeply satisfying. They are putting their faith and trust in you. And they are willing to pay.

When a client would call up his lawyer and tell him to send all his files over to Finley, Kumble, that lawyer would be livid. His financial well-being and ego were under attack because his client, someone with whom he thought he had a special association, had just been stolen. At Finley, Kumble, we went from virtually no business to 14,000 active matters. You can imagine how many unhappy lawyers there were across the country. You can also imagine the happiness and enthusiasm with which we were greeted when we pulled into a new community and said, "Here we are, boys." They looked on us as they would look on an outbreak of the bubonic plague.

Finley, Kumble picked up new clients in a variety of ways: in a social context or even on the other side of the table in negotiations. We'd get word-of-mouth recommendations. We'd write. We'd lecture. The firm, in its hiring, put a premium on the ability to attract clients. Most of the partners in the firm were socially adept. I suppose there are a lot of lawyers who don't know how to socialize with people, to get along with clients except on a purely business level. That was not the case with us. Almost universally, the people in the firm had qualities of personality and enthusiasm that allowed them to mix socially with clients. They had the incentive to develop business relationships with people they met. And they did it with a vengeance.

Early on, we began to operate on the notion that clients give their loyalties to lawyers, not to law firms. We concluded that the notion that a client was a client of the firm was misplaced. We noticed that lawyers who were leaving other firms to join us were bringing their clients with them. So, we began to operate on the assumption that if a lawyer left to join us, his clients would follow.

A further burr to the legal community was the style of the Finley, Kumble lawyers. Law is an adversarial profession to begin with, and we were enthusiastically adversarial. We tried hard in litigation. We tried to do the best for our clients, within the boundaries of ethics, but we were vigorous and aggressive.

And hated.

Some of it was pretty raw. One former associate with the firm, whose wife is an attorney as well, recalls a Christmas party at his wife's boss's home. They were standing around chatting and he was introduced to an older man, a lawyer. He asked the young fellow what he did. The associate told the older man that he, too, was a lawyer. When the older man asked who he was with and heard it was Finley, Kumble, he set down his drink, held his hands out in front of him with his two index fingers forming a cross, like you see in vampire movies, and backed away. He wouldn't talk to our associate for the rest of the evening.

We were tough and it caused some problems among our own people as well. One version of how things went comes from a lawyer who spent a couple of years with us and then left: "I think that lawyers in the firm gave good service to their clients and cases were won or lost on their merits. But the way they went about it, the style was abusive. I think hardball is fine, but they went beyond that. If you were on the other side and you wanted a delay because your wife was having a baby, they'd tell you to go to hell."

"They were always killers," says a litigator who dealt with our lawyers. "There is a certain reasonableness and decency that you usually find among lawyers, but these guys were madmen. They wouldn't give an inch even on little issues. You'd ask for a delay of a couple of days and they'd object. Things like that, that had no bearing on the outcome. They were mean-spirited. You got the impression that winning was not enough, that they were trying to kill you. It didn't win them any friends."

That may be, but such behavior has become common in the high-powered practice of the law, and the notable practitioners are not nice guys. Look at Skadden Arps. They do everything rough and tough, and who do they represent? Major American corporations. They managed to get a lock on the takeover business, and it was something the old, established Wall Street firms would not touch. Now, they would love to have that immensely lucrative business. In the mid-sixties, when Pennzoil sued Texaco for $12 billion contending that Texaco had illegally horned in on Pennzoil's agreement to take over Getty Oil, who did Texaco hire to defend them? Weil, Gotshal and Manges. They're not white-shoe. And who did Pennzoil hire? Joe Jamail, a man who got his start as a personal injury specialist.

When you look at big, important cases these days, who do you see? Wachtel, Lipton or Fried, Frank or Paul, Weiss. These firms were not considered part of the New York establishment fifteen or twenty years ago.

Steven Brill used to refer to Finley, Kumble, Wagner, Heine, Underberg, Manley, Myerson and Casey as a bunch of salesmen. And when the firm went under, the story in the *American Lawyer* ran under a headline that read, "Death of the Salesmen." It was one of the things people resented about us. We had a facility for selling ourselves. *Forbes* magazine called me the quintessential rainmaker. Other people said that I had developed this great idea about how to sell services. I can't conceive that I invented this. It is so elementary. The difference was that we actually did it. We had no rules against it; no culture that would prohibit it. We expanded the ways of getting new business and, as a result, there has been a sea change in the legal business, a change in attitude across the range of firms.

SEVEN

L ong before attitudes about the conduct of the practice of law changed, Marshall Manley had become one of change's prophets. He said out loud, in public, before witnesses that the law is a business.

Nobody wanted to hear that. Least of all, his partners in the California law firm of Manatt, Phelps, Rothenberg, Manley and Tunney.

Before Steven Brill founded the *American Lawyer*, he wrote for *New York* magazine and *Esquire.* It was to him that Marshall Manley spoke candidly on the subject of the law as a business, in an article *Esquire* ran in 1978. He told Brill, for example, "We come up against older guys who interviewed us for jobs when we were coming out of school and we kick the shit out of them." Despite the vindictive, even brutal tone of that statement, and Manley's assertion that he had "no qualms about stealing lawyers and clients from other firms," and that such practices formed the "keystone of our program," the piece seems tame by today's standards.

At the time, though, it was the buzz of the profession. Everyone was talking about it. I read the piece, and one day not long after it came out, Neil Underberg, I think it was, said that the fellow in the article was going to be in town and would I like to meet him. I said sure; I thought it would be interesting.

One of our important real estate clients was moving to California, and we wanted to open a California office as a way of keeping this client and as a way to grow. One of Neil's friends out there was a lawyer who had worked in New York and knew Marshall. This fellow had introduced Marshall to Neil a year before as a possible recruit for us, but Marshall was not interested in moving at that time.

Underberg heard that after the *Esquire* piece, Manley's partners at Manatt, Phelps had thrown him out of the firm. The *Esquire* article precipitated it, but it was probably coming anyway. Marshall's attitude, then as later, was that the only thing that matters is getting the business. And he pushed his weight around, demanding more and more and more money. In any organization, he could be overreaching.

Manley was born in Newark and grew up in Brooklyn. After Brooklyn College he had gone on to New York University Law School where he had done quite well. His first job after law school was in Los Angeles with McKenna and Fitting, where he quickly acquired the reputation of an incredibly hard-working and aggressive young lawyer. Both attributes paid off in the form of partnership in the firm, despite his having alienated older partners. But for Manley, whose forte was bringing business in the door, the reward of partnership was not enough. Manley let his partners know that he also deserved more money than they had put him down for.

Marshall's next stop was Manatt, Phelps, Rothenberg and Tunney, where the senior partners agreed with him that his compensation should be tied to his rainmaking abilities. Manley was on a vertical trajectory and his ability to initiate business made the firm one of the hottest practices in the country for a time.

Neil suggested that we meet with Marshall when he next came to New York. He was coming here because he had created such animosity with Los Angeles firms that his only hope was to make a deal with a non-LA firm that wanted to open an office on the West Coast.

From reading the *Esquire* article, I had a mental image of Manley as a man in a checked sports jacket, a real loudmouth. He was completely different from what I expected. He was dressed in a dark blue suit, a dark tie, black, well-shined shoes. He was well-spoken and quiet. In fact, during part of the first meeting I had to strain to hear him talk. He was very businesslike.

He talked in a way that I had not heard from many lawyers. He talked about law as a business. I was pleased because he talked about the law as I did; about business expansion and growth and the means to achieve them. He talked about what the short-, medium- and long-term goals were; where we could open new offices. He was very forward-looking, and I was impressed.

We made a deal. He would build the firm on the West Coast, and we would stake him.

When Marshall Manley left Manatt, Phelps, his main client was City Investing Co., which was headed by George Scharffenberger. The company was technically headquartered in New York, but the main operation was in Los Angeles. City Investing was a conglomerate that had been built up and run by Scharffenberger, a man who had bootstrapped himself to immense wealth. Manley had taken on a difficult case for the mogul in the early 1970s while still at McKenna and Fitting and so impressed Scharffenberger with his tactics and aggressiveness that he began throwing Manley a ton of business.

Scharffenberger had assured Marshall when he switched firms that City Investing would continue its relationship with him. Problem was, Manley had no office, no staff, nothing. The deal that he struck with Finley, Kumble was that we would provide the cash and other support necessary to start building a local firm in Los Angeles.

When Manley first joined us, he made his business home at City Investing's Beverly Hills office, at the corner of Wilshire Boulevard and Doheny. But even there, he really had no space that was his own, and he floated around. It worked for a while because City Investing itself was moving back to New York, and there was quite a bit of empty space. And he would use whatever space was available to meet clients and to work. It was certainly not a proper law office and it made recruiting difficult.

His first move was out to Century City where, as the California business began to grow, Manley and the new staff and partners set up shop in a beautiful suite of offices. Eventually, they outgrew that space and moved back to Beverly Hills and took over the space that City Investing had vacated.

That office was spectacular, the kind of thing you would expect the senior officers of a multi-billion dollar conglomerate to occupy, but not a law firm. It was plush. The furnishings bespoke money. And the place was decorated in great style and taste. The walls were done in fabric. The door frames were of polished steel.

For himself, Manley took over the old office of City Investing's chairman, George Scharffenberger. It was a knockout, with walnut panelling—a portion of which would slide away to reveal a wet bar—oriental rugs. As part of the suite, Manley had a private bathroom and changing room and a private dining room.

It was far better than our office in New York. We moved into new quarters at 425 Park Avenue at about the same time we recruited Manley. It was fine for a while, but because of our rapid growth we became so cramped that one of the criticisms leveled against the firm was that it resembled a sweatshop, where even partners toiled in windowless tiger cages. We later remedied that, but at the time, the difference was striking. Eventually, we expanded at 425 Park and took on two additional floors in the building. We then decided to spend some real money fixing up the offices. We knocked down walls, ordered all new furniture, built a new library, and installed a sophisticated computer system. It was a huge expense and was well done. But it never compared to the palatial digs the Los Angeles office occupied.

The leases, refurbishing, furnishings and equipment, and other costs involved in growing from a one-lawyer operation in Los Angeles to one with more than 150 attorneys were staggering. But the growth was remarkable, and the investment had a tremendous payoff. If the firm as a whole was, for a time, providing the financial juice that made the growth possible, it was Manley who was out hustling new lawyers and new business. He was terrific about promoting the firm and about using the City Investing relationship to romance new clients.

Some people think Manley and I should have been friends. Heine, for example, has said that since Marshall was a charismatic and strong leader, he and I should have been kindred spirits since we were both "very aggressive, very dynamic, very bright." Then he trashes us both. "And they really had no feel at all for any professional qualifications, strictures, restraints. When you talked about the legal product, each of them would say, 'What does it matter? The client is not smart enough to know whether it is good or bad.' "

There is no basis in fact for that criticism, but Heine's comments notwithstanding, Manley and I found, at least initially, that we had a lot in common. But after a while his grand business style and use of perquisites began to jar, and I thought he was doing things that sent the wrong signal to the other partners and the associates. Finley, Kumble paid very well, but we had always been careful about the perks the partners received. I felt strongly that they projected the wrong image. It is inconsistent for a lawyer to be driven around in a limousine while clients are struggling to make their payments on their bank loans. So, we discouraged that sort of thing. I was always big on avoiding first-class travel, for example. How can you travel first class when the client is sitting in the back of the plane? The way you lived was one thing, but the way you functioned professionally reflected the firm's image.

To give him his due, Manley was extraordinarily able as a recruiter, seeking out lawyers with impressive connections and clients and then parlaying them to expand both the firm itself and its business.

One of the more interesting lawyers he brought in to Finley, Kumble was Alan U. Schwartz.

Schwartz was well-known in the literary and entertainment law area. He started out at Greenbaum, Wolff and Ernst, the firm that distinguished itself in several areas, including representing the United States publisher of James Joyce's *Ulysses* after the book had been banned here. Schwartz had a reverse Midas touch with the firms he worked for. As of this writing, all but one of the firms he has worked for no longer exist. Greenbaum, Wolff and Ernst blew apart in a very public way. Schwartz was for several years a partner in New York's Barovick, Konicky, Schwartz, Kay and Schiff, which later merged with a Los Angeles firm to form Fulop & Hardee. The merged firm went bankrupt in 1982. Shortly after that, he came to Finley, Kumble. Despite his ill-starred choice of firms, Schwartz's resume is enormously impressive. His credentials as a human rights advocate and civil rights lawyer, particularly in the area of the First Amendment, are impeccable. And his client list reads like a who's who in the literary and entertainment areas. While he was still at Greenbaum, he represented Svetlana Alliluyeva, Joseph Stalin's daughter, as she made her way through the American literary maze after she defected from the Soviet Union and wrote her autobiography. The Russian novelist, Aleksandr Solzenitsyn, was also a client for a time. He has represented British playwright

Peter Shaffer for more than thirty years. He had Truman Capote as his client until his death, and subsequently represented Capote's estate. Writer David Halberstam is a client, as is director and producer Mel Brooks, who is also a close friend. When Brooks made the movie "Spaceballs," a send-up of "Star Wars," the shibboleth that ran through the movie was "May the Schwartz be with you." The Schwartz was Schwartz.

Getting him to Finley, Kumble was quite an accomplishment. He had no interest in joining us, but after Fulop & Hardee failed in 1982, Schwartz, who had recently relocated to the West Coast, felt like a displaced person. He was concerned about Finley, Kumble's reputation, but Manley was able to persuade him to come on to head up and build an entertainment practice for the firm.

He did a good job but was never a star at bringing in huge amounts of business. One of the problems was that he was preoccupied. In addition to practicing law, he found himself, at age fifty, facing the prospect of taking and passing the California bar exam. He had been practicing law for about twenty-five years, all except a few months of that time in New York. But if he was going to stay in California, he would have to be admitted to the state's bar. Any lawyer can tell you that preparing for and taking the bar exam—even when one is fresh from law school and the facility for memorizing trivia is at its peak—is a grueling and daunting experience. By the time a person hits middle age, that facility and the inclination to put up with the grind of preparation have fallen off considerably.

But if Schwartz wanted to practice, he had to pass. He took the exam once. He failed. He took it again. He failed. Finally, he basically had to retire from the practice of law for a while so he could cram for the exam, and he passed it on the third try.

Even though Schwartz never brought in the kind of business the firm's most productive members were able to develop, he added a luster and credibility to Manley's Califor-

nia operation that could be used by the office there to
attract attention and clients. Manley knew what he was doing.

And what he was doing was not unlike what we had done
elsewhere. But in Manley, more than with anyone else I had
brought into the firm, I had found my own true nemesis.

Like some who preceded him and others who followed
him at Finley, Kumble, Manley would come to mean trouble. One woman who watched the rise and fall of the firm
from an intimate vantage has said of me, "For all his ability
to deal with people on some levels, I don't think he was very
sophisticated psychologically. He deeply misperceived not
only some of the people he brought in, but their ability to
work for a larger cause. He brought in men who were of the
same stripe as he was: highly ambitious, ballsy, totally directed, and with an instinct for power; men who were interested only in their own work and their own prestige."

In a way, she's right. I thought I could manage all these
egomaniacs. It was a serious misjudgment, and in time, the
inmates took over the asylum.

The office in California was built by and dominated by
Marshall. He had recruited most of the people, and he ran
the operation with a carrot-and-stick approach. He used
the stick of compensation. The carrot was extra money. He
would give people money, lend them money, put them on a
board he controlled, get them on the management committee of the firm. He was constantly doing favors for people
and wanted them returned. I got the feeling after a while
that he was like a Mob godfather, and I took to referring to
him as "Don Vito." He did a favor for you; you returned the
favor. That may be standard practice in the godfather business, but it's not such a great idea in a law firm.

Marshall Manley was brilliant at certain things. He had a
sixth sense about people. He could see their weaknesses.
He was like a dog who can smell fear. And he exploited
those weaknesses to his advantage. Andy Heine needed a
friend in his dealings with me, and Manley became that

friend. Harvey Myerson needed money and the trappings of money, and Manley was able to provide that for him. Bob Washington wanted power and the appearance of power, status. And Marshall Manley was able to make those available for him.

People say that the California office was loyal to him. Whether that loyalty was a virtue or just the result of his masterly manipulation of the troops is something one might quibble about. I think it was manipulation.

But because of the loyalty he engendered, any confrontation that would have resulted in his departure would also have meant the disappearance of the whole West Coast operation. And while that was not obvious to me at the beginning, it became crystal clear as time went by. So, when I had disputes with Marshall, the question was always in the back of my mind: Do we want to lose the West Coast?

The answer was a resounding no. It was that simple. And the commitment to keeping the West Coast intact gave Marshall Manley safe haven, strengthened the base from which he could wield power, and became a major factor in the destruction of the firm. Manley was the kid who owned the football. And his partners at Finley, Kumble wanted to play.

After relations between Manley and me began to chill, I felt less than welcome on the West Coast and spent less and less time out there. Andrew Heine became the firm's liaison with the California operation and in the process allied himself with Manley.

So, the firm eventually tilted toward the West. But long before it did, I moved to bolster the firm in the power centers of the East and Southeast.

EIGHT

Each year on the second Saturday in November, the Washington International is run at Laurel Race Course, the Maryland track not far from the capital. The run on the turf attracts top horses from all over the world, and while it may be just another day at the races for capital-area horseplayers, it is one of a handful of crucial social and business occasions that brings together the currycombed international set.

It was an important event on the business calendar kept by Peggy Vandervoort, an internationally known thoroughbred breeder and bloodstock adviser. In 1978, I accompanied Peggy, whom I had met a few months before in Florida, to the race. We were the guests of her friends, John Schapiro, who owned the track, and his wife Ellie. Over the weekend, Ellie Schapiro and I chatted sociably, and she mentioned that her brother was a lawyer, too, practicing in Washington. "Perhaps you know him." she said. "Joe Tydings."

"You mean the former senator?" I replied. The very one. I said no, I didn't know Tydings, but I'd certainly like to meet him. But I never called him.

A year later, almost to the day, Peggy and I, then newly married, were once again at Laurel for the running of the Washington International, and Ellie Schapiro and I again were chatting. She said to me, "You know, my brother is here and I'd like to introduce you to him." So, I met Joe Tydings.

To my eye, Joe Tydings looked and sounded the way every senator should look and sound. He's a tall, distinguished-looking guy with a deep voice, an impressive man, well-connected socially. His father was U.S. Senator Millard Tydings. His grandfather, Joseph Davies, was ambassador to Moscow during World War II and was married to Marjorie Merriwether Post. Joe had grown up living the good life, and it showed.

I told him that I was in Washington on business frequently—which was an overstatement—and that maybe we could have lunch one day and talk about the possibility of doing something together. He asked what I had in mind, and I said maybe joining forces somehow. I didn't want to use the word merger.

He asked me, "Do you mean the possibility of combining our firms in a merger?"

I said, "Yes." And he said, no way, absolutely not, no interest at all, not a chance.

I took it more as a challenge than as a rebuff, and I persisted. Later, on some flimsy pretext, I made it a point to visit him in his office at Danzansky, Dickey, Tydings, Quint and Gordon, where he was the managing partner. It was a well-known Washington firm with 44 lawyers. At this time, Finley, Kumble had a total of about 135 lawyers.

Because Washington is the seat of government, it has always been a place where any major law firm must have a presence. Virtually all American companies have at least occasional contact with the federal government, either because they are regulated by some arm of the government or because they do business with the government. In either case, they need legal representation when dealing with the labyrinth of federal agencies. And while it is true that many law firms can handle that kind of business without being in Washington, there is a perception in the business community that negotiating with the federal government requires being represented by a firm that has influence with the federal government.

At certain times in history, who you knew was probably as important as what you knew. Today, with the spotlight on questionable arrangements with the Washington bureaucracy, things happen by and large on their merits. Still, companies want to be represented by a firm that knows its way through the bureaucratic maze and even though they might be convinced that things are decided on the merits, deep down they might not be so sure. So, their impulse is to hire a top-flight firm that also knows its way around the capital.

Most of our clients understood intellectually that we could handle their work concerning the government. But they still felt that they should be represented by a firm with a Washington presence. There is a Washington mystique, and it is encouraged by everyone who operates inside the Beltway. They really think that everything that goes on in Washington and everything people say in Washington is vitally important. And capital lawyers are no exception. They encourage the idea that only an attorney based in Washington is qualified to handle issues relating in any way to the federal government.

It is like the old joke about the judge who got a call from a plaintiff's lawyer: "If you decide in my client's favor, he'll give you $25,000."

The judge, taken aback, hung up on the lawyer. While he was weighing the proper course of action, the phone rang again. It was the defense counsel: "Your honor, if you find for my client, he will pay you $50,000."

The judge hung up and called the plaintiff's counsel. "I've been thinking about your offer. You're going to have to come up with an additional $25,000 . . . So I can judge this case on the merits."

In Washington, when you are up against another group represented by a politically well-connected firm, you believe you have to go out and hire an equally well-connected firm so the case will be decided on the merits.

By the time that I went to my second Washington International, in November 1979, the senior partners in Finley, Kumble had talked many times about the desirability of opening a D.C. office. Our firm was successful. The California operation was coming on strong. The New York office was doing very well. The foray into Florida, despite problems there, was turning a profit. And the firm was gaining notice for something other than having had a partner that went to jail. The upstarts were on a roll. Why not expand to Washington?

We reasoned that Finley, Kumble had the professional expertise to handle most matters dealing with the federal government, but since we had no Washington presence we were referring business to D.C. firms, or losing it to them outright. It was business that we had to find a way to keep. There were several ways to do that. One possibility was to send people down from New York. Another was to hire lawyers out of the bureaucracy. A third was to merge with a firm already there. We had explored all of those things, but it had come to naught.

Joe Tydings was then running Danzansky, Dickey, a fifty-year-old Washington firm that was, interestingly enough, principally involved not in dealing with the federal government, but with the local business of Washington. They had substantial clients and represented Giant Food, Potomac Electric Power Co., the National Bank of Washington, and a large group of other local clients including several major real estate developers.

The firm was also well-connected to the local political

scene. Robert B. Washington, a partner in the firm, had been chairman of the Democratic Committee of the District of Columbia and was a member of the National Democratic Committee. He was close to Washington mayor, Marion Barry, and was, in addition, a leader in the city's very important black community. Not much happened in the District of Columbia that Bob Washington did not have his finger in.

In addition, the firm was moving toward stronger connections at the federal level. They had a couple of former politicians. Frank Ikard, the former Texas judge and congressman was there, and, of course, Tydings, who had been brought in to give them additional muscle with the federal government. Unfortunately, Joe did not have much government-related business.

Tydings's main business was plaintiffs' anti-trust litigation, a legal specialty in which he represented entire classes of allegedly aggrieved parties who might have been damaged by activities that violated anti-trust legislation. It was a great source of business, but it created awful cash flow problems. It required a ton of work and generated enormous fees. But it took years to resolve, and the fees were contingent. Meanwhile, the firm had all these people working on these cases, absorbing a huge amount of cash. As a result, his firm was hurting financially.

Not long after our meeting at the track, I called Tydings, saying that I was going to be in Washington and invited him to lunch. I had no other reason for going except to talk to Joe. We had several such lunches as I pursued Tydings and his firm as merger partners. He was not at all enthusiastic about getting together with Finley, Kumble, but as time wore on, and the fortunes of Danzansky, Dickey, Tydings, Quint and Gordon continued to languish, he saw more and more benefit in our marriage. We could bring in out-of-state business and help create a solid federal government practice and improve his firm's fortunes.

I began to float the idea in New York. And as the conversations progressed, I expanded the circle of people who were involved. The negotiations were difficult, and it took nearly a year to come to an agreement. Under the arrangement to merge, we picked up all their debt and paid it off. Balancing that, we acquired their work in process and accounts receivable. One problem was that the plaintiffs' antitrust cases were the biggest single item on their books. They generated hefty fees, but only if you won. We decided not long after the merger to get out of that business. We'd finish the cases we had, but not take on anything new.

The details worked out, the two firms combined on February 1, 1981. Forty-two of the forty-four lawyers at Danzansky came along. Conspicuous by his absence was Stephen Danzansky, the son of Joseph B. Danzansky, the late head of the firm, who had subsequently become the chairman of Giant Food and then of the National Bank of Washington. I was not unhappy about young Danzansky's decision not to come along. I was told that Steve was too heavy for light work and too light for heavy work. His family name was on the firm, but he found himself working for a man who had taken over his father's role in the firm. He couldn't see himself in a continuing subservient position to Joe Tydings, and our agreement called for Joe to continue running things. So, Steve Danzansky saw himself losing both the firm name and any hope of real power. We had concluded that we didn't want young Danzansky, but for the sake of keeping the peace, Joe asked me to make an attempt to get him to come along. I met with him to try to convince him, but I failed in that effort. That was the good news.

The bad news, although I did not really care, was that we could not use the old firm's name. Initially, the merged Washington entity was to be known as Finley, Kumble et alia, but for a period of several years, the letterhead of the Washington office would have the former firm name printed in parentheses just below the Finley, Kumble name. Danzansky threatened to seek an injunction to prevent that.

So, the firm skipped the parentheses. It meant something to Tydings and Bernie Gordon and Milton Quint, whose names would disappear. But it didn't mean a thing to us.

What was important was that it was a merger of significant size. The combinations that Finley, Kumble had concluded prior to the Washington merger were minor compared to the cross-border takeover of the Washington firm. It was, at the time, one of the biggest law firm mergers ever. We were suddenly catapulted into the big time. And once again, I assumed that I could keep it all under control.

If there is a Washington mystique, and if among its practitioners are Washington lawyers, then there was little reason to expect that the same lawyers operating under a different name would change much. The Washington group that joined Finley, Kumble were and remained a cohesive group, loyal to each other and focused on their parochial presumption of their own importance.

The D.C. people merged with us as a result of my relationship with Joe Tydings, but because they were older and had been together for a long time, they retained a tremendous amount of autonomy and were close-knit, if not clannish. It was difficult to enforce a national system. Their loyalty was to each other, although for a time they were largely in our camp. That began to shift when Tydings' star began to decline.

It took a long time for us to develop a federal practice for them. And part of the problem had to do with Tydings himself. One of the things I discovered was that Joe was not the high-profile litigator I assumed he was. Even though he had been United States Attorney for Maryland, he was not a famous trial lawyer. And though he had been in the Senate, he did not have a big book of federal government-related business. In fact, Joe had little business besides his plaintiffs' anti-trust cases.

That whole practice created innumerable problems. The Danzansky firm had come close to going under because of the anti-trust work. Such cases were questionable enough, even when the anti-trust laws were actively enforced. But with the coming of the Reagan Administration in 1981, there was a widespread feeling, by no means discouraged by the administration, that anti-trust enforcement would be less than vigorous.

It was clear that the anti-trust practice had no future, and Finley, Kumble decided not to pursue the business further. I did not realize the impact that the decision would have on Joe. I assumed that he would be able to develop a thriving federal practice based on his connections and past experience. I was wrong. We took away his business and left him with nothing. This eroded his authority and power, and he was forced to go out at a late stage in his career and develop a whole new line of business for himself.

Joe and I had become friends. When I traveled to Washington, I stayed at Tydings's home. When Tydings stayed in New York, he stayed with us. After his separation from his wife Terri, Peggy arranged dates for ladies' man Tydings with, as she puts it, "really super, darling girls."

Whether or not the blow to Tydings's business was the motivation behind it is unclear, but when I was deposed, it was the former senator who lead the delegation that told me of the coup against me.

In Finley, Kumble, money may not have been everything. But it was close. The amount of business a lawyer brought in the door was dominant in setting compensation and was a good barometer of power and influence as well. After the senior people decided that the firm would take on no new anti-trust work, Tydings wasn't bringing much new business in the door.

Although Tydings was the D. C. firm's point man, he really did not control it. And as Tydings's fortunes fell, his authority in the office slipped. After a time, the management responsibility shifted. The man who came to run the D.C. office was Mitchell Cutler, a well-respected real estate lawyer. Cutler emerged as the big rainmaker in the office. Although he was first and foremost a Washington guy, his relationship with the rest of the firm was very good. He had a leavening effect on the attitudes of the Washington people vis-a-vis our other offices. He was a man of stature in the Washington legal and business communities and was respected throughout the firm as being something of a statesman. He had good judgment. He was mature and a good lawyer. He generally had the enthusiastic support of the people in the Washington office. But he did not like the administrative job. It took him away from the practice of law.

And as Cutler backed away, the task of running the D.C. operation began to pass to Robert Washington.

Mitch was a year younger than I was, but he looked ten years older. He was terribly overweight. He smoked heavily. He was a connoisseur of fine wines, and he loved good restaurants. He was big on rich desserts and fancy living. One day, he just fell over dead in his office. His loss was deeply felt throughout the firm. As a leader, he had no equal in the D.C. office.

At that point, Bob Washington took over the reins and pretty much isolated Tydings. Washington, a man well-known and well-connected in the nation's capital and beyond, had become a major player in a law firm that was rapidly achieving mega-firm status. He was a black man in a firm and a profession dominated by white men. A native of Blakely, Georgia, he was raised in Newark, New Jersey, had gone to college and law school at Howard University, and later done advanced legal studies at Harvard Law School. He lived in a grand house in the Foxhall section in northwest Washington, where his neighbors included his friend, the former presidential aide and political fixer, Michael Deaver.

Robert Washington was known around town as a man of vast charm, whose well-cut pinstripes and homburg set him apart. He has been described as "smooth as silk." He is also tough and clever and thick-skinned, as any politician must be. Controversy rolled off his back like rain off oilskins.

Well before the Finley, Kumble combination, he had been publicly criticized for his role as counsel to a federally subsidized small business agency that put up $450,000 to back a wine-importing firm in which Washington had a stake. Although he stepped aside as the agency lawyer while it was considering the matter, he returned to the post after the venture was approved. He told the *Washington Post* at the time, "I'm cleaner than Caesar's wife."

Whether or not Calpurnia would find the comparison complimentary, some of her husband's other intimates might have admired Washington's ambition and skill in rising to influence and power. In 1971, a year out of law school, he became staff counsel to the United States Senate committee on the District of Columbia. In 1973, after a stint in academe, he was named staff director and chief counsel of the House District Committee. In that position, he had a key role in drafting the home-rule legislation for the District of Columbia which became law in 1975. The change in status for the District from congressional fiefdom to self-governing city not only gave its citizens the right to run their civic life, but provided an enormous boon to well-connected lawyers. Before 1975, local businesses seeking advantage or backing for their causes and projects would lobby the Congress. Now, they found it necessary to seek out the locally-elected mayor and city council. It was a need they found they could best fill with the help of the city's cadre of black lawyers. Robert Washington, with close ties to the city council's chairman and his position on the D.C. Democratic committee, benefited more than most.

In 1975, Robert Washington joined Danzansky, Dickey, Tydings, Quint and Gordon. With the firm's extensive network of local business and financial connections, and with his own ties to the black establishment and its nascent political power structure, Washington, then in his early thirties, was on the fast track to becoming one of the city's most important lawyers.

By early 1981, when the Danzansky firm was merged into

Finley, Kumble, it was not only Washington, D.C., that had seen the exercise of black political muscle. No major American city has so great a proportion of black citizens, but many American cities had elected or were on the verge of electing black mayors. All those black mayors were Democrats. And Robert Washington knew them all.

Bob Washington's importance in the firm and his practice took an important turn with the rise of black politicians in the United States. Finley, Kumble had for a long time been trying to get into the municipal bond business. It was a prestigious—and at that time a very lucrative—area of legal practice. It was a big plum, and we did not have a piece of it.

Among the difficulties in getting such business is a Catch-22 in qualifying as a bond counsel. There is a publication called the *Bond Buyers' Guide,* a publication that, among other things, lists all the law firms and all the lawyers within those firms whose opinions can be accepted by underwriters of municipal securities. If an attorney wants to issue legal opinions on the securities, his name must be inscribed among the *Bond Buyers' Guide* elect. The way to get his name on the list is by having rendered opinions that are accepted by municipal underwriters.

If we couldn't render an opinion unless we were in the Guide, and if we couldn't be listed in the Guide without having rendered opinions, how could we get into the Guide? We thought about this and decided to find someone who was in the Guide and bring him into the firm. We'd recruit our way into the Guide. So, we took on a fellow named Jim Normile from Mudge Rose, the firm where the late John Mitchell had been one of the nation's premier bond counsels before joining the Nixon administration. Normile helped establish our firm's credentials. As he began rendering opinions as a member of our firm, he would include the names of other lawyers from the firm who were working with him. After a while, we had a whole string of lawyers at Finley, Kumble who were listed in the *Bond Buyers' Guide.*

That was half the battle.

The other half is that the municipal finance business is political. Very political. It is not for nothing that major Wall Street investment banks and securities dealers are among the major contributors to the political campaigns of candidates for such seemingly innocuous offices as state, city, and county treasurers and comptrollers. In many places, those who hold such offices have a great deal to say about who underwrites the billions and billions of dollars worth of public finance that is issued each year. Nor is it for nothing that such firms go out of their way to hire people who know their way around the political clubhouses and county buildings and statehouses across the country. Old politicians never die. But instead of fading away they go to work for Merrill Lynch, or PaineWebber, or Shearson Lehman Hutton, or Kidder, Peabody.

Among law firms, it does not hurt to have in the firm a former mayor of the City of New York as a name partner. Nor does it hurt to have in the firm the former governor of the State of New York, or the former governor of Nevada. Or the daughter of the former president of Cuba. Or the fellow who ran the unsuccessful gubernatorial campaign of the mayor of Los Angeles. Or a former congressman with close political ties back home in Texas or Florida. Or a man who knows every black politician worth knowing in the United States.

Not only does the firm have to be in the *Bond Buyers' Guide,* but it must also have a reputation. And equally important, it must have cordial relations with people who run for office. It is a cordiality that is enhanced mightily by contributing to their campaigns—with dollars or sweat or both.

For Finley, Kumble, the final ingredient was Bob Washington getting in the fold. The mayor of Chicago was black. The mayor of Atlanta was black. The mayor of Los Angeles

was black. The mayor of Philadelphia was black. The mayor
of Washington, D.C., was black. When our firm had its
annual meeting in Los Angeles, Tom Bradley was the fea-
tured speaker at our dinner, and he issued an official proclamation declaring Finley, Kumble, Wagner Day. And another year, when we had the meeting in D.C., Marion Barry
was invited to speak and he, too, issued a proclamation
declaring it Finley, Kumble Wagner Day. We did not look
like carpetbaggers.

We did whatever we had to do to make the world go
around.

It went around very well for Robert Washington and for
the D.C. office of Finley, Kumble. Added to his ability to
bring in local business, Washington's rainmaking prowess
now extended well beyond the Beltway. His stature grew.
The business origination for which he was credited surged.
And Tydings, the patrician who had been an intimate of the
Kennedys, found himself pushed further and further into
the background.

Eventually, the municipal bond business became a cropper. The reform of the United States tax code, which culmi-
nated in the passage in October 1986 of the Tax Reform
Act, was killing the municipal bond business as Congress
slashed away at the number and kinds of projects that could
be financed with tax-free securities. The more celebrated
effects of the changes in the law were seen in the disappearance of new issues of industrial development bonds and in
the withdrawal from the market of so important a player as
Salomon Brothers, Inc. But through the middle years of the
1980s, business was brisk, and in 1985 and 1986 the antici-
pation of tax reform led to a staggering rush to market that
enriched both underwriters and lawyers.

It was not only local businesses that needed influence
with the local establishment in the city of Washington. One
notable example was Citibank. The 1927 McFadden Act
had forbidden banks from crossing state lines to do a full-
range of banking business. But over the years, changes in

the law had set the stage for interstate banking. Chief among those changes were laws that allowed states to set up reciprocal agreements among themselves to allow banking companies access to their markets. New York, whose huge banking organizations want to blanket the country, passed a law that allowed banks headquartered in any of the other forty-nine states entry into New York. Other states combined to structure regional pacts to keep out the New York giants. Virginia and Maryland did not want the likes of Citibank opening retail offices in Arlington and Chevy Chase, and their laws reflected that.

But the District of Columbia was another matter. So what if many of the affluent retail customers that Citibank was pursuing lived outside the District? They may have lived in the suburbs, but hundreds of thousands of them worked in Washington itself, and the power of deciding which banks might cross the border into the capital city belonged to the D.C. Council. Citicorp wanted to have the rules in the District of Columbia changed to allow out-of-state banks to operate there, so they hired Finley, Kumble. There was one reason. Bob Washington.

Initially, Robert Washington seemed content to practice law. He had become a major rainmaker in the firm, but as Tydings's business fell off and Cutler wanted less and less responsibility for the running of the firm, that began to change. Andrew Heine, whose war with me was heating up, sought out Washington. As he tells it: "I was the first one who pushed him to get into the administration of the firm instead of running off to Nigeria and Antigua and London and various places. We were having a management commit-tee meeting in Washington, and I had been out to dinner with some people. As I came back to the hotel, I ran into Bob in the lobby and invited him up to my room for a drink, and we stayed up until four in the morning talking. I told him where he was going in the wrong direction and that he should get more involved in the operations of the firm. I told him that he was the wave of the future. He was younger than we were, very dynamic and very smooth. And really, in D.C. there was no one else to compete with."

I do not know what was in Heine's mind at the time, but that may have been the foundation-laying for the cabal that would eventually take over, and destroy, the firm.

During the same period of time that we were completing the negotiations with Tydings and the D.C. firm, I had begun a series of conversations with Hugh Carey, who planned to step down as governor of New York at the end of his second term at the end of 1982.

Hugh distinguished himself over seven terms in the U.S. House of representatives before returning to New York in 1974 to run for governor. He was a close friend of Bob Wagner's, and while Carey was winding down the last months of his long public service career, Wagner, with my blessing, encouraged him to talk with Finley, Kumble. We met and began to talk seriously about his joining the firm.

He and I hit it off. It was clear that he was a man of great magnetism and intelligence and spirit and decency. He had a dozen kids; he had lost his first wife to cancer and two of his children in an automobile accident. During the time that he was governor, New York City went through its fiscal crisis, and it was Hugh Carey, more than any other individual, who saved the city from bankruptcy.

Bringing him into Finley, Kumble was a rare opportunity for us. We had several conversations and I felt that he would make a genuine contribution to the law firm.

He did make a large contribution to the firm. His intelligence, his abilities as a leader, his legal acumen all made a great difference. Because of his long political experience, he had unrivalled knowledge of the inner workings of business and municipal finance, and he was forever coming up with sound ideas about how to solve difficult problems. He was a resourceful and creative lawyer.

But it did not stop there. Obviously, having the former governor of the State of New York as a partner could be expected to bring a cachet and prestige to the firm that clients would find attractive. Part of his appeal was that business would come to us because he was in the firm. But when he did come on board, Hugh Carey was not content to let business seek him out. Even though he had been governor, he did not feel it beneath him to get out of his chair and work actively to develop new business for the firm, and he was a substantial business originator.

I like and respect Hugh Carey, and in the years that we were partners, we became close. Hugh served as a lieutenant colonel in the Army and was decorated as a hero in World War II. He was one of the first Americans to enter and liberate the Nazi concentration camps. He was a courageous man and faced trouble head-on as a soldier, as a congressman, and as governor of New York. When Finley, Kumble developed the serious problems that would finally destroy the firm, he sought solutions to those difficulties. It was an endeavor doomed to failure since we did not know that the structure, philosophy, and business of the firm had been undermined by the personal and financial relationships among a small clique at the top. He could have run the firm better than I, because he was a gifted leader. But the problem was that the four horsemen of the apocalypse were not going to be led by anyone.

NINE

For many New Yorkers, Florida is a state of mind, a place where they spent holidays as children. It is Miami Beach or Fort Lauderdale or a dozen other spots where their parents, retired from business and tired of New York, have fled and now live year-round. It is New York South with a Latin flavor, complete with Bronx-accented speech tinged with Yiddishisms.

To my mind, that is a naive and inaccurate view. There may be a lot of Jewish expatriates from New York living in Miami Beach and other Florida communities. There are important Cuban communities as well in Miami proper. They are a significant part of the economic lifeblood of the city and substantial legal business comes from those segments of the community. But Miami is still a southern city, in a Deep South state. It is run by the old establishment. The members of that establishment are southerners. They vacation in Georgia and the Carolinas. They go to WASP heaven, Hilton Head, in the summer. It is a whole different scene from what New Yorkers might imagine. And you don't get piped in, really piped in, to the Miami community unless you are part of that establishment. It's not Miami Beach. It's not Palm Beach. It's not black. And it's not Jewish or Cuban. At bottom, Miami is a good-old-boy village. And if you understand that, then you can survive there.

A New York law firm parachuting into town to show the local boys how to practice would look like a bunch of carpetbaggers. And they would not succeed.

It took us several years to understand that. The firm had learned the painful lessons taught by a pair of false starts. We had established several significant business connections. And, on the personal side, I had married a woman whose engagement announcement, detailing her accomplishments and background, filled half a page in the *Miami Herald*. In 1982, with all of that in place, Finley, Kumble at last came to grips with the south Florida culture and began the highly successful pursuit of the practice of law there.

I had first cast my eye South early in the firm's life. One of my initial, and most important clients, one that I brought with me from Amen, Weisman, Finley and Butler when Finley, Kumble was formed, was Richard Cohen. He was a big shopping center developer, a very successful young fellow, who was married at the time to Victor Posner's daughter. Victor appointed him vice chairman of every company he owned or controlled.

Posner's corporate empire, which by the mid-1980s began to unravel, was then on a roll. He was busy swallowing up companies using the creative financing techniques for which he became famous, if not infamous. He was a controversial and colorful figure, whose financial machinations skirted the line of legality. The SEC and the Justice Department were engaged in a seemingly endless investigation of him and his activities. At the time, however, the daring, and, many feel, exciting Victor Posner was viewed with a certain romanticism as a latter day buccaneer. It was not

until a decade or more later that it would become clear that
some of his dealings may have fallen across the line of
legality, and his name would be linked to one of the biggest
financial scandals of the century. While still serving a
community service sentence on a tax fraud conviction in
mid-1988, Posner was named in the vast SEC-Justice Department inside-trading investigation involving Drexel
Burnham Lambert and former stock arbitrageur Ivan Boesky.

Still, even in the mid-1970s, Posner's style had earned
him an army of establishment enemies. Because of his manner and character, Victor was having a difficult time dealing
with the banks, so Richard Cohen became his spokesman
with institutional lenders. I had a close association with our
own banker, Frank Wright, and introduced Posner to
Wright and the Manufacturers Hanover Trust Co. It was an
introduction that led to the bank doing hundreds of millions of dollars worth of business with Posner.

Finley, Kumble handled the legal work on those financing deals. They involved not only traditional corporate
lending work—term loan agreements and the like—but
also a great deal of due diligence work on specific companies. Under due diligence rules, before financing can be
provided, a company is investigated to insure that it is in
fact organized under the laws of the state in which it is
doing business; that it is qualified to do business in the
states where it does business; that the loan agreement has
been approved by the board of directors and anyone else
from whom approval is needed; that if the agreement gives
the bank a lien on assets, the assets really exist and are
properly valued; that the agreement is not inconsistent with
any other agreements or loan documents the company has
entered into; and that it is a legally binding obligation of
the company. The reason for such detail is simple enough:
if a company later defaults or otherwise refuses to repay the
loan, the law firm that has expressed the opinion that the
loan documentation has been done properly can be sued

and held liable if the agreements are faulty. So, it is very important to be certain that the legal work, including due diligence, has been done properly.

Due diligence done, however, a lawyer who expresses such an opinion in Florida must say that all those things are valid under Florida law. Not being members of the Florida bar, we had to rely on a Florida firm for the opinion. That firm would insist on repeating the work we had already completed. Why give someone else a fee? Why not do it all ourselves? Why not have a Florida office?

Posner also figured in the second line of reasoning leading to the establishment of a Florida office. We were doing a lot of legal work for Victor. Posner was a man who attracted a phalanx of well-wishers who were interested in getting business from any of the companies he controlled. He gave out hundreds and hundreds of thousands of dollars worth of legal business. Firms that were around, that were on the scene, would be more likely to get some of that business. We decided it would be appropriate for us to have a permanent presence there, so we opened a small office with two or three fellows, led by Bob Mallow.

Much of Mallow's practice had been in representing lending institutions in real estate deals. As it turned out, we staffed the Miami office with the wrong kind of people. We should have had corporate lawyers and litigators, but instead had real estate lawyers. We thought we could build on what we started with, but it proved to be impossible to get Bob Mallow to do the recruiting necessary to build up the office. After a couple of years, he left to join Morgan, Lewis and Bockius.

I began again to look for someone to head up a Miami operation. A woman who worked for our firm as a secretary called to say that she was leaving to go to work for a Miami lawyer she had worked for in the past. The lawyer, she told me, was thinking of leaving Fine, Jacobson, the firm he was with, and might be available. Would we be interested? I told her we would. It made sense. It would give us an instantaneous presence and credibility in the Miami area.

I met with the lawyer, J. Arthur Goldberg, to discuss a potential merger. He reported that his firm itself was not interested in merging, but he and several other lawyers from the firm would like to join us. He suggested that we take them on as a group. I thought that was a terrific idea and sold it to my partners. Andy Heine and Neil Underberg and I negotiated the package deal by which Goldberg joined Finley, Kumble to head up a Miami practice with his group.

Goldberg insisted all along that he was no administrator and had no interest in being one. He told me that if I thought he was going to be responsible for day-to-day management, I was wrong. I decided he was just being modest. It turned out he was absolutely correct. He was one of the worst administrators I've ever met. He would occasionally show up in the office wearing blue jeans, an open shirt showing off gold chains around his neck, no socks. I was always on him about time sheets and cash receipts and his failure to supervise the growth and progress of that office. It was profitable, but only marginally. It was a struggle to get him to conform to the requirements of the firm in terms of time-keeping and billing.

It got worse over time. I am a stickler on such things, and Goldberg was just not interested. Other issues surfaced. I tried one day to call the Miami office from a pay phone. I didn't have the number with me and called information. The operator told me the office had an unpublished number. A law firm with an unpublished number? Unbelievable.

It was difficult to bring lawyers of substance into that operation. After a while, it became clear the problem was Goldberg. People would not join us either because they didn't like Goldberg, or because they didn't want to work in an office he was running. He didn't have the kind of image or stature necessary to recruit a lawyer with a big book of business, and he refused to share authority. Finally,

Goldberg and his people weren't even returning phone calls. I kept finding it necessary to intervene in the administration of the office. We were constantly arguing. The arrangement was unsatisfactory from their standpoint and from mine and the rest of the firm's. After Goldberg realized I was working to replace him, he left.

The way he left made Finley, Kumble and me the laughingstock of the Miami legal community.

One Saturday morning, about ten o'clock, I got a call at home from Phil Bloom, one of the partners down in Florida. He said to me, "I'm in the office, Steve. Something strange has happened."

"Yeah, Phil, something strange? Strange like what?"

And he said to me, "All the furnishings are gone. All the pictures and diplomas are off the walls of the offices."

I said, "What do you make of that?"

And he said, "Well, either we're redecorating or they've moved."

And I said, "Wait a minute. It's ten o'clock on Saturday morning. Were you in the office yesterday?"

He said, "Yes."

"What time did you leave the office?"

"Six or six-thirty."

"You mean between six last night and ten this morning, they moved, and you didn't know that was going to happen? Who's left?"

And he said, "Me. And Mike Maher."

"You mean they pulled a truck up in the middle of the night and moved?"

Well, that is exactly what had happened. They had been planning this move for months, and I think it was a couple of days later that we got a notice of withdrawal from J. Arthur Goldberg and two or three other partners and all the associates. They had opened a new firm and had taken all the client files and records. We ultimately had an arbitration proceeding to determine what they owed the firm. It was a mess.

It was, to a great degree, my doing. I found Goldberg, and I was the one who helped build the office. Their midnight exodus was greeted with derision. One newspaper cartoon showed me flying down to Miami to an office building that was all boarded up.

The day after I got the call from Phil Bloom, I flew to California for a management committee meeting scheduled for Monday. I went to a partners' cocktail party at Manley's house in Malibu on Sunday night, but I was so embarrassed about what had happened that I couldn't tell anyone about it.

The next morning, I stood up at the management committee meeting and said, "Before the meeting begins, I have an announcement. Remember all the problems we were having down in the Florida office? Well, the problems are all gone." Then, I told the story.

Joseph Tydings, who at this time was an ally, supported me, saying the firm should see the midnight departure as a clean sweep of the problems in Miami and an opportunity to fix the situation there.

I was humiliated and disappointed. Goldberg should have given us notice, and when the matter went to arbitration, he and the others who left lost their entire interest in the partnership and had to pay us a significant amount of money. We were very tough in those proceedings. I wanted to discourage anything like it from happening again, so it was a way of sending an important message: If you can't get along, you can leave, but the fair thing is to do it in a professional way, not in the middle of the night when the moon is down.

I found the situation in Florida discouraging. I had married a woman from south Florida, from Coral Gables. Her father was an important executive at Southeast Bank, and she was well-known in the Miami community. Her name appeared regularly in the society columns of the local papers, and she knew all the big hitters in the Miami area. I was running around trying to develop business in some measure through her contacts. So the failure, for the second time, of our Florida office was humiliating.

Some of my partners suggested we give up on this Florida idea. They felt that Miami was a backwater town and really had no room for a New York-style firm. I was disheartened. They asked, why focus on a place where progress was impossible? Still, Florida was appealing to me. In addition to the business the firm already had in Florida, there was potential from the state's economic strength. I knew if I found the right combination of people, it would be a home run, as indeed it turned out to be.

Forty or fifty years ago, Florida was, in fact, a backwater, whose only appeal to New Yorkers was as a vacation spot. But that is in the long-distant past. By the early 1980s, it had become one of the two fastest growing states in the union. It was a dynamic, growth-oriented place. It was a right-to-work state. Energy costs were low. It had a vibrant business climate, and the state itself, as well as many localities, was very aggressive about attracting new business. It was the U.S. center for banking and trade with Latin America. It had tremendous population growth. If the trends continue, it will be the third most populous state by the end of the century. It is a great place for a law firm to prosper.

If that law firm can put things together.

After Goldberg's departure, the only partner we had in Florida was Bloom, and I began another search for lawyers to join the firm and staff the Miami office. I interviewed a whole raft of people. I went through Martindale-Hubbell's Miami listings and made cold calls. The conversations were awkward because I was calling people who were successful and happy where they were, telling them I wanted to take them away and bring them to a place where we had failed twice, the second time in an embarassing and public way. I didn't get a great reception. People were not saying, "Gee, we can hardly wait for you to come down. We'll meet you at the airport with a brass band."

I was looking at Miami from the outside, but I was married to someone who was an insider. And it suddenly dawned on me that if we were going to be successful in Miami and south Florida, we would have to build a firm with the look, the image, and the feel of a genuine Miami outfit. So, I set about finding a group of lawyers who would fill the bill.

On one of my regular trips to the firm's Washington office, I was visiting with one of my partners, the late Mitchell Cutler, bemoaning my lack of success in finding the right people for Florida. Mitch told me he knew a fellow down there who was a terrific lawyer with a boutique firm, Tew, Critchlow, Sonberg, Traum and Friedbauer. He said he had a great deal of respect for this man, but was certain he would have absolutely no interest in becoming part of Finley, Kumble. But, he said, he'd be a great person to talk to and to seek out advice about good people in Miami. I didn't think there was much sense in talking to another lawyer about moving into his community and trying to take business away from him. But I talked to the fellow anyway, the first time on the speakerphone in Mitch Cutler's office. It was Tom Tew. And in that first conversation, he made all the right sounds.

I had read about his firm in the *American Lawyer*. The publication had run an article on outstanding small firms, and his was one of them.

Tew grew up in south Florida. He played football at Coral Gables High School and graduated from Dartmouth and the University of Miami Law School. Peggy knew him and remembered him as "this dreamboat high-school football hero." When I called, Tew knew about Finley, Kumble's failures to establish a beachhead in Miami, but he also knew who I was in local terms as well—Peggy Basten Vandervoort's husband. He was not so uninterested as Cutler had predicted.

So, I went down to Miami to meet with him, and after several meetings, convinced him to join Finley, Kumble. There was instant chemistry between Tom Tew and me, at least from my standpoint. He was an extremely bright, alert, hardworking individual, who was, among other things, a distinguished and successful lawyer. He had not made it to the big time, however, and his firm was getting by, but not flourishing. He was making only about $130,000. Why were they not making significant money? Because they were not following the kind of plan Finley, Kumble had, and they did not have access to some of the big clients and big businesses in Florida.

What they did have was a far more collegial concept of the practice of law than at Finley, Kumble. Tew was more of an egalitarian than anyone I knew. He was low key. He did not believe in fancy offices or in great differentiation between partners in compensation levels. He really took care of his people. He was also given to consulting with his partners at length on decisions affecting the firm. He arranged a meeting between me and a group of his partners.

They had something closer to a democracy than we did, and he had to consult with every one of his partners. I met with them, and the reception was chilling. I talked about Finley, Kumble and tried to explain away our difficulties in Miami. We had lost Goldberg. We had lost Mallow. They still remembered Bob Persky's indictment and conviction. They were worried about our reputation. I said we had made mistakes, and I accepted the blame for all of them. But I told them, and I believe this to be true, that a lot of the criticism against Finley, Kumble was the result of envy on the part of other firms we were beating in court or whose lawyers or business we were taking away. Our offices in N.Y., L.A., and Washington were becoming a huge success.

And I convinced Tom and his partners.

Not long after I made contact and started negotiating with Tew, Critchlow, I began to romance another Miamian, John Schulte, a partner at Smathers and Thompson, the very establishment firm of Senator George Smathers. Once again, there was the connection through my wife. Peggy had known Schulte's wife since high school. They had,

moreover, gone to Indiana University's distinguished
school of music together, where Peggy studied voice and
Joanne Schulte piano and organ. Later, the connection
continued with Joanne playing the organ at the Episcopal
church where Peggy's sister and brother-in-law ran the music program.

During the negotiations with Tew, Critchlow, I pursued
Schulte. He was leaving or thinking about leaving Smathers
and Thompson, and we started talking. The conversation
expanded to include Harry Durant, another partner in
Smathers and Thompson, who was a member of the firm's
executive committee and a person of some reputation in
the community. These two men represented a number of
banks in south Florida and bringing them on board seemed
to me a clear way into the establishment pipeline in Miami.
The problem was that Tom Tew and John Schulte knew
each other. And there was not a chance in hell these two
men would ever be willing to practice law together. Not in a
million years. It was just one of those things. In some re-
spects they were much alike. They were both bright and
ambitious and good lawyers. In others, they were very different. Tew was low key and egalitarian. Schulte was flamboyant and something of an elitist. He was always talking
about the Riviera Country Club and the Surf Club and the
kind of clubs that don't admit people like me—New York,
Jewish. John was very proud of the fact that he belonged to
the Riviera.

Miami is a very clubby place, much more than New York.
And there is one club in Palm Beach, the Everglades Club,
that is the most WASP club outside South Africa. Jews and
blacks could never be members. But, more important, a Jew
or a black, could not even go into the club; could not walk
in the front door. Schulte often talked about his desire to
belong to the Everglades and was amused by the sour expression on my face when he mentioned it.

He always had the finest clothes and Mercedes automo-

biles, and when he traveled, it always had to be first class.
Tew would travel economy.

Convinced that neither man would want to have anything
to do with the other professionally, I nevertheless persisted
in this dual negotiation.

I saw in Schulte a way for the firm to get into the Miami
establishment, and I felt that having these two lawyers together in the same firm would be a coup. We would create
something out of whole cloth, with a whole book of banking
business and, boom, we'd be right there. This all sounds
crazy, but it is exactly what I did. As I negotiated with Tew, I
subtly hinted that I was talking with John Schulte, but im-
plied that nothing was likely to come of it. And when I was
negotiating with Schulte, I hinted in the same way that I was
talking with Tom Tew.

As we got farther down the road, I disclosed more to
each of these groups about how I was negotiating with the
other group. But I never really brought them together until
I made a deal with both.

Then I left town. I made a deal with the two disparate
groups and literally ran away. It was explosive. At the beginning, they were in the same firm, but I left it to their own
conclusion whether they were really partners of each other
or of Finley, Kumble or both. The office had built into it the
possibility that it could implode at any moment. John didn't
like Tom's way of doing things. Tom didn't like John's way
of doing things. And neither of them liked Harry Durant.

Harry thought he was running the firm. I said to him,
"You and Tom and John are going to run the firm."

And he said, "Yes. But I'm the senior person, right?"

"Absolutely," I told him. He was certainly senior in age. I
never said anything about that to Tom and John, but I
hoped that when I left town, having made the announce-
ments about the Miami firm, they would get along with each
other.

It didn't happen quite that way. Very shortly thereafter,
Harry attempted to formalize his sense of seniority, and it

became clear that the other two were not buying it. The phone to New York never stopped ringing. I'd get phone calls from each of them every day in the weeks that followed whining and complaining about the others.

One of our first efforts was to have a big party, a dinner at Grove Isle, a private club, for the big hitters in the Miami community. In addition to the Miami people, we planned to have several of the key players in the firm—Bob Wagner, Hugh Carey, Joe Tydings—go down for the dinner. It was a press draw, a way to impress clients and potential clients, and get the office off to a roaring start.

But I had not bargained on the Miami people feuding as much as they were. I really did not know the extent of the discord until one night I was awakened from a sound sleep at two in the morning by a call from Harry Durant.

"Hello. Steve?"

"Yes. Who is this?"

"This is Harry. I'm very upset. The boys insist on having chicken. I told them we should have beef."

"What are you talking about?"

"For the dinner. They insist on having chicken for the dinner and I said it looks cheap, and they are trying to ride over me on this chicken thing."

I don't remember now what we had, but I do remember later on that morning calling Tew and Schulte and insisting we have whatever it was Harry wanted. Otherwise, he was going to abandon the firm.

Another stone in my shoe was Phil Bloom. I had recruited Phil, and he worked with the Goldberg group after they joined us in the second incarnation of the Miami office. He was a litigator, but better known among his partners as a tennis player. Goldberg and others made jokes about him behind his back. After Goldberg and his people departed in the dark of a Friday night and I recruited Tew and Schulte, I insisted, despite their resistance, that Phil be part of the new office. As time passed, Tew and Schulte began to heckle me about Bloom. They didn't think much of him and were forever suggesting that I help Phil find a new home. It was something I was reluctant to do because of his loyalty during the earlier problems with the Florida office. I supported him over their clear objections. The problem was solved when Bloom ran for and was elected to the circuit court bench. He's still a judge.

Despite the disasters that marred our first two attempts at expanding to Florida, and despite the creaky and potentially fractious beginning my own intrigues created, the third Miami manifestation of Finley, Kumble became a textbook example of what I was trying to create all along.

With the imposition of Finley, Kumble's sometimes ruthless time-keeping, billing, and collection system, the firm started making more money quickly. The idea of a local firm with ties to New York, California, and Washington came to fruition. The social connections, exploited to the hilt, began to pay off.

One thing I did was use my wife's social position and stature to help promote the firm. In Miami, Peggy was well-known and well-connected. She was right at the top of the social ladder, and I'm sure her family stood on their heads when she brought home this divorced, New York Jewish lawyer.

Peggy was chairman of the Flamingo Ball, one of the most prestigious social events in south Florida. It was held the night before the Flamingo Stakes race at Hialeah to benefit the American Cancer Society. It attracted socialites from all over the United States, and for the local Miamians who were invited, it was a big deal. So, when we went down to Miami and did the merger to get the office going, I knew John Schulte would do cart-wheels over being invited; he'd just die. We'd take two tables and invite John and his wife and the Tews and several of our other Miami people and the mayor of Miami. And then we'd also have Bob Wagner or Hugh Carey or Harry Helmsley down from New York, and there'd be photographers all over our tables and pictures in the paper the next day. It was the sort of thing that would impress clients, or if not clients themselves, clients' wives.

The next day, there in the papers for all to see, were the black-tied partners of the Miami office of Finley, Kumble, not only lawyers of some reputation, but now social lions as well. We had it all figured out. And the firm promoted itself not as the Miami office of a New York firm, but a Miami firm with offices in New York, Washington, and California. The trick was to create a local firm with local people who acted in line with local mores and were plugged in to the local power structure and establishment.

Some of my former partners criticized me for out-WASP-ing the WASPs in Miami. I think it's just a question of blending in, of promoting an ecumenical look. Jerry Kowalski, for example, complained that the firm did not hire young lawyers with good credentials that he had recommended because, although they had graduated high in their Harvard or Columbia Law classes, they had been undergraduates at Yeshiva and all I wanted in the firm were WASPs with Roman numerals after their names. I find the criticism totally off-base. Six of the firm's eight name partners were Jewish as were scores of other partners, including Kowalski.

I was a firm believer that when in Rome, you wear a toga. If you are going to deal with good-old-boys, you might just as well have some good-old-boys to do the dealing. I was always careful to match clients with attorneys, just as I would not seat together at a dinner party two people who did not like each other or who I thought would not get along. Law firms are reluctant to talk about it, but in those days, no firm would send a black man to open its office in Johannesburg or someone named Goldberg to open its office in Damascus.

Less controversially, I disliked beards and mustaches in a business context. I couldn't stand them. I admit it. I hated lawyers in the firm to wear beards because I was concerned that clients might not like it. Some clients might not mind;

others might. But nobody objects to a man with no facial hair. So, I said, no beards. I got a lot of flack over that. The issue points to the importance we placed on image, on getting clients up to the door and doing nothing that would turn them off before they even got into the room.

There was a time when Wall Street firms were considered bastions of anti-Semitism. And I suspect that came from the feeling of those running those firms that their clients would not be receptive to people who would not be welcome as members, or even as guests, at their clubs, and who would not fit from a social point of view. Fortunately, that attitude is no longer evident.

Miami, today, has a distinct Latin flavor, but Miami, and Florida generally, are still hotbeds of old southern attitudes. In the recent past, there were whole sections of Miami where Jews, Cubans, and blacks could not buy homes. While Jews and Cubans have made tremendous contributions to the business and artistic life of that city, my sense is that the establishment group, with its old-boy network, has not welcomed them unreservedly. I personally detest that attitude, but I am not about to change the world. My belief, and our practice, was to hire the best, most competent lawyers, irrespective of their religious or ethnic background. But we also wanted to have people who would blend in well with the business climate.

Our strategy for practicing big-time law in Miami was to develop a local look and to put forward the Tom Tews and the John Schultes and the Jim Jordens. That was our image there.

With the ecumenical mix we in fact had, the Miami office received the acceptance the Florida people wanted to and did achieve. It was local. It was piped in. It was part of the community. And they built and developed a great law firm with that image. Unfortunately, blacks were not part of it. Cubans were. And that became a point of contention in their relationship with Bob Washington, a senior D.C. partner and later a co-managing partner of the entire firm.

There is a very important Cuban community and economic presence in Miami, and we had in Finley, Kumble a good and important representation of the south Florida Cuban-American community. The lawyers we had were from some very fancy families, including the daughter of the former president of Cuba and a fellow whose grandfather had been that country's attorney general. These were people who, in their former exalted circumstances, might not have been sitting down at the same table with us.

Miami was putting out first-class work at every level, and I was proud of the offices there. What they couldn't do themselves, we would help them with from New York. Tom Tew, brought in the International Gold Bullion case. And as soon as he landed it, Gary Blum, one of the best bankruptcy lawyers in the country, flew down from the New York office to help him. Gary worked with Tom to structure the case. Tew did a great job. Then he got the Colombian Coffee case. And Gary helped on that as well. It was the way things were supposed to work. There was a real synergy between the offices. When the ESM Government Securities bankruptcy case broke, Tew was initially called by one of the principals in the case. After a quick look, he turned them down as a client and returned the retainer. Then, he pulled off a great coup by becoming the bankruptcy trustee in the case.

ESM Government Securities, Inc., was a Miami-based financial company engaged in the little-understood, but crucially important government securities trading and repurchase business. Each day, tens of billions of dollars in United States Treasury bonds are bought and sold on a short-term basis—mostly overnight—as a means of borrowing and lending money. In a typical repurchase agreement, or repo, a cash-rich institution "buys" such bonds from another institution that needs or wants greater short-term liquidity. The price is the securities' market value, minus a small margin to account for the risk of a change in market value. The seller agrees to "buy" back the bonds.

The price at which the bonds are repurchased reflects the market value of the bonds, plus a premium that is, in effect, an interest rate. The buyer of the bonds is said to be "doing a repo." The seller is "doing a reverse."

Most such transactions take place among the bluest of blue-chip operators, the huge money center banks, which, along with a handful of securities dealers, hold the coveted status of primary dealers granted by the Federal Reserve. They are inordinately sophisticated in their dealing and pricing, and their creditworthiness is of the highest order. But also operating in the largely unregulated market are dozens of smaller dealers whose main customers are small banks and other savings institutions and hundreds of public entities—county, city, and town governments, school boards, and the like.

Municipal institutions, particularly, have uneven cash flows. Taxes are paid in semi-annually, leaving the institutions with significant amounts of cash that they must put to work until it is time to pay their bills. Under pressure from taxpayers and superiors, the treasury officials of such bodies have sought to get the most from their cash positions. Since they are restricted, in most cases, to investing safely —bank accounts and Treasury securities are acceptable— doing repurchase agreements seemed like a good idea.

But the people in charge of those institutions often have nary a clue to just how complex the transactions can become, or how important is the creditworthiness of their counterparties. Most important, they fail to insist on the most basic protective measure in doing such business: delivery of the securities that they are investing in, either to themselves or to a bona fide depositary institution.

They took ESM's word that the securities were on hand. They were not. ESM was involved in a giant juggling act that got bungled and the company was forced into bankruptcy. Among the victims of the backwash from their insolvency was an Ohio thrift institution whose failure came close to bankrupting the state-sanctioned deposit insur-

ance fund. News of the fund's precarious position set off a
run on the rest of the Ohio institutions that were covered
by it, and the national network news shows treated Americans to the first pictures since the 1930s of round-the-block
lines of people in several cities queued up to get their funds
out of their banks.

Tom got all kinds of publicity on that case and was even
called to testify before the Ohio State Legislature. It was
great for him. It was great for the firm. The firm made
millions of dollars in trustee's fees, and Tom did a superb
job.

I could see from the beginning that something exciting
was going to happen in Florida, and that despite their dif-
ferences, with Tew and Schulte spearheading the effort
there, we could prosper. A couple of years after they got
going, Tom and John told me that there was a Miami lawyer
in another firm who represented insurance companies in
the securities area. They thought he would add a lot to our
firm. We recruited Jim Jorden and he came on as co-equal
with Tew and Schulte. He brought with him a great book of
business. He's a terrific lawyer and an outstanding individual. From an image standpoint, he was just the kind of man
we wanted. He also served as a leavening factor between
Tew and Schulte. The three of them together were dyna-
mite, and there was no legal business we could not go after.
We were moving in a big way into the establishment. At the
same time, Finley, Kumble's Florida operation was growing
from the 14 lawyers it started with to 145 and from one
office to four. Through Schulte's initiative we opened an
office in Palm Beach, and through Tom Tew's efforts we
opened a Tallahassee office.

One of the firm's Washington partners, a former con
gressman from Orlando, Lou Frey, decided to run for the
Republican gubernatorial nomination. Tew was one of his
principal advisers and campaign managers. Frey lost, but
Tom handled things so skillfully and deftly that after the
primary, he was able to shift his support to Bob Martinez,

the successful Republican candidate who eventually won the governor's mansion. Tom became a real power in the State of Florida, and so we opened an office in the capital by merging with a firm there.

Florida was one of the shining stars in the firm. We had good people. It was highly productive. Morale was high. It had a glowing image. And it was built out of whole cloth in five years.

But when Finley, Kumble fell apart, the first major defection was Florida. The reasons for that are complex, having to do with the infighting that was going on elsewhere in the firm. But one of the reasons the partners in Florida were able to pull out so easily was that they had created a distinctive local identity.

Building a local firm that is part of a broader firm, however, requires that the local operation have a much greater degree of autonomy than is common in large law firms. That necessary autonomy, is often coupled with the egomania that is frequently part of the lawyerly personality. Added to it in Finley, Kumble were the greed and selfaggrandizement that characterized many of the partners. It created a fabric of inter-relationships that was stretched so tight that when it was pierced it would tear irreparably.

There is a curious paradox that attaches to major law firms in the United States. They are all partnerships. But almost all of them are, at the same time, autocracies. In each firm, there is one man who runs it. At Jones, Day in Cleveland, everyone knows that Richard Pogue is the man in charge. At Skadden, Arps, Joseph Flom is the man to pay attention to. At Cravath, Swaine and Moore, Sam Butler is in the catbird seat. Sam Butler speaks for that firm. They have committees and so forth, but there is little publicity about friction unless it is the friction generated by Sam Butler rubbing his hands together. That may not be very democratic, but in a business like a law firm where there are so many strong personalities, it is the only way to go.

For other firms, offices in cities away from their home

Steven J. Kumble

Photo credit: (Pamela Craig/The National Law Journal, 1983)

In happier times, (L-R) Andrew Heine, Steven Kumble, Neil Underberg.

Long after he left Finley, Kumble, Norman Roy Grutman (L), who had for many years represented *Penthouse Magazine* was hired by right-wing religious leader, the Rev. Jerry Falwell (R).

Photo credit: (AP / Wide World Photos)

Photo credit: (Bert and Richard Morgan Photographers)

Part of the genius of Finley, Kumble was the combination of business and social life. Here (L-R) are Harry Helmsley, Phyllis Cerf Wagner, Leona Helmsley and Robert F. Wagner.

For many years, at work and at our ease, Alan Gelb was one of my very closest friends.

Ready for an evening cruise out of Miami are (L-R) Leon Finley, Alan Schwartz, Joseph Tydings, Robert Washington and Steven Kumble.

Joe Tydings and his former wife, Terri.

Photo credit: (Bert and Richard Morgan Photographers)

Photo credit: (Bert and Richard Morgan Photographers)

In the paddock at Hialeah, Peggy Kumble, (L) is joined by the late Elaine Wright, Frank Wright, and Phyllis Cerf Wagner. Peggy's social, business and racing connections were a potent force in helping the firm grow, particularly in Florida.

Again in the Hialeah paddock, (L-R) John Schulte, Steven Kumble, Amy and Jim Jorden, Donna and Tom Tew, Evangeline and Hugh Carev.

Photo credit: (Bert and Richard Morgan Photographers)

Joe Tydings and I were very close, socializing together regularly. At the end, he became the point man in the effort to move me aside.

The Viscayan Ball is one of Miami's most important social events. Here at the Ball, (front, L-R) Steven Kumble, Evangeline Gouletas Carey, Donna Tew, Hugh Carey; (rear, L-R) John Schulte, Joanne Schulte, Peggy Kumble, Tom Tew, Nola Washington, Bob Washington.

Marshall Manley, in more prosperous days, was co-managing partner of Finley, Kumble and president of the Home Group. He helped destroy both enterprises.

Photo credit: (© Sherrie Nickol)

Photo credit: (Chester Higgins TR)

Steven Brill, whose gossipy monthly, *The American Lawyer*, changed the way journalists covered the law and lawyers.

Peggy Kumble.

Photo credit: (Bert and Richard Morgan Photographers)

Hugh Carey, Evangeline Gouletas Carey, Peggy and Steven Kumble. Hugh's friendship was another casualty of the law firm's breakup.

John Schulte and Tom Tew at the time they opened Finley, Kumble's Palm Beach office.

Photo credit: (John Pineda)

Hugh Carey helps Peggy Kumble from a carriage on the way to a ball at Saratoga. Steven Kumble at rear.

Photo credit: (© Carl Glassman, 1987)

When Harvey Myerson, with cigar, joined Finley, Kumble's litigation department from Webster and Sheffield, he, along with a gaggle of loyal disciples, referred to themselves as the "A-Team" and lorded it over the lawyers already in place in the department.

Photo credit: (Barton Silverman/The New York Times)

By 1984, Finley, Kumble was a powerhouse of American law and the second largest law firm in the country. This picture accompanied an extensive story in *The New York Times* **in October, 1984, that described Finley, Kumble as "the fastest growing firm in the U.S."**

Harvey Myerson gained control of the firm's New York office. Toward the end, I told him that my meeting him was the sorriest day of my life. I told him to his face, "You destroyed this law firm." More than any other person, he did. He subsequently went on to destroy Myerson and Kuhn, the firm he founded with former Baseball Commissioner Bowie Kuhn after Finley, Kumble imploded.

Photo credit: (© Carl Glassman, 1987)

Photo credit: (AP/Wide World Photos)

Paul Laxalt, former governor of Nevada, former Senator from that state, and "First Friend" in the Reagan administration. He joined Finley, Kumble at the beginning of 1987 for $800,000 a year and moved into new, plush digs in Washington's newly renovated Willard Hotel. He promptly announced that he was running for Republican nomination for the presidency. One of those who ran against him was Alexander Haig, whose son was with the firm's D.C. office.

Photo credit: (AP / Wide World Photos)

More than any other man, Sen. Russell Long, the Louisiana Democrat, was responsible for the passage of the Tax Reform Act of 1986. Here he is shown smiling at his colleagues' applause in October 1986 on the Saturday night that the joint House-Senate conference committee approved the bill. (L-R) Rep. Daniel Rostenkowski (D-Ill), Sen. Robert Packwood (R-Ore), Long, Sen. John Danforth (R-Mo). Long left politics at the end of that year to become an $800,000-a-year Washington partner of Finley, Kumble.

The story that heralded the destruction of Finley, Kumble ran under this picture as the lead piece in the Business Section of *The New York Times* on Sunday, Nov. 15. (L-R) James Jorden, Steven Kumble, Harvey Myerson, Robert Washington, Alan Schwartz.

Photo credit: (Vic De Lucia / The New York Times)

base were satellites. Finley, Kumble chose to pursue a different route, and however perfectly or imperfectly the idea was realized, the notion that the firm was to be a local firm in each place demanded considerable autonomy.

It was probably a mistake. And the reason for it was my recruiting and growth philosophy. I wanted Finley, Kumble to be a Florida firm in Miami and to have the look, the feel, the taste, the smell of a Florida firm. The same was true in California and Washington. As a consequence, we had to give a great deal of leeway to those offices and had to establish the fellows running those offices, not only as leaders of the particular office, but also as leaders of the firm. And having done that, we could not back down. In one way, it made a great deal of sense. They had broad authority to recruit and to move quickly. But ultimately it led to schisms and splits and the politicization of the firm.

Maybe such a style of operation can be made to work, but it requires a sense of common purpose and the universal commitment to achieve it. But once you introduce people like Marshall Manley and Harvey Myerson into the mix, it cannot succeed.

TEN

By the early 1980s, in the midst of our phenomenal growth and success, other currents began to swirl that would ultimately undermine the never-strong foundations of the firm and bring it down. Long-simmering difficulties between Andy Heine and me were on their way to becoming an all but public feud. Marshall Manley revealed himself as a man intent on doing things his own way and answerable to no one. The signs were clear that trouble would be the end point, but I continued in my belief that I could control these disruptive forces.

I had grown increasingly annoyed at Andy's penchant for bad-mouthing me and criticizing the firm. By itself, it might have been a manageable issue, but Andy's resentment continued to grow and eventually found an outlet.

As our falling-out deepened to a permanent rift, Heine continued to do stupid things. When, in the late spring of 1984, the firm called in the press to announce that Harvey Myerson was leading a litigation group that was joining

Finley, Kumble from Webster and Sheffield, a group of our senior people were gathered, together with Myerson, to meet with reporters individually. I took pride in orchestrating these kinds of things and had carefully cultivated members of the press. When it came time for Andy to talk, he said he felt it was important for the reporter to know that Harvey had been thrown out of Webster and Sheffield. He said it to be controversial; to get attention. And he knew the reporter would focus on his remark. I knew the reporter's next call would be over to Webster and Sheffield and that the story, instead of being this nice puff piece for the firm, would say that Myerson had been kicked out of Webster and Sheffield and found a home at Finley, Kumble.

I asked Heine, "Andy, why did you do that?" He said, "Well, it's true." I asked him again to keep his mouth shut and his response was, "Don't you tell me what I can and cannot say."

From then on, any time there was a media event, I would structure the whole thing and not tell Andy until afterwards. I'd say, "Sorry. The guy called, and he came up here and you weren't around." I'd tell him late enough so that he couldn't call the reporter to add some off-the-wall quote.

But it got to the point where the press would call Heine because they knew that they could get some kind of nutty comment from him. They knew that there was a loose cannon at Finley, Kumble who would give them some offbeat, screwball, stupid comment; someone who was a name partner in the firm.

I was trying to figure out how to sever the wires to his phone or block access to his office. But there was nothing I could do.

Others see it differently. A close friend of Heine's, who was aware of what was happening in the firm, recalls, "When Steve went on his public relations campaign, I don't think he realized that it was going to offend other senior people in that firm. At that point, in the late seventies,

Steve was still running the firm and Andy was managing the corporate department. To Andy that meant that they were running the firm together. Andy was still more a practicing lawyer than Steve, looking after the legal component while Steve carried the managerial load. I think Andy truly felt that meant they were sharing the responsibility for running the firm. That is why, when Steve went out unilaterally on this p.r. campaign, Andy was so angry."

Other people were angry, too, although, I was not so aware of it at the time. One of my partners now says, "Psychologically, Heine believed that Kumble had taken too much credit for everything that was going on. Every article mentioned Kumble, Kumble, Kumble. Take a look at what was written about the firm from 1980 until 1986 and the only name you see is Steven Kumble. Many people said to themselves, 'I'm as important to the firm as Kumble, but to the world I do not appear as important as he does because he is getting all the publicity.' "

In fact, I never considered the potential adverse effects of some of my actions.

"I don't think it dawned on Steve that other people would take offense," says the Heine friend. "Steve thought it was something that was going to be helpful to the firm. He gave them all compliments in all his public statements. He certainly gave a great deal of praise to Andy. But Steve went out into the world at large and presented himself as Finley, Kumble. And Andy saw red. Steve was presenting himself as the mainstay and master builder, which he was. But he just didn't realize the impact it was having. I don't think he ever asked anyone else about how to go about it. He never went for consensus. He just went ahead and did it. Andy was outraged. He wanted double billing. He was never going to get it at Finley, Kumble. It never occurred to Steve that Andy should have it. I don't know if they ever talked about it. Instead, they reacted after the fact. Andy never got over Steve not taking him along with equal billing

on the public relations campaign. That was the start of their
real war.

"Rather than finding a constructive way of handling
these things or developing channels for dealing with these
kinds of disagreements, they resorted to personal warfare;
to vendettas and politicization and anger and retaliation for
stuff that was small and silly. And the larger enterprise
suffered."

Andy's way of equalizing things was not to promote himself, but to diminish me. It got to the point that he was
disparaging me in the firm and outside the firm. He gave an
interview in which he said, "We don't give ethical problems
to Steve to handle." Incredible. What could I do? Sue my
own partner for libel?

The night that article came out, I was at a party at Heine's
home, his birthday party. I saw the piece and the reference
to me about an hour beforehand. I was angry about it, but I
didn't know how to respond. I have a delayed reaction to
these kinds of things. So, I went to the party and was pleasant and made a little speech wishing Andy a happy birthday.

But that night and for the next couple of days, I kept
turning it over again and again in my mind. I had been to
his home in the country the weekend before, and I could
not understand what was going on. During the weekend
and at the party that evening, he had been the perfect host,
and I could not imagine what he had in mind when he said
what he had to the writer.

Finally, a couple of days later, in an attempt to settle the
matter, I met with Heine and Neil Underberg at the Mayfair
Hotel for a drink. And it took me a long while to bring up
the issue. I told him that I just could not get over it. "Forget
that you and I are friends. How can you piss on your partner and piss on your own firm in print. You're always talking about improving our image and then you do something
like this. It is something for everyone to read and joke
about and ridicule us for. If the firm were a corporation,

you would be fired. No one would want to keep you around. They just would not tolerate it."

His response was to ask me whether I really believed that he had said what he was quoted as saying.

I said, "Yes. Steve Brill is too smart to publish something like that unless he has it on tape."

Then I asked him, "What can we do to prevent you from doing this kind of thing. I don't know how I can function with you speaking to the press."

Andy's response was that he would talk to whomever he pleased. He was not the kind of guy who would ever let on that he was sorry.

In partners' meetings, he was very disruptive with his constant disagreement with everything I said, so I became careful not to say anything that he could disagree with. I would ask him what he thought and then make sure to work his view into my comments so he couldn't disagree.

For some men, self-aggrandizement does not stop at having more than they can ever hope to enjoy, and competition does not stop at winning. They must kill their opponents; if they are, by some definition, civilized, the killing is usually figurative. Andy is competitive to the point of being self-destructive. If he can't win, then it is important that you lose.

I suppose the final fuel for Heine's enmity toward me was that beginning in about 1984, I started to try to ease him aside.

The world had changed and with it corporate law. The advent of the Reagan administration transformed free-boot capitalism—if not greed itself—from something that was looked down on by the government into a civic virtue. The economy and the financial markets were expanding. Inflation was well under control. Interest rates had seen their highs and were noodling along in single digits. Credit was loose. Optimism reigned.

Throughout the 1960s and 1970s, a form of financing known as bootstrapping had been commonly, though not notoriously, used in taking over companies that were having trouble, were badly managed, or were, for some other reason, undervalued. It was a fairly simple process. Identify and buy the company, borrowing heavily, usually via a private placement of securities with an insurance company. And then—because the covenants that went with such securities were so detailed and restrictive—with the lender virtually sitting behind you looking over your shoulder at every moment of the day, run the company. Slim it down. Get rid of staff. Sell off some assets to raise cash. Tighten the management. If it worked, cash flow could be improved dramatically after a time and the company sold for far more than it cost. The lenders were paid off and the equity holders who had done the deal enriched.

The subjects of such transactions were generally smallish companies, and the prices paid for them rarely got beyond $20–30 million. Most such transactions were for far less. They were the bread and butter of the merger and acquisition business that accounted for tens of thousands of business deals each year.

Banks were almost never involved in such deals. And certainly the public securities markets were beyond the reach of such companies. Borrowing in the bond markets was something reserved for big companies with good track records and the attendant credit quality that merited the stamp of approval from Moodys' and Standard and Poor's.

But the tectonic plates of finance had shifted. Several streams converged. The deals—leveraged buyouts by another name—got bigger. And then in 1983, former Treasury Secretary William Simon and his partner Ray Chambers did a deal that set deal-makers to salivating. In 1982, Wesray Capital, as the Chambers-Simon group was known, bought Gibson Greeting Cards from RCA. RCA thought the company was a dog and sold it for $120 million. Simon and Chambers, along with their co-investors, who included a handful of secretaries in their Morristown, New Jersey, offices, put up $1 million for the equity and borrowed the rest. As it turned out, Gibson was not a dog. It was, more than anything else, a cat, a cartoon cat named Garfield. When Wesray took Gibson public eighteen months later, the company sold for $290 million. Simon and Chambers, who had each put up $330,000, each netted over $66 million on the deal.

A second stream that powered the change was the junk bond. And whether you look upon Michael Milken as an ogre or a flawed genius, the change that he worked through the invention and marketing of the high-yield bond was revolutionary. His idea was simple. Many companies—because of their size, their relative youth, their lack of a track record—cannot access the securities markets. Yet, it is clear that great numbers of such companies are terrific credits. They can borrow from the the banks, but banks don't like to lend for very long terms. And the banks, like the insurance companies that finance private placements, are always nosing around, telling you how to run your company.

So why not pay a higher rate of interest, float bonds that the rating agencies would not call investment grade and make your company grow?

That was the start. By the mid-eighties, such bonds had been transformed and were coming into wide use in the financing of hostile takeovers which burgeoned as a result.

The third stream was the computer. The number and size of the deals that were done in the 1980s would never have been possible without the computer. In the hands of highly sophisticated investors, the computer was used to identify likely takeover targets. At the other side of the deal, the same technology was used to come up with the strangely mutant and exotic strains of securities that were used in the transactions.

Those factors came together in the hands of a group of driven and talented men who changed the face of global finance, among them Carl Icahn and Saul Steinberg and Ronald Perelman and T. Boone Pickens. What they were doing also changed the practice of law. Suddenly, lawyers were called upon to help structure these complicated deals, to help plot strategy that increasingly relied on a barrage of litigation, to act as negotiators in this complex world.

It was clear to me that Andy was not the man to bring the firm foursquare into that new era in corporate work. He was never able to develop substantial new business of any consequence in the area of leveraged buyouts and mergers and acquisitions, and when other people in the firm would bring such business to the firm, Andy was so arrogant and full of himself in dealing with those clients that they would soon look elsewhere for their corporate finance work. They included Steve Roth, a client of Neil Underberg's, who was involved with the Bass brothers and who took over Alexander's; Ray Chambers and Bill Simon from Wesray Capital; and Donald Trump who had hired Harvey Myerson to represent the United States Football League in its anti-trust suit against the National Football League and the television networks.

The big dealmakers in the takeover business are not people who come to a law firm as supplicants. They are dynamic and ballsy and have huge egos. Any lawyer, no matter how good he is, has to understand that and has to sublimate and subordinate his own ego to the will of the client.

Andy couldn't bring himself to do that. He would second guess the client on the business aspects of a transaction. It is one thing to say to a client that there are two or three approaches to structuring a particular deal, and go through them and point out the risks and the costs of each, and then recommend one of the options. Not Andy. The worst example was when Trump came in with something. Andy had looked at it, and when they met, he said to Trump, "How come you're paying so much for this? I looked at that for myself a few months ago, and it's not worth it."

Trump would not use us on his takeover deals. Ray Chambers at Wesray Capital would not use us. And Steve

Roth, even though we did all his real estate work, went to Sullivan and Cromwell for his corporate work.

The feud between Heine and me got worse. His sniping, his nutty comments to the press and privately voiced calumnies, his intrigues; they were more than I could tolerate. By the end of 1985, we were literally not speaking to one another. Our friendship was long since over. I wanted nothing to do with the man.

One of the stunts he pulled went beyond his usual rantings and had the potential for serious damage. The way it was portrayed publicly still annoys me. Basically, Heine accused me of underhanded dealing and attempted to convey the impression that I had played fast and loose with the securities law.

In late 1981, I had a series of conversations with Leonard Toboroff about joining the firm. I had met Lenny years before while I was still at Amen, Weisman and he represented the Carvel Corporation. He had, over the years, made a great mark for himself in the area of commodities law, representing brokers against Jake Simplot when the Idaho potato magnate had tried to corner the potato futures market and against the Hunts in their attempt to corner silver. At the time of our conversations, he had won a landmark commodities case in the Supreme Court of the United States. He was looking for a change.

Toboroff had his own small firm with several other lawyers. He was then and still is a big stock trader and dealmaker. Essentially, he wanted to become counsel to a big firm and devote his time to trading and deal-making, not to the practice of law. He had talked to Joe Flom over at Skadden, Arps, Slate, Meagher and Flom, but because so much of the business Skadden, Arps was involved with was takeover related, trading and deal making were not allowed to lawyers connected to the firm.

He and I talked. We struck an agreement whereby he would come to Finley, Kumble as counsel, bringing his clients and his deal business to us. One of the only restrictions we placed on Lenny was that he would have to drop his representation of the brokers who were suing the Hunts because the Hunts were clients of Finley, Kumble. Lenny complains to this day that he got screwed because his former clients won a $240 million judgment against the Hunts, and he would have gotten a substantial piece of the recovery as a fee.

One of Lenny's important clients was a young commodities broker named Neil Leist. By the time he was barely thirty, Leist had made a fortune as a trader and had used part of it to acquire a substantial minority interest—it was over fifteen percent—in American Bakeries, a big midwestern baking company. Lenny was handling Leist's proxy fight for control of the company.

At the American Bakeries' annual meeting in early 1982, Leist managed to get himself and a group of his allies—including Toboroff—elected to the company's board of directors. Leist was subsequently elected chairman of the board.

In the early hours of Monday, May 24, 1982, Leist was involved in a serious automobile accident on Long Island. His companion was killed and Leist was rendered a comatose vegetable. He died a couple of years later. Toboroff became chairman and chief executive officer of the baking company. Lenny and several others, including Heine, Underberg and I from the firm, financiers, Gerald Tsai and Carl Lindner, and executive, Garrett Bewkes, bought out Leist's stock position.

When we purchased that stock, Heine, the corporate lawyer, decided that we should not file a 13-D with the Securities and Exchange Commission characterizing the purchasers as a group with five percent or more of American Bakeries stock. His reasoning was that we did not agree to hold, vote, buy or sell shares in concert. We had no understanding of any kind consistent with acting as a group. And in fact, I sold my shares two or three months later for a small profit. And that was that.

Sometime prior to Leist's accident, the firm had intro-duced Lenny to Gary Bewkes, who had taken early retire-ment from a high-level post at Norton Simon and was inter-ested in running his own shop. Lenny didn't want to be a full-time baking company executive and Gary was invited to run American Bakeries. I subsequently became quite friendly with Gary and would meet with him from time to time. He told me what a mess American Bakeries was and the problems he faced in running the company. The prob-lems were huge, but I was impressed with Bewkes as a manager. And so occasionally, when I had some extra money, I would buy common stock in the company in open market transactions. I continued to do that for a couple of years and accumulated over 100,000 shares.

When I met with Bewkes, I would always insist that he pay for lunch, telling him that I was one of his big stock-holders. Because Toboroff and Heine were on the board of directors and because Finley, Kumble represented the company, American Bakeries was required in the proxy statements it filed with the SEC to report the number of shares that members of the law firm held collectively. Peri-odically, I would furnish our corporate department with precise information about my shareholdings, and that in-formation was included in the American Bakeries annual proxy statement.

By the spring of 1985, my stockholdings in American Bakeries were just below the five percent reporting require-ment level. I became aware of the possibility that the com-pany might buy back its own shares on the open market. I was about to leave the country for an extended European trip and was concerned that if American Bakeries did in fact buy back a significant number of its shares, my stake in the company could exceed the five percent level. If that were to happen, I would be required to file a 13-D with the SEC. So, to be on the safe side, I decided to file, disclosing the number of shares I had even though it was less than five percent. In the filing, I also disavowed any characterization of group ownership with any other partner of Finley, Kumble. I told Bewkes and Toboroff what I planned to do and asked the people in the firm's corporate department, the department that Heine headed, to prepare the papers. While they were doing so, Heine heard about it and exploded.

He was offended because he had been telling everyone American Bakeries was his company; that he was in control of the board and it was his deal. In fact, the filing would make it apparent that I had about twenty times as much stock as he did.

His response was to send memos accusing me of embarrassing him, acting in bad faith and of violating SEC regulations. It was nonsense.

There was some talk that Andy was going to file his own 13-D, but he would have looked ridiculous since he owned only about 6,000 shares.

I tore up the memos. I filed the 13-D. I took my trip.

Andy went on and on about how I had traded on inside information and screwed Bewkes. The facts are otherwise. Long afterwards, in September 1986, when Bewkes led a management buyout of American Bakeries, he invited me to join him as an investor as part of the buyout group. Heine went to him and tried to persuade him against including me. If Gary felt that I had betrayed him, he certainly would not have included me in the deal.

In the spring of 1987, nearly two years after the 13-D filing and the exchange of memos, the *American Lawyer* ran an article about my fall from power. In the article, the magazine included reference to the internal memos. In addition, the SEC received copies of the "confidential" memos, with the dates whited out, making it look as though my purchases of the stock were contemporaneous with the company going private. Only Heine could have supplied them with those memos. Some partner.

The Commission investigated. I supplied them with information, and they were ultimately satisfied that there was no basis for Heine's accusations.

For Heine, the final stroke of retribution had to wait until early 1987, when, in the culmination of a strategy conceived and developed over a period of years and perfected in late 1986, his allies killed me off, engineering my removal from any effective control of the firm.

Heine is disingenuous about it. He says that he was not in on the planning of the coup. "There were many meetings before that, but they asked me not to participate because it would just look like a vendetta. I think they were right."

At the meeting where I was deposed, the members of the management committee agreed to a policy of silence about what had really happened; to put the best face on what had occurred lest the firm's bankers, among others, become alarmed at the turn of events. For the most part, the vow of silence was maintained, and even partners who were not on the management committee were left in the dark about what was really going on. They found out about it in late Spring of that year. They read about it in the press.

Killing me was not enough for Heine. He could not control himself. Heine was so happy about the turn of events; that he had succeeded in busting my ass, that he wanted it known generally that I had been emasculated. And he leaked a story to the *American Lawyer* that was ultimately picked up by *Forbes*.

If not seeing that Heine, among others, were put off by my taking credit for the growth of the firm was a fault, a greater fault lay in my belief that I could control all these tremendously ambitious men whose interests, like mine, were directed to their work, to power and prestige. During the period of time that my relationship with Heine was undergoing a slow and corrosive deterioration, I was also beginning to see clearly that serious trouble was brewing on the West Coast.

Things went well enough there for a time, but as Finley, Kumble's California operation grew, Manley began to push. There were a number of things about Marshall that bothered me. The the most telling was that I did not trust him. I cannot say that was true from day one, but after a while things happened that I knew or suspected were rip-offs. And each one, while not in itself a calamity, character-ized his attitude.

For example, we opened an office in Newport Beach. Now, Newport Beach, California, compared to Beverly Hills, is WASP heaven. All the genteel people had decided to move to Orange County, and a number of companies were opening offices there, moving headquarters there. Manley decided to follow them. We had a partner, Jerry Miles, who was a real estate lawyer, and he opened our new office in Newport Beach. After nine months or a year, we decided it was not working out, and sublet the space to another law firm.

In the meantime, Manley's girlfriend, later his wife, Dassy Kallenberg, had gone into the executive search busi-ness, legal headhunting, and she and her firm put us to-gether with a firm out in Newport Beach that we subse-quently merged with. We paid a substantial finder's fee.

As it happened, the firm she put us together with was our tenant, the same lawyers we had sublet our space to. The California people negotiated the deal and I didn't find out about the previous connection until some time later. It was pretty raw. Dassy's firm got a big fee for introducing us to our own tenants, who thereupon stopped paying us rent because they were no longer our tenants but our partners. To top it all off, the lawyer who headed the firm neglected to tell his own partners about the merger. And a few days after the merger took place, they left. So, we paid this huge fee basically for one lawyer. The fee was not contingent on their staying for a stipulated period of time.

Another time, we had a client on the West Coast who owed us a lot of money and couldn't pay. As a good faith gesture, he gave us his new Mercedes Benz with the understanding that if he didn't buy it back within a certain time, we could sell it to settle the bill.

On one of my visits to the California offices, Manley picked me up at the airport in this big, beautiful Mercedes. "Nice car," I said.

"This is the one we got from the client," he said. I asked him, "Why are you driving it? Why haven't you sold it?"

He came up with some lame excuse.

Then there were our messenger expenses for the California offices. Our head messenger out there was getting $35,000 a year. A messenger. The reason he was getting that kind of money was that he was wearing a chauffeur's livery and driving a limo. If that expense had been highlighted as a car and driver for Manley, his New York partners would have rejected it, but it was being expensed as messenger services.

After a while, whenever I talked with him, I was reminded of the old joke: How can you tell when a lawyer is lying? When you see him move his lips. I came to assume there was nothing he was involved with that was not suspect, and was sure that if I turned over a rock he had been sitting on that I would find something unsavory.

Maybe the worst situation arose when we moved from Century City back to Beverly Hills. After the move, I asked Neil Underberg to take a look at the lease. Every time we would sign a new lease, Neil, who was the head of the real estate department, would review it. So, I asked him to look at it. Underberg hadn't gotten the lease. I kept asking. He kept telling me he hadn't gotten it. I said, "What the hell is going on, Neil?" He told me he kept asking for it and never got it.

The firm was paying the rent. We had paid $500,000 for furniture and improvements. I said, "I want to see the lease. I want to see it, and I want you to review it."

We finally got the lease. It became clear immediately why we were being stalled. The lease was not in the firm's name. It was in Manley's name. That meant that if a dispute arose, and we decided we wanted to throw him out, he could throw us out instead.

When I cornered him on it, he just laughed.

I did not do anything about that situation. And if I have any regrets, that is one. But I don't know that it would have made any difference.

Manley is a man who, if not stopped, would push and push and push and take and take and take. When, finally, I tried to stop him, my attempt backfired, and Manley ended up as co-managing partner of the firm.

Like many firms, we had a practice at Finley, Kumble that allowed for partners' personal legal work—wills, simple matrimonials, property closings and the like—to be handled as a matter of internal courtesy. It was not usually a big deal. Throughout 1983 and into the spring of 1984, Marshall Manley and his estranged wife were involved in a protracted and increasingly bitter divorce proceeding that the firm was handling. And although time charges were not ordinarily levied against partners in such matters, the time itself was logged, along with expenses.

Manley had been married once before. When I first knew him he was married to a woman named Tonya, a former model. Marshall was jealous and possessive and concerned that she was running off or doing something she should not have been doing. It was so bad that he had this powerful telescope in his office through which he could spy on his own house, almost a mile away.

Eventually, they got divorced. It was very painful, as all divorces are, but unlike others it became an important legal matter in the Los Angeles office. It was a real mess. Marshall was determined that he was going to get sole custody of their son, Chase. It was a monumental task, particularly for a father, and he did a job on this woman. He had an unlimited legal budget because he was having the firm do the work. And under those circumstances, he could just wear the other side down.

I watched as the numbers got larger and larger. The cost

of Manley's divorce grew to over $400,000 in time charges and an additional $60,000 or $70,000 in out-of-pocket expenses.

I thought it was outrageous. So, I sent him a memo saying that we could discuss the fee at some other time, but he really should reimburse the firm for the out-of-pocket expenses. He never responded. Instead, I got a call from Dick Osborne, a Los Angeles partner who was Marshall's big champion at the time, asking me who the hell did I think I was, and didn't I realize how much Marshall had done for the office and what a great guy he was and what right did I have to do this?

I told Dick that this was my job. I also told him the firm had never done a will for me, or my mother's will, without being paid. I had my own matrimonial done outside the firm and paid for it. And I founded the firm.

The most important thing for me was the law firm. It was my life. That attitude sometimes caused me trouble. When my wife put together a very important thoroughbred syndication and hired Finley, Kumble to do the legal work, she was ready to kill me when she got the bill. It was for hundreds of thousands of dollars. She complained that it was too high, and even though I might have agreed with her, I would not negotiate the fee because it might appear that I was playing favorites. I insisted on that. And in any work the firm did for me or my family, I paid a hundred cents on the dollar.

I asked Osborne, "How the hell can Marshall run up nearly half a million dollars worth of time and expenses on the firm and not pay anything for it?" He told me it was none of my goddamned business.

Rather than continue what was an unproductive conversation, I ended it and went to talk to Heine about it. He had the job of liaison with California. He allegedly knew everything that was going on out there. I asked Andy, "How can the guy who's making the highest compensation in the firm take another $400,000 or $500,000 without asking? I understand that the firm has a policy of doing minor things for partners, but this is a full-time job for lawyers out there. This is a significant percentage of our billable hours in that office."

Heine's version leans toward Manley's side. He puts this face on the incident: "Marshall was at the time responsible for the dynamic reputation of the California office. He had built it from nothing to well over one hundred lawyers in a relatively short period of time. Steve was angry or jealous of Marshall, and he complained that Marshall was using the office in his divorce and running up huge bills in terms of time and disbursements. Steve wanted the firm to get paid. He sent a memo to Marshall telling him that the firm should be paid. It was around the time they were going to trial on this very unpleasant divorce. Steve told me he was going to send the memo. I told him not to because, one, the firm should represent its partners, and, two, it was not the right time."

As liaison between California and New York, Heine was going out there every month. He and Marshall were quite close, and Heine knew that Manley was upset about my challenging him. Heine says Marshall never trusted me. Marshall told him at one point that if he, Manley, ever stumbled, I'd be right there to push him down.

Andy came back and said that the billing issue was taken care of. In fact, it was not. But Manley had decided he did not care to co-exist in a firm where anyone could tell him what to do.

Among his grievances against me, Manley felt he was cut out of administration and I was taking too much credit for the firm's growth and success.

Manley expressed the intensity of his anger over the memo soon enough. About three weeks after I'd sent it, Heine got a phone call about eleven o'clock on a Wednesday night. "I was in bed, just falling asleep. It was a call from one of our Washington partners who had heard from one of our California partners, the head of real estate out there, that there would be a meeting of the California partners the following Sunday about taking the whole office into Shea and Gould." Shea and Gould was a competing law firm in New York that was anxious to open a Los Angeles office.

We had held a management committee meeting in Washington, one at which we were introducing our new litigator, Harvey Myerson, to the committee. The evening before the meeting, as we always did, we had a big cocktail party for the committee members and for the attorneys from the local office and their spouses. It was a way of keeping this far-flung firm knit together.

No one from California showed up at the party. And they did not show up until late the next day. They had a variety of reasons and excuses, but the fact was, as we later discovered, they had spent the entire weekend and part of Monday in New York negotiating with Shea and Gould to become their California office. It did not work out.

We had within the firm a deep throat who tipped us off a couple of days later that Manley was livid about the divorce expenses and was set to move the entire California operation out of the firm, and it was going to happen within a week. I made a few quick calls, determined it was true, and a group of us flew out to California the next day. Manley never acknowledged that he had held those negotiations, but he did say he was very unhappy about my attitude concerning his divorce.

Joe Tydings and Hugh Carey said that we should throw him out of the firm, and that if he took the California office with him, so be it. But Underberg, Heine and I were the cooler heads. We showed up in Los Angeles unannounced. John Schulte came out from Florida. We spent an entire day negotiating with Marshall. The next day we had a meeting with all the West Coast partners, and at that time everyone was told there was an ugly rumor that had no truth to it. We said the California people were making a great contribution and they deserved greater recognition.

The meeting seemed in my mind to have pacified Manley, and I thought we had put the problem behind us.

What I did not realize was that we had set the stage for the destruction of the firm.

Manley concluded, as a result of that meeting, he could get exactly what he wanted. He had worked out a deal with Heine whereby he paid nothing of the $400,000 in time charges or $60,000 in expenses connected to his divorce. More significantly, at Heine's urging, we agreed that to show the world that we were a truly national firm, we would formally name Manley co-managing partner with me. I reluctantly went along with the idea. Manley was not interested in building the firm. Manley was interested in California and did not know what was going on in the rest of the firm. At bottom, Manley was interested in Manley, period.

Marshall now understood he had a solid base on which to exercise his power. While he might not be able to get what he wanted immediately, he could get it over a period of time. We were weak, irresolute, and willing to pay attention to the squeakiest wheel. And that, in my judgment, was the beginning of the end of the firm.

Carey, the former congressman and governor of New York, and Tydings, the former United States senator, were more politically astute than the rest of us. They recognized what Manley was about and the importance of getting rid of him. Hugh was opposed to accommodating Marshall. He's got an Irish temperament and in many ways is completely fearless.

And Joe Tydings regarded himself as very principled. He'd talk himself into a principle and then go to the ends of the earth for it. He believed that Manley was taking advantage of his partners and thought it would only be a matter of time before we had an irreconcilable problem with him.

They both said, "Let's bite the bullet now."

And I could not accept the idea of destroying this beautiful organization we had built. I was so concerned about the growth and the image and the esprit of the law firm that the public humiliation and financial loss of cutting California loose entailed more pain than I could deal with. I was not thinking clearly. It was like having gangrene in your leg. You know that it is eating away at you, but you won't allow the leg to be cut off. Letting California go was like that for me.

It was fatal decision. There was a moment when we could have dealt with the problem cleanly. We could have done what Manatt, Phelps had done. We could have pushed, and Manley would have been gone. It would have been very expensive, costing us millions of dollars and several years of growth. But I could not bring myself to believe the problem could not be solved some other way.

The only way to deal with a man like Manley, I think now in looking back, is simply to get rid of him. Because if you don't get rid of him, he'll kill you. I should have recognized that. But I had the ego to think I was going to be able to contain Manley.

It became clear that Marshall Manley was in absolute and total control of the California office. While the partners in Los Angeles were partners in the national law firm, they were first Marshall's people. The person most directly involved and most influential in terms of fixing their compensation, was Manley. Everyone in that office knew that very well.

I never saw Manley at work making deals and playing godfather, but I saw how people related to him. One of the reasons he did not like me is that I kept talking about the best interests of the law firm. It was not a term that he understood.

Several factors weighed heavily in the rather elaborate system Finley, Kumble devised to set compensation—billable hours, supervisory responsibility, business origination. But in California all those factors were overshadowed by a slavish loyalty to Manley. If Marshall did not like you, or if he thought you were somehow disloyal to him, your contribution to the firm in terms of hours spent, administrative work, and the rest would mean nothing. He would say, "He creates problems. He's disruptive." It happened again and again, and, although the other members of the compensation committee would wonder at the disparity between the hard numbers on a lawyer and Marshall's assessment, he was the man on the scene and sufficiently persuasive. It was difficult to overrule him.

Conversely, there were people who Marshall liked and who were loyal to him who were exceptionally well paid, far better than they deserved. The most outrageous example was Richard Osborne. Dick was a partner in the firm and an outstanding trial lawyer, but during most of 1985, Dick was out ill a great deal of the time. He was subject to recurring pain and brutal headaches that were diagnosed as being caused by a problem with his jaw. To alleviate the pain, he underwent reconstructive surgery. As a result, his contribution to the firm, his hours, his business development fell off dramatically.

At about the same time, Finley, Kumble was facing a disciplinary proceeding in California. One of our clients had paid a retainer of $100,000 to the firm and subsequently demanded it be returned on the grounds that it had not been earned. The firm was very slow about repayment. The client complained to the California Bar Association. A disciplinary proceeding was started. The target was Marshall Manley.

Osborne agreed to accept responsibility for the foul-up and received a disciplinary letter from the Bar Association.

He also received a six-figure increase in his compensation. It was not justified by his contribution to the firm, and there was heated discussion about the increase, with Manley arguing forcefully for Osborne. It made no sense to me, but Manley prevailed. Osborne had taken the fall for him, and Marshall, like Don Vito, was taking care of his loyal capo.

From mid-1984 on things began to change at Finley, Kumble. Within a matter of months, from the time that

Manley had wrested at least part of the control of the firm from me, the Washington office had undergone a realignment, and Tydings had drifted to the back. In New York, Harvey Myerson's arrival as head of the litigation department coincided with Manley's accession to power. It created deep bitterness in that department and cost me not only allies but also friends. Both events coincided with the escalation of hostilities between Heine and me.

Once Manley had managed to secure his position of power, there was no stopping him. He is a man described by turns as Machiavellian and politically astute, but he was clearly a man with a nose and an instinct for power and money. As soon as Marshall became co-managing partner, he began the struggle for complete control of the firm. He was very patient and methodical about it.

Several years before, as the firm began to grow beyond the New York base, Finley, Kumble established a management committee. The partners set it up it as a way of disseminating information, as a means of gathering intelligence, and as a help in making quick decisions on matters that affected the whole firm. For many years the committee functioned much like a Quaker meeting, though somewhat more raucously. Issues were raised and talked about. And a sense of the members, a consensus, was reached. There were no votes taken. If members of the committee expressed strong dissent on one issue or another, the issue was dropped, at least for the time being.

The management committee was not truly representative of the firm. It was never meant to be. The weighting of the committee was somewhat skewed. But over time, it became, largely because of Marshall's doing, the highly politicized governing body of the firm.

Over the years, Manley had grown close to City Investing's chairman, George Scharffenberger, and had done a great volume of legal work for the company. When, in 1985, City Investing bought the Home Insurance Group and began to liquidate itself, Scharffenberger asked Manley to run the company during the transition, a move that enabled Scharffenberger to pull the ripcord on a golden parachute worth $17.8 million. The assignment was temporary. Or so Manley told his partners.

He did less and less for the firm as the City Investing/ Home job became more and more time-consuming. When City Investing spun off the Home Group as an independent company in September 1985, Manley was named president. And it led to yet another confrontation between Manley and me. The firm had agreed to allow Marshall to hold both his partnership in the firm and what we thought was a temporary position with Home. But the firm's partnership agreement also stipulated that all earned income belonged to the firm.

We had a policy, clearly stated in the partnership agreement, that as a member of the firm, all of a partner's work was to be on behalf of the firm. All compensation for any professional service that he would render, any consulting, acting as a trustee, executor, broker, finder, or director, it all belonged to the firm. That should have included the $300,000 Manley was supposedly getting from Home that first year.

Manley disagreed, insisting that he would keep the money. I told him it belonged to the firm. The partnership agreement was unambiguous.

As part of his deal with Home, Manley had to relocate from Southern California to New York. He argued that it was going to cost him a fortune to move and to maintain a house in California and a house in New York. It was reasonable that we should take his expenses into consideration. I suggested he announce to the firm that he believed the compensation from Home would barely cover the extra expense, with the result that after taxes and all, there would be little or nothing left. So, he told the management committee that to the extent that compensation from Home exceeded his expenses he would turn the excess back to the firm. They agreed. As it turned out, the compensation was not $300,000, but closer to a million dollars. And that did not include the perks, the travel on the company jet, the car and driver, and so forth. That was all in addition to his substantial compensation from the law firm. He never made any accounting, and the firm never got the money.

I continued my attempts to get Manley to back off from some of his more outrageous actions. It did not sit well with him. The only person who would negotiate with him, who would go toe to toe with Marshall was me. And he saw in me the only real threat to running the firm for his own benefit. At first, he negotiated in the context of something that was good for the firm, taking a responsible leadership position. Later, he dropped the ruse.

He decided every question, not on the basis of whether it was good for the firm, but whether it was good for Marshall Manley. That was the only criterion. He was taking anything he could possibly take. It was like the king saying he will take whatever he wants and never thinking that being the king demands taking less, leaving something on the table for the common good; investing in the future. There is no evidence that such a thought ever occurred to Manley.

Several factors conspired to allow Manley to act as he did. Over the next couple of years, his power in the firm grew, even as he spent less and less time working for Finley, Kumble. For one thing, he remained co-managing partner. Secondly, he and Heine joined in the common cause of getting me out of the way. He had, further, co-opted Robert Washington, who had become the head of the firm's Washington office, by putting him on the board of directors of the Home Group's reinsurance company and by arranging, through Scharffenberger, an old Ronald Reagan pal, for Finley, Kumble to do the President's will. Heady stuff for a young black man from Georgia by way of Newark. Manley had also, both personally and through notes—with highly favorable terms—from a bank he controlled, lent hundreds of thousands of dollars to Harvey Myerson, the flamboyant and high-living New York litigation partner.

And, probably as important as all of those factors, was Manley's use of the power he gained to dispense legal work through what turned out to be his very permanent, very full-time job outside the firm as president of the Home Group.

The Home Insurance companies hand out to outside counsel fees of over $100 million each year. And Home was a very important client of Finley, Kumble. In fact, it was the firm's most important client. Manley regulated the amount of business Home gave to us because, if the business that the Home Group gave to Finley, Kumble, amounted to five percent or more of our revenues, the Home would have had to disclose that in its proxy statements. So, Marshall always saw to it that the number was kept below five percent. As our revenues from all sources grew, the revenues from Home increased as well. Had the firm not stumbled in 1987, its final year, we would have grossed over $200 million, and the Home Group would have accounted for about $10 million of that total.

Revenues from the Home were huge and they kept increasing. Where did the revenues come from and why was the business so significant? The Home, as a property and casualty insurer, has two basic aspects to its business: selling insurance and taking the premiums, and then, on the other side, doing everything it can to avoid paying out claims. Home insures against all kinds of risk. They're very big in accounting and legal malpractice insurance, for example, as well as property and casualty insurance. They hire law firms to defend the company and its policy holders, parcelling out the business all over the United States.

That, however, was only part of it. In addition to the direct line of business that Manley was pushing to Finley, Kumble, he was also able to pick up a great deal of business because of his position in the Home Group. Insurance companies these days tend to be extraordinarily sophisticated financial companies with huge pools of capital to invest. And they do a vast amount of business with investment banks and securities dealers. That gave Manley, and through him, Finley, Kumble, significant leverage in getting business from the securities firms. For example, we had been anxious to do business with PaineWebber. And Manley could say to Donald Marron, the PaineWebber chairman, "We at the Home do a lot of business with you. How come PaineWebber doesn't give any business to my law firm?"

PaineWebber wasn't using Finley, Kumble, but when Manley suggested that they do so, it was a no-brainer for them to take his hint. And Manley got credit for the origination of the work. So, in the last year of the firm, although he was doing not one billable hour of work for the law firm, he was to have a total compensation and expense package of $1.75 million, seventeen times what the most junior partner of the firm was earning. And the $1.75 million was in addition to the more than $3 million total that Manley was getting from the Home Group for performing his full-time job there.

With the management committee in his pocket, there was no way to enforce the partnership agreement and compel Manley to turn over his Home Group compensation to the law firm. But I could never understand why one of the stockholders of the Home Group did not sue to compel Manley to turn over his law firm compensation to the Home Group. In a sense, it was nothing more than a referral fee.

It had become Manley's plan to take control of the firm and ultimately his style and his priorities permeated Finley, Kumble. The only thing of any importance to Marshall was to originate business, and he was the biggest business originator in the firm. If a lawyer were doing a lot of work, putting in a lot of billable hours, particularly if he were putting in billable hours on matters that Marshall had originated, he would get some credit. But on a scale of one to ten that would be a one and the ability to originate the business was a ten.

And so, over time, the people who contributed the most

in business origination found themselves more strongly allied with Marshall. Ultimately, bringing in the business became the overriding concern. And everything else counted for a lot less.

As disruptive an influence as Heine was, and as greedy and power-hungry as Manley was, no one better exemplified what came to be wrong with the firm, or better shows my misplaced confidence in my own ability to control, than does Harvey Myerson. For it was Myerson, once steeped in the same morass with Heine and Manley, who finally served as the catalyst of the firm's eventual destruction.

ELEVEN

Somewhere deep down in the human spirit, there is a voice constant and persistent, sometimes loud and sometimes barely perceptible, but always there. "More," it says. "This is not enough. More."

It is a central fact of our lives, the grail of our quests, puny and grand. At Finley, Kumble, the choral voice in the firm's collective psyche may have been louder, more persistent and more effective than elsewhere. When Finley, Kumble began in 1968, the firm was small by any measure. It was a small fish in a big pond, but it would have been a small fish in any pond. By the middle of the eighties, the opposite was true. The firm had become a killer whale, on its way to becoming the second largest law firm anywhere. Our top people were making more money than they could have made anywhere else. We had more clients and more active matters than any other law firm. We had more wood paneling in our dining rooms and conference rooms and partners' offices than did any other firm. We had a museum-quality art collection hanging on our walls. And while Finley, Kumble by no means had a corner on partners and associates whose lives were distorted and whose personalities off-center, we had more than our share.

But none of that was enough.

"More," said the little voices, contrapuntal in their collectivity. "More."

What we got was Harvey D. Myerson.

One of my fondest fantasies is to make a movie about the firm and cast Danny DeVito as Harvey Myerson. DeVito has a knack for playing short, chubby men with a loopy, arrogant, and utterly distorted sense of their good looks, charm, attractiveness, and sexual magnetism.

Personally, Harvey gives new meaning to the word abrasive. Physically, he's built like a fireplug. He's short, stocky and perpetually bathed in sweat. He wears a curly, black toupee that looks like one of those old football helmets that Knute Rockne used to wear, the leather ones. And he has it in different sizes and shades and lengths. As the month would go on, he'd change the toupee and then say something about needing a haircut. Then he'd start the cycle all over again.

Harvey is a mystery to me. He is married to a lovely woman and between them they have eight daughters, two from their marriage and the others from their previous marriages. He is a very persuasive man. A number of people think that Harvey is a charismatic leader.

I am not one of those people. Myerson has a raspy voice, an absolutely wild temper. When he got overwrought—something that happened regularly—he would scream at the top of his lungs. He was forever making wild threats. I recall one time he threatened some young guy in the accounting department that if he did not issue reimbursement checks for some out-of-pocket expenses he was going to come upstairs and chop off his fingers. I think the guy believed him.

It always seemed to me that Myerson thought he could

intimidate people or persuade them by yelling. That may work with clerks. It may sometimes work with juries. But it certainly does not work with judges or with lawyers on the other side of the fence. They do not view such behavior with alarm. More likely, they rightly take it as a sign of weakness.

Watching Harvey eat was an experience in itself. He would devour food, stuffing his mouth hand-over-hand. And talk all the while, so that food would be falling from the sides of his mouth and occasionally shooting out at his table companions. There was nothing subtle about the man.

Nor was there ever a sign that he had any regard for anything or anyone but Harvey D. Myerson. On one occasion, several people had come in for a meeting with him and they met in one of our main conference rooms. Harvey was running the meeting and, as was his practice, was smoking one of his ten-dollar Havanas. As the meeting started, he stoked up his cigar. If anyone in the room objected, tough.

As the cigar burned down, Harvey flicked the ashes. Onto the walnut table; onto the carpet; into his lap. People stopped paying attention to the substance of the meeting and just watched the show of Harvey and the cigar ashes. Finally, one of the outside lawyers at the meeting could stand it no longer. He excused himself and left the conference room.

A few minutes later, he returned with a large ashtray he had appropriated from the reception area and put it down in front of Harvey. Myerson paid no attention. The ash on the cigar grew. He flicked in on the carpet.

A former lawyer with the firm, who remembers it as low comedy, sums up Myerson: "Harvey wears suspenders, purple shirts. He looks like a bowling ball. He looks like Garry Trudeau did him. He's always got a cigar that's the size of his arm in his face, and he always has the driver and the car that's about sixty feet long waiting downstairs with the motor running. He's got five houses, two wives, eight daughters. You could not make him up. He's like a cockroach. He'll never die."

I told Myerson, as the firm was crumbling, that the worst mistake I'd ever made was bringing him into it. It may have been. With Tyding's star falling and Robert Washington's in ascent; with bad blood between Manley and me; and with the open warfare with Heine, I had no need for enemies. But it was what I bought with Myerson.

I am not alone in my view that Harvey was the catalyst in the firm's destruction. Several former partners in Finley, Kumble trace the beginning of the end of the firm to Myerson's arrival. In retrospect, I see that was the case. It was in Harvey that Heine found a formidable ally in his vendetta against me. It was in him that Marshall Manley found a man with financial needs that he could help fulfill and someone with the political instincts to help Manley in his quest to gain control of the firm. Finally, after I had been toppled and Manley had faded into the background and Heine himself was stripped of power and on his way out, it was Myerson who presided over the firm's collapse into insolvency, a condition on whose brink Myerson personally often seemed perched.

Myerson's quick rise to power at Finley, Kumble was built in part on the firm's willingness to drop-kick out of the way partners who had been in the firm for years. Finley, Kumble had found no graceful way to move people aside.

Every business goes through stages and phases of development. And the management style and the capabilities necessary to run a ten-man firm are different from those necessary to run a twenty- or fifty- or one-hundred- or seven-hundred-man firm. Most firms grow through those stages via a gradual metamorphosis and, to a certain degree, sensitive to the positions of all the people who were helpful and important to functioning when the firm was at a different level.

It happens to every law firm and every company. Take a man who is president of a middle-sized corporation. Over the years, the company grows and prospers and brings in people beneath and around him who are vital to transition. By the time that man is ready to retire, the company has reached the next level where someone much younger and more vigorous is needed to take his place. That metamorphosis and the changing of authority is handled with some decorum and some sensitivity for the man who was at the top. He's made chairman emeritus and given an office and a secretary to make his exit less painful.

Other times, someone rises in the organization but events pass him by. He has to be moved aside. It is a wrenching experience.

At Finley, Kumble we had none of the first and a lot of the second. There was no slow metamorphosis. Growth and change were telescoped into a brief and meteoric life, and to some degree we ran roughshod over the sensibilities of people who were necessary and important at earlier stages of our development. Our people often had the feeling that they were keeping the seat warm for the next occupant.

We grew so fast and expanded so quickly that we had to replace people, including department heads, more often than other firms. We were always on the lookout for the next, best lawyer. As we grew, we needed people with different backgrounds, higher levels of professional experience. That process, and the way we handled it, created a lot of resentment in the firm.

Alan Gelb and I had been close for many years. He was the man I sought out when I had problems. When my first wife and I divorced, I used Raoul Felder. But when it came down to settling the matter and stopping the litigation that was going on interminably, I turned to Alan, and he got it settled. Gelb was one of the small circle of a half-dozen intimates who were invited to the ceremony when Peggy and I were married.

After the Grutmans had walked out in a huff in 1976, Gelb became the head of the firm's litigation department. He was a man to whom many of his colleagues turned for counsel, both legal and personal. His team of litigators, particularly the younger among them, thought the world of him. At least one had gone so far as to change his will, naming Gelb as executor of his estate and guardian of his children.

Robert Smith, a Boston lawyer who, like many associates, fled Finley, Kumble in pursuit of his sanity, remembers Gelb as a man of civility in the midst of barbaric personal and professional relationships. "Doors would slam. People were always yelling. And the level of personal abuse that partners heaped on their juniors was shocking. Everybody in the place was depressed. I was lucky in that I worked very closely with Gelb. Toward the end of my three years there, he turned me loose to work on important matters, and most of what I was doing, I was doing for him. I learned a lot. He taught me a great deal about argument and writing. He is a brilliant guy and a great lawyer."

Jerome Kowalski, a young litigation partner who later fell out with Gelb over the issue of making peace with Myerson, describes his former boss as a man with "significant leadership qualities and standards. He was the guy people came to with their own problems. On legal questions, he was a lawyer's lawyer."

But I had misgivings about Gelb's ability to be a star litigator. I was genuinely fond of the man, and have great respect for him professionally. He is bright. He is a good lawyer. He is a good litigator. He is articulate. He drafts well. Despite all that, he was never able to develop the professional persona that would be an independent attraction to outside clients.

Alan and I started going our separate ways. I did something later that Alan never forgave me for. But at the point we started going in separate directions, it was my feeling Alan Gelb was not maturing in a way that would bring Finley, Kumble top status and stature in the litigation area. He was the number-one lawyer in the department, but I don't know if he commanded the respect that a real leader should. Alan and I drifted apart. We didn't see each other so much socially. I didn't invite him to as many parties, and he did not invite me to as many, although I still regarded him as a friend. But when, at my insistence, the firm brought in Harvey Myerson, we did so over Gelb's clear objection. The effect was to reduce Gelb to a distant number two in the litigation department.

Andrew Heine, who has the uncanny knack of making brutal comments putting down even those people whom he classifies as his friends, did not think much of Gelb. He says of Gelb's heading the litigation department, "We had all decided that Gelb could not handle it. Not dumb by any means. He would not take challenges. We had been looking since day one, since I joined the firm for a great litigator. The department had no growth potential at all. It was a service department that could not generate any business on its own and in some instances could not handle the business that it was given."

My view is different, though the ultimate outcome was the same. Alan Gelb was an effective litigator, but he did not bring in much business. He did not have the reputation, the personality necessary to attract litigation business. The litigation work the firm did, at least in New York, arose from representing clients in other matters. In Florida, Tew and Schulte had good reputations as litigators. In California, we had Dick Osborne. In Washington, Carroll Dubuc had great stature as a litigator in the aviation field, and Paul Perito was a widely respected criminal lawyer and litigator. But in the New York office, we had no one with the stature to attract the kind of business we wanted.

The litigation department in most corporate firms is a service function. You can't run a big company these days without being involved, from time to time, with the courts, with government agencies, with people under investigation, and the like. In addition, litigation is an important tool in any kind of corporate maneuvering.

At Finley, Kumble, we had a substantial real estate and

corporate practice, and had our share of litigation. But all of it arose from our existing clients. And occasionally, because we did not have a superstar litigator on staff, those clients would go outside the firm for counsel when they got into deep trouble. That was part of the problem.

The other part is that litigation on a large scale is a tremendous producer of income. When a firm gets involved in a major piece of litigation, it means monthly bills in the hundreds and hundreds of thousands of dollars, the kind of revenue that can keep a firm thriving.

And our firm was not getting its share. A client from outside New York, or a client who wanted to turn to another firm for a major piece of litigation work, would not think of us.

If you can get that business, it feeds on itself. If you handle important cases, you get a reputation, and the reputation brings in even more cases. And in terms of public identity, there is nothing better for a law firm. People write about litigation. It captures the public interest in a way that simple business transactions do not.

By the early 1980s, the world of litigation was changing. The glamour end of high-powered corporate law was increasingly tending toward the world of corporate takeovers. In that area, a strong litigation department was necessary. Litigation is an important part of the total takeover or defense strategy, to delay things, to throw the other side off balance. It's like a big chess game. That brand of the law was not Finley, Kumble's long suit.

Gelb's undoing was a case involving the takeover of GAF. Samuel Heyman had retained Finley, Kumble to help him wrest control of the company through a proxy fight. As is the case with many such battles, any and all means, fair and foul, were used.

Sam Heyman, who had gone to Yale Law School and knew Heine, asked Finley, Kumble to represent him. Heyman owned about five percent of the stock, and the management group at GAF owned relatively little. Heyman felt that the performance of the GAF management had been miserable and went after them. Heine represented Heyman, and did a creditable job. But the GAF board and management, represented by Skadden, Arps, claimed that the proxy material filed by Heyman was deficient because it failed to disclose that he had been accused of fraud as a trustee in a case involving his family. The case had been sealed by the judge to protect the privacy of one of the family members. There was really nothing to the GAF claim. It was a ruse to delay the close of the proxy vote. Gelb litigated the challenge, and the other side prevailed. Heyman was beside himself and the first thing he said was that it was the lawyers' fault.

In fact, the court had come up with a bad decision. It's not so unusual. But on the appeal, Heyman switched from Finley, Kumble and hired Arthur Liman at Paul, Weiss, Rifkind, Wharton and Garrison to represent him. Heyman won the appeal, the votes were tabulated, and he took control of the company. But our relationship with Heyman had been damaged.

As a result, Heine was more determined than ever that we should get a strong litigator, someone with experience in the takeover field, and he came up with Harvey Myerson. How he came up with him, I don't know, but I think through a headhunter. Myerson was considering leaving Webster and Sheffield and had been out on the street looking. If Harvey could be believed, he had several offers.

None of us knew Harvey. Heine's recollection is that he was sent to us by an executive search firm. When he first came by, Underberg and I were not in so Heine talked to him and then talked to Neil and me about him. Heine described Myerson as a charismatic man, with a great sense of humor.

The idea that Myerson is charismatic is a joke. The first time I met him, I found him difficult to like. He was loud. He was coarse. He was adversarial. He was rough-hewn and unattractive. At the same time he was bright, very aggressive, determined, tough, and I discounted his adversarial manner as the mark of a litigator.

To listen to Harvey talk, you would have thought that he was the most well-known trial lawyer on God's earth. He represented Shearson-American Express and several other clients, but I had never heard of him and no one else was familiar with him. By his account, he was running Webster and Sheffield. By other accounts, he was running one section of their litigation department. By Myerson's account, he was supporting the firm, bringing in the money that allowed the firm to meet its payroll. By other accounts, his partners at Webster and Sheffield were anxious to get rid of him.

His former partners at Webster and Sheffield won't talk about Harvey D. Myerson. They entered into an agreement at the time he left for Finley, Kumble in June 1984 not to talk publicly about Myerson. It is an agreement which, as far as I know, none of them has broken. "We do not think it appropriate to talk publicly about the internal affairs of the firm," says managing partner, Donald Elliott. "We did not talk about him when he left. We have maintained silence since. It is a matter of firm policy. Harvey Myerson was a partner here. We were not unhappy to see him leave. We really wanted him to."

Finley, Kumble in the persons of Heine, Underberg, and I, three of the four most senior people in the firm, had several discussions with Myerson. His principal concern, after considerations of money, of course, was where he would stand in the firm. At the time, there were four of us who controlled things: Manley, Heine, Underberg, and I. Myerson wanted to be sure he would be part of an expanded five-man executive group and would have a title that indicated not only that he was running the New York litigation department, but also that he was in charge of the national litigation practice. It was just before Manley became co-managing partner, and I told Myerson that nobody had titles. I said people who were leaders rose to the top, and if he was terrific, he would rise to run the litigation practice. He insisted that it be clear he was running the litigation department in New York and the litigation practice for the whole firm.

Myerson also insisted that his name be added to the firm.

There are many firms—Davis, Polk, Shearman and Sterling, White and Case, Sullivan and Cromwell—where a lawyer who joins the firm, no matter how important he may be, does not get his name added to the firm name. For example, when Cyrus Vance joined Simpson, Thacher and Bartlett after serving as Secretary of State, they didn't change the firm name.

But at Finley, Kumble, things were different.

When we started the firm, it was known as Finley, Kumble, Underberg, Persky and Roth because that was the way our names appeared on the complaint that the Weismans filed against us in their attempt to prevent us from leaving the old firm. It was a nice touch.

When Norman Roy Grutman joined us, he insisted on having his name in the firm, and we added it at the end. When Andrew Heine came with us, he, too, insisted on having his name in the firm name. After getting Neil Underberg's consent, I added Heine's name just before Underberg's.

But the name was getting unwieldy. So, I went to Herb Roth and said, "Herb, the firm name is getting much too long. We have to shorten it, and the only way to do that is to eliminate a name." When I told him that we had decided to cut his name, he looked at me kind of funny and said, "R-O-T-H?"

When Grutman left, we took his name out. When Persky left, we took his name out.

And when Manley joined the firm, he wanted his name included. After all, he argued, he had been a name partner at Manatt, Phelps. I told him we would have to review it at some point in the future, but if things worked out, we could add his name then. Eventually, after he had built up the

West Coast office, he began insisting that his name be in the firm. We did that simultaneously with adding Bob Casey's name. Bob had just joined us from Shea, Gould, Klemenko and Casey. Casey argued that he had never been in a firm that did not have his name in it.

At that point, the name of the firm was Finley, Kumble, Wagner, Heine, Underberg, Manley and Casey.

It was a joke. Tydings's name was not in the firm name. Carey's name was not in the firm. Yet, they were both men who had important public identities. When Myerson joined the firm, he insisted his name be added to the firm. At that point, I'd give a speech someplace and and by the time the guy who was introducing me finished saying the name of the firm the audience would be yawning.

There was talk that we should have our firm letterhead done on corrasible bond so we could add or delete names more easily. It would have saved a fortune in printing bills. It was a real pain in the ass. So, I told Myerson no. We already had the longest name in the profession, and it was dumb to make it even longer. He complained that he was bringing over a lot of business and besides, he had talked it over with Manley and Heine and Washington and they said it was okay with them. We added Myerson's name.

The name and the capriciousness of changing it was a sign of what was wrong with the firm. It evidenced the inability on the part of several partners to work in a unified way, and it pointed up the fact that we had a lot of people going in different directions, unable to go forward under any banner other than their own.

The prospect of Myerson's joining the firm created an uproar in the litigation department. Some of the younger partners there had found the years from 1982–1984 an almost idyllic time, but it came to a quick end when they got word that we were talking to Myerson. Nobody in the department had heard of him, and when they snooped around, they heard only scary news: He had a reputation at Webster and Sheffield as very hard to get along with. A group of the litigation partners decided to oppose bringing on Myerson and challenged us on the choice.

It was a pretty gutsy thing. We had a reputation as people our juniors had better not cross. Jerome Kowalski, who was outspoken about Myerson, recalls the time from the vantage point of those who fought against taking Myerson into the firm: "It became a real war. As the issue escalated, Gelb sat with us and said—it was a very emotional speech—he said, 'You guys all have wives and kids and mortgages. You have everything to lose. I'm single. I live in a rent-controlled apartment. I can survive. I have worked with these guys for twenty years. They are bad guys, and they will win. And after they have won, they will get you. So, don't do it. Don't put your welfare at risk on my account.' "

In response, Kowalski says, "We met without Alan being present and decided to do the right thing."

They had done a lot of intelligence work on Myerson. He would work only with selected people. He was disruptive. Myerson's big pitch was that he could bring Shearson in. In fact, he had been representing them only for a couple of months, and not on their major matters. And his partners at Webster and Sheffield were trying to throw him out of the firm. The younger litigation partners had done their homework. I wished later I had heeded their warning.

In the course of the hiring process, Myerson went to Washington, D.C., to a meeting of the firm's management committee. For the most part, they were unimpressed. And if memory serves, although I did not know it at the time, the day we interviewed Myerson in Washington was the same day that Manley and the California members of the management committee had flown down from New York where they engaged in the all-night negotiation session at Shea and Gould. I have no idea whether they were interested in Myerson. They had one foot out the door.

The issue soon became one of making a clear-cut selection between Gelb and Myerson. Myerson appeared to have a great deal of business; Gelb had none. Myerson had a substantial client list; Gelb had none. Myerson claimed a great deal of experience in takeover litigation; Gelb had little or none. It came down to a pissing match between Myerson and Gelb. I had known Alan Gelb for many years. I had done some things over the years that Alan did not like. I was always kind of rough with him. I saw it as my job to be a taskmaster. I don't think that sat very well with him. Still, I regarded him as one of my closest friends.

But here I was taking the firm's litigation department away from him. To demote a man halfway through his career and to leave him with no hope of ever getting back to the position again is a bitter pill.

It was a pill that Gelb strongly resisted taking. Gelb didn't want Myerson at all, and Myerson wanted the whole pie, complete with fancy titles. I wasn't keen on the titles, but I felt that the firm should get Myerson. Logically, it made sense. At the time, Myerson filled our need for a relatively young litigator with an important client roster and experience in the takeover field. I felt it would be in the best interests of the firm to take Myerson.

There was a big meeting of the New York partners where the question was whether to approve or not approve Myerson. Gelb and other people were lobbying vigorously against it. And my instincts, my desires, my personal friendship with Alan all told me that I should pass on Myerson. But business logic told me that he would be a good man to have in the firm. It was another case where I should have followed my instincts, but did not. The meeting was going badly for Heine, Underberg, and myself who were proposing Myerson. It looked as if we were going to have a revolt on our hands. The litigation partners, Gelb, along with Jeff Fillman, Larry Blades, and Jerry Kowalski were all dead set against bringing on Myerson, particularly as head of the department.

Gelb gave a very emotional speech at the meeting. He said, "You owe it to me to turn this down." The battle at the meeting continued for several hours. Finally, I asked if it would go down better if we brought Myerson in as co-head along with Gelb. Everybody agreed to go along with it if he fulfilled promises to work cooperatively with all of us. Everyone agreed except Jeff Fillman who said Myerson would never be able to co-exist, and that it was foolish to think he would or could. Underberg, Heine, and I did not think Myerson would agree, but we promised to call Myerson and offer him the terms. After the meeting, I had to break the news to Myerson. I told him, "You got everything you wanted except running the litigation department." I told him he could come in, not as head but as co-head, and that I thought in time he would run it. Amazingly, he bought it.

I regret that now. I wish to God he had not bought it. I told him in later years that my meeting him was the sorriest day of my life. I told him to his face, in front of other people, "You destroyed this law firm."

We reported back that we had talked with Myerson and he had agreed. Gelb told his people he did not trust us and went to Underberg demanding that he get Myerson on the phone to verify the conversation. Underberg refused. So, Gelb called Myerson himself and got a different version: Myerson was coming on as head of the department. Gelb and Myerson subsequently met several times and worked out an arrangement about sharing responsibilities. The arrangement did not hold.

I believed that once Myerson came on, he would—because of his personality, his aggressiveness, his book of business, his muscle—in short order be running the litigation department. I didn't care about the title. He could be the national director of litigation, or the coordinator of national litigation, or the national chairman and president of the men's room committee. No one in any of the other offices would pay any attention. So, we gave him the title, whatever it was.

When Gelb was interviewed for a newspaper story on Myerson joining Finley, Kumble and asked how he felt about it, he replied, "When Steve Kumble talks to me about money, I talk to him about loyalty."

Gelb was hurt and offended at my bringing in Myerson over his objection. It caused him some humiliation and some embarrassment. And I regret that. At first they were constantly at odds. There was a group of old litigators and a group of new litigators, and the two never really got together. Myerson kept the old group out of the new Myerson business, although ultimately some of the old litigators shifted their allegiance to Myerson because they saw that was where their future lay. Gelb and Myerson had kind of a loose truce for a while, but there came a point when Gelb determined that his future lay with Myerson and not with me. In fact, Gelb acutally became Myerson's most visible spear carrier in the campaign to give Harvey absolute authority. I suppose that was understandable. After the firm collapsed, he went to work with Myerson in the new firm, Myerson and Kuhn, that Harvey started and ultimately destroyed.

For those in the old litigation group, life was tough. It was the old group versus Myerson and the people he had brought over with him. Associates were told that if they worked with the old group, then they would be working with the B-team, and they would not get any work from Myerson's group, the A-team. By 1987, Myerson's people would not talk to the people who were part of the firm before their arrival.

Alan Gelb, meanwhile, joined Myerson's camp. Sometime in late 1986, something I have yet to discover, happened between Myerson and Gelb. Prior to that time, the out-group were quite open in their criticisms of Myerson, but before the end of 1986, Alan Gelb became a staunch advocate for Myerson, telling people that the future of the firm was with Harvey.

What a future.

But for a time, it worked. I had wanted a hot litigator, someone who would bring in business and get the firm good press. Myerson eventually got enormous attention representing the publicity hound Donald Trump and the United States Football League in an anti-trust suit against the National Football League and the television networks that broadcast NFL games.

The United States Football League was born of the idea that a pile of money could be made from what seemed to be the nation's insatiable hunger for football. The idea was to fill the late winter and spring airwaves with big-time football, thus avoiding competition with the National Football League. The only area where the new league would compete with the older organization would be for personnel. After the formation of the twelve-team league was announced in 1982, ABC agreed to a two-year, $18-million contract to broadcast USFL games for the 1983 and 1984 seasons.

The league boasted former Washington Redskins coach George Allen as the owner-coach of the Chicago team and the New Jersey Generals franchise was able to snag Heisman Trophy winner, Herschel Walker.

In the first season, 1983, the owners lost a total of $40 million and several sold out. Donald Trump picked up the New Jersey Generals and Walker hired Walt Michaels, the former New York Jets coach, and started spreading money around. In a matter of months, the USFL had become a madhouse of high-priced bidding for top talent. Even with the costly talent, teams still lost money in the 1984 season.

The USFL owners began to push for a fall season, but the major broadcasting networks sat on their hands. The NFL had a lock on the medium. Led by Trump, a man whose corporate takeover schemes had added to his fortune, the young league fought back with a lawsuit, and in October 1984 the USFL went to Federal District Court in New York charging anti-trust violations and seeking $1.3 billion from the NFL.

Their lawyer was none other than Harvey D. Myerson. Harvey was in his glory. His office soon filled with signed footballs and other sports paraphernalia. Here was a guy, who as a kid had assembled a collection of the bubble gum cards of Jewish baseball players, suddenly hobnobbing with the likes of Howard Cosell and calling as his first witness the near-legendary commissioner of the National Football League, Pete Rozelle.

After the highly visible trial began in May 1986, Harvey began appearing in the *Times* and on the television news programs on a regular basis. He ate it up. He had always been a legend in his own mind and now here he was with the media's seal of approval. His runty swagger became even more pronounced.

The trial went on for more than two months, with final arguments on July 23. Six days later, a previously dead-locked jury reached a compromise verdict. Yes, the NFL, as Myerson had argued, had muscled out the upstart USFL. But the damage verdict was not what Myerson was expecting. Instead of the $1.3 billion Trump and the other USFL owners asked for, they got one dollar. Since it was an anti-trust case, they were entitled to treble damages: three dollars.

People win and lose cases. The USFL case was difficult to begin with, and Myerson made the best of it. I never faulted him for his handling of it. A great number of people in the firm worked on it, and the bills, which were fierce, were paid on a regular basis.

Well before that highly publicized trial, Myerson became the beneficiary of my ability to generate press coverage. Heine may have objected to my getting a great deal of publicity for myself, but the fact is that I had managed to promote the firm quite effectively.

I was not crazy about Harvey. But once we made the decision and once he came on board, the idea was to orchestrate the most flattering story that we could.

In the legal profession, it doesn't require a genius to make somebody well-known. All you need to do is to get his name in the papers. There is a glut of papers writing about the legal business, and they are all dying for copy. Give them a story about reorganizing your Xerox room and it would have a shot at seeing print. I would get calls almost every day from people asking me what was new, whether there was anything going on. And if there were something that was interesting in our firm, or if I heard something, I'd pick up the phone and call them. For our own publicity, I would prepare a release. Then, I would call the *American Lawyer,* the *New York Law Journal,* the *Legal Times,* the *Wall Street Journal,* the *New York Times.*

Over the years, I did whatever was necessary to demonstrate our openness and accessibility to the press. I tried to establish personal as well as professional relationships with people in the media. Early on, it was Steven Brill of the *American Lawyer* and James Finkelstein who owned the *New York Law Journal.* In later years, the list included reporters from the *Wall Street Journal,* the *New York Times, Fortune,* and *Business Week.* I had them to my home for dinner. I'd invite them to parties—anyone who wrote about the law. And it paid off. I always went direct. I'd always tell them the truth. And if I didn't want to comment, I'd tell them I didn't want to talk about it. At certain times, we would try to control the damage when we sensed a story about the firm was going to be unfavorable. But I would always pick up the phone and talk directly with these people.

When Myerson joined the firm, what we did was typical. We prepared a glowing press release about Myerson. I showed it to Myerson. He insisted on rewriting it, giving himself titles and a bigger role in the firm. Then I took it back and got rid of his changes. But it said that Myerson was a great litigator and a great human being and a variety of other wonderful things about Harvey. Following that, there was a boilerplate section on the firm that detailed the number and location of our offices, the number of partners and some puffery on the well-known members of the firm such as Bob Wagner and Hugh Carey and Joe Tydings. Then, I called up the publications—we timed it so they all

got a fair shot and none would be beaten to press by another—and invited them up. We scheduled meetings for
every two hours, one reporter at a time, and suggested that
they bring a photographer.

As on other occasions, we orchestrated the interviews.
I'd say to our people, "Look, you say this and Andy, you
talk about that and so forth and I'll keep quiet." So, the
fellow would come up and I'd give him the release and he'd
read it over. Then, I'd introduce him. This is Harvey Myerson and this is Governor Carey and this is Mayor Wagner
and this is Andy Heine, the head of our corporate department, and this is Neil Underberg, who heads our real estate
practice. Then, the writer would talk with Harvey for a
while, and Neil would bring in the real estate department,
and Carey and Wagner would talk so the reporter would
have something interesting to write.

In addition, I decided that Myerson was sufficiently colorful that I could mount a larger campaign than usual to get
Harvey and the firm's name better known. I was going to be
like Professor Henry Higgins in Shaw's "Pygmalion." I
would promote him every chance I got. I was looking for
national press coverage because I was trying to make Finley, Kumble a household name. And the way to do that was
not in the *American Lawyer.* But if a story were sufficiently
interesting, reporters for the general press would pick up
on it. So, I was constantly promoting Harvey to the press.
Not surprisingly, he ate it up.

I also found myself promoting Myerson to the firm's
bankers. Shortly after Myerson joined Finley, Kumble, he
told me he had liquidity problems and asked me to introduce him to some banks. Since he was a new partner in the
firm, I said I'd be glad to do it. I had no idea at the time how
desperate was his personal financial situation. At the time,
this was in 1984, he owned three homes and had a collection of very expensive cars. He was a man who chain-
smoked ten dollar Cuban cigars; a real high flier. But he
said he was having "liquidity problems," so I introduced

him at different times to different banks the firm did business with. Since they also got valuable referrals from us, they were anxious to accomodate the lawyers at Finley, Kumble.

All the banks had private banking groups that served so-called high net-worth individuals. The firm had hundreds of lawyers, and the banks wanted their business. I introduced Harvey to Citibank, to Manufacturers Hanover Trust, and to Bankers Trust Co. He borrowed money from all of them. What I did not realize then was the extent of his other borrowings. It was only later that it became clear that we had a desperate situation on our hands. Harvey is a profligate spender. He can't help himself. He is to spending money what Ray Milland was to alcohol in "The Lost Weekend."

Harvey's assets were tied up in things that were not income-productive. In fact, most of his investments were income negative. At one point in 1986, he owned five homes, including a house in Bedford, New York, one in Jamaica, B.W.I., another in Martha's Vineyard, his apartment in the Towers of the San Remo on Central Park West, and a house out in the Hamptons he had bought from Donald Marron, the chairman of PaineWebber, for $2.2 million. He had all these fancy sports cars and stock in a couple of private companies. He was forever getting involved in private investments, not blue-chip stuff. I'm not suggesting there is anything wrong with private investments, but they're not all that liquid, so it is not a great idea to borrow money in order to make the investment. Harvey's way of servicing the loans was to borrow more money. The trouble is that eventually the sources of new money run out. I suggested that he reduce his non-liquid assets to the point that his income from the firm was sufficient to live on and to carry some loans. He once had about $5 million in mortgages alone. The question in my mind was how could he support that kind of financing. He was drawing no more than $500,000 or $600,000 from the firm, so the interest on the real estate loans alone equalled his draw. How he did it, God knows.

It was a question that would later be asked by several banks, some of his partners, the Federal Deposit Insurance Corporation, and assorted other bank supervisory agencies.

By the beginning of 1988, Myerson was in default on over $700,000 in loans from the National Bank of Washington—on whose board sat his partner, Robert Washington—and had been in hock for several years for six-figure loans from Heine and Manley, among others. I myself never even considered lending Myerson money, although I suppose if I had, it would have put me on a level playing field with Heine and Manley and Washington. For the eternally strapped Myerson, loans were like mother's milk, the stuff of survival. At one point, he came to me again asking for my intercession with the firm's banks. When I called on his behalf, one banker told me, "No way. The last half-million we lent him is gone. It's going out the door too fast." And that was the reaction I got from all the banks.

The portent was serious. When, in 1987, the banks found out that Myerson had been put in charge of the firm's checkbook, previously approved credit lines of the firm itself—always considered a blue-chip banking client—dried up.

I may have seen myself as playing Henry Higgins to Myerson's Liza Doolittle and acting the part of Rumpelstiltskin to his need to create gold from straw. But I was less keen about sharing the power with Harvey. And that contributed to the political rifts that would destroy the firm.

The New York office became politicized. The deal we made with Harvey was that he would be at the same level as Heine, Manley, Underberg, and me. We would have meetings, but I didn't always invite Harvey to these meetings. Heine complained that we had made a deal with Myerson and we weren't living up to it. Heine said if I didn't invite Myerson, he would boycott the meetings.

Heine says that when he complained, I replied that we didn't want Myerson in on the decisions and now that he had joined the firm, he really had no place to go. I dispute that recollection.

It pulled Heine and Myerson closer and closer together, an alliance that proved to be difficult to deal with.

I eventually drove additional wedges between myself and Myerson. Myerson turned out to be a major rainmaker for us. The first year after he joined the firm in 1984, he generated between $2 million and $3 million in business. Within three years that had grown to nearly $9 million. Because at Finley, Kumble a great premium was put on bringing business in the door, Myerson's compensation level grew quickly. So did his expense account limit. The firm had a system for senior people that allowed them huge amounts for business-related entertaining aimed at drumming up business. Myerson's ERL, or expense reimbursement limitation, eventually grew to over $200,000. And what I saw as clear-cut abuses led to a further falling out between us.

We had a policy at Finley, Kumble that the firm would reimburse each partner for expenses incurred to promote new business, hold existing business, or any other expense that could be classified from a tax standpoint as a legitimate business cost, provided that a lawyer had the proper vouchers and supporting backup. But because it would have been virtually a full-time job for Peat, Marwick to supervise the validity of such expenditures, we simply put a ceiling on them. But up to that limit, provided that it appeared to be a legitimate business expense, no one would question the expenditures. It was kind of an honor system.

The ERL was also supposed to bear some relationship to an individual's historic ability to originate business, and we used a percentage of the business a lawyer had originated the previous year as a benchmark to establish the ceiling.

I, for example, for 1986 had an ERL of $90,000. For 1987, it was $60,000, of which I spent $30,000. What was it spent on? Mr. Jones is our client. We know that it is his wedding anniversary. We send flowers to Mr. and Mrs. Jones. They cost $100. Or I'm invited to a charity ball. I buy two tickets for $1,000. Do I care about this charity? No. But an important client invited me and my purpose is to please that client. If I had paid for the tickets out of my own pocket, I could have taken it as a tax deduction, but here the firm pays for it, takes it as a business expense, and it is not income to me.

Or, a long-term client calls me from Oklahoma City and tells me there is an interesting business opportunity down there, and he asks me down to talk about it, but says he doesn't want any bills. I don't know if we want to go forward on this situation, but I get on a plane and go to Oklahoma City. That's $700. We have dinner. That's another $150. I stay over for a night. That's another $200. I've listened to his idea. It's nothing, a zero. And I've spent over a thousand dollars to find out. I come back to New York. I put in a chit for the expense. I don't charge the client. Although the next time we do a deal for him, we send him a bill that reflects those expenses.

Or, straight entertainment. To my mind, taking two or three couples out to dinner at 21 is a big waste of time.

Instead, I would invite eight or ten couples to my home. We would have some very special people and do a lot of social engineering to ensure the right mix of guests. We'd have a few musicians and a little music for dancing, a catered dinner, flowers, booze. It would be gracious and beautiful, and it would cost a couple of thousand bucks. I charged it as a business expense, not the use of my home, but the cost of the evening. If I had taken those people out to dinner on five different occasions, it would have cost me $5,000. Either way, it is possible to run up a lot of big tabs that way, but the benefit comes back very quickly.

Other partners did similar things, and they had a general understanding of what the expense and ERL funds were for and how they were to be used.

But not all of them.

In the middle of the USFL trial, I got a call from Bill
Lang, the firm's administrator, saying he'd gotten two chits
from Myerson: one for $25,000 worth of jewelry and the
other for $15,000 worth of furs. Lang told me that he
wasn't going to sign off on them, but I could if I wanted to.
So, I went to see Underberg. Keep in mind that Harvey was
on the management committee and a muckety-muck in the
firm, so I talked to several people about this because in
matters of this nature, I did not want to handle it all by
myself. I was always the one saying no, and I knew that
Myerson was going to be upset about my not approving
reimbursement.

He called up Lang asking why he hadn't gotten the reimbursement checks. Lang told him to talk to me. Myerson
called up screaming. I said, "Hey, Harvey, the firm is not
going to pay this. Write the goddamned checks yourself."

He said, "I'm too busy. I'm breaking my ass for the
goddamned law firm. I'm bringing in tons of money every
month and I'm in the goddamned hospital having my stom-
ach reamed out. I'm all upset and nervous and I'm collaps-
ing from exhaustion from this trial. And you, you son of a
bitch, you won't even approve this thing. I don't have time
to be writing checks. I'll take care of it when I get back."

I said, "No, Harvey. If you have time to write the chits,
you have time to write the checks. I won't approve it. It's
not a firm expense." He ultimately paid those bills.

It was at that point that I decided to help Myerson work
out his financial problems. I went over his financial situation with him when he finished the trial. But the banks
demurred. It was about the same time that he bought his
million-dollar co-op in the San Remo on Central Park West
and spent another several hundred thousand dollars decorating it. I don't know where he got the money.

The argument over the furs and jewelry was not the last
such incident. At another point, Lang called me about another chit from Myerson, this one for $16,000 for four
months rental on an apartment on the Upper East Side.

Again, a confrontation developed. I asked him what the bill was about, and he told me it was for an apartment. I said to him, "Harvey, you already live in a lovely apartment on the West Side with your wife and family." He said it was for visiting clients, for lawyers who were working late. I said, "Not a chance, Harvey. It's for a woman. You want to screw some woman, pay for it out of your own pocket. Don't screw the firm." He said it wasn't for a woman. And I said that it sure looked like it to me, but in any case, the firm wasn't going to pay for it.

The final contretemps over expenses came around the same time, in late 1986. Harvey was trying to work out a merger with a London firm. It was a crazy idea to begin with, and it was all the worse because Harvey did not know how to go about it. Recruiting requires putting yourself in second position. Nevertheless, Harvey was shuttling back and forth to London on the Concorde. And at Thanksgiving, he brought his wife and two or three of his daughters to London, on the Concorde, and ran up charges of tens of thousands of dollars. When the bills came in I said to him, "How can you justify this?" And he said, "I'm breaking my ass flying back and forth and ruining my Thanksgiving weekend and I wanted my family to join me. Don't you think that's fair?"

I said, "No. It's a boondoggle for your family. It's nice and all that. And it shows your kids that you're a big man, but why don't you pay for it?" I told him, "Harvey, you can't keep doing this. Stop. Stop. Stop."

TWELVE

When Alan Gelb said, "When Steve Kumble talks to me about money, I talk to him about loyalty," the comment cut to the heart of what I thought was an important aspect of the business enterprise known as the practice of law. Money was important. And it was something that I understood and managed well. I don't know how true it is, but friends and business associates say that my ability and comfort with numbers is such that had I taken a different turn in life, I could have had a successful career in one of the Big Six accounting firms or a major investment bank, instead of one of the largest law firms in the country. Over the years, I became equally at ease with financial statements as I became with legal drafting.

It was a skill that in ways both straightforward and arcane made it possible for Finley, Kumble to grow. It is expensive to attract talented lawyers, house them in offices, provide the service staff to work with them, and to pay the substantial overhead that they incur.

But Finley, Kumble did that and did it successfully for many years. In part, we did it because there was, at least until the last year of the firm's existence, someone who paid attention to the numbers and leaned heavily on everyone to get bills out and hound the clients until the bills were settled. The one who fulfilled that role was me. But the force behind the vigor with which I pursued the smooth operation of that system, and the ethos it encouraged, had its roots elsewhere. I believed that as long as the system worked, the concept of the firm would work. It could continue to grow because financing that growth would be possible. It could continue to grow because it could attract good people, paying them more than they could get elsewhere. It could pull off mergers with whole firms of talented lawyers by promising, and delivering, better bottom-line performance.

But I also knew that if the system faltered, the firm would falter. Heine always like to put a negative face on my emphasis on the business side of the law. He has told people, "Steve's favorite saying: Everyone is motivated by two things and only two things, greed and avarice. That really was the guidepost in his life."

It's true that I would stand up at partners' meetings and make a speech in which I said, "You are all here for many reasons, but one of those reasons is to make more money than you can anywhere else." That bothered some people. But I was the one who was seeing to it that they made the kind of money they expected to earn.

By the time the firm failed, we owed the banks from which we had borrowed—Bankers Trust, Citibank, Manufacturers Hanover, and National Bank of Washington $83 million dollars, including $23 million in loans to the individual partners for the financing of their capital contributions to the firm. The size of the number shocked a lot of people, and some—including Norman Roy Grutman, a less-than-disinterested former partner who was representing several of the firm's junior partners—and *Business Week* magazine took to defaming Finley, Kumble's financing as a "Ponzi scheme."

That's a naive and unfair view. I am not alone in my conviction that had the firm held together, we would probably have found it necessary to stem the accelerated rate of growth, but it would have survived and prospered.

The financing, all of it bank loans, was of four varieties: working capital loans in the form of revolving credit lines; long-term capital improvement loans; partnership capital contribution loans that the firm guaranteed; and loans collateralized by firm accounts receivable that had been sold to a firm-owned corporation.

All four types had been used for many years, although the size of the borrowings increased over time. The financing was structured by the banks and by Peat, Marwick, the firm's auditors. It was not unique to Finley, Kumble.

As a firm, we did not borrow money from banks to any significant extent until the mid-1970s. Then a couple of things happened. First, we had to make some substantial capital improvements in our offices, and the money had to come either from capital contributions or from bank borrowing. We used both.

Every business needs a certain capital base to operate from. A law firm can't go to the public markets, so it must look to the partners, either by requiring them to leave part of their profits in the firm or by having them make an additional capital investment in the firm. The problem with doing that was that in the days of the fifty percent federal tax rate (and New York was another nine or ten percent), if a partner left $1,000 of his profit distribution in the firm as capital, he'd have to pay an additional $600 in taxes on money he'd not actually received. We thought that was not an appropriate way to do it.

So, we said we'd create equity in the firm by fixing the capital requirement for each partner depending on where they were in the financial pecking order. And we developed a way for partners to borrow the money from the bank, contribute it to the firm as capital, and repay it over time.

But we found as the firm grew that increasing the capital position of each partner was not sufficient to cover the firm's spectacular growth. So, the firm itself would borrow on a long-term basis. For example, when we put in a new computer system, it cost us $1.5 million. That is not the sort of thing one pays for out of one year's revenues. So, we took a bank loan and paid it off at the same rate as we depreciated the equipment. The result was that on our books, the bank loan would have the same net value as the equipment. All businesses do that.

At the end, Finley, Kumble occupied close to 400,000 square feet of space in 18 offices around the United States and in Great Britain. Our rent was $7 million a year. We had on our books about $30 million in capital improvements for those 18 offices. We also had on our books paid-in capital of about $33 million.

Something else was happening as well. The firm was getting big, and our cash flow was seasonal. We'd start from zero in February and then it would go to the top of the line by the following January. But we had to pay salaries and draws and rent on a routine basis. We found it necessary to even out the cash flow. So, starting in February, we would borrow money to meet our working capital needs and around August we would begin paying down those working capital lines. That was something we did up through 1981. By the end of each year, our working capital loans were completely paid off.

Toward the end of 1981, the final mode of borrowing was put in place at the suggestion of Peat, Marwick. The purpose was to increase partnership distributions by selling a small portion of the firm's accounts receivable to a separate corporation owned by the firm, borrowing at the bank against the receivables, and then using the cash to distribute just enough money to ensure that each partner received a total annual distribution equal to the projection made at the beginning of the firm's fiscal year.

I thought it was important to make those distributions because I projected to the partners at the beginning of the year that they should make X dollars for the year. At the beginning of the year, I would come up with these numbers and say "Mr. Jones, this year you can expect to make X." And at the end of the year, I wanted to make sure that Mr. Jones made that amount.

Not everyone thought that was a great idea. For example, one of my former partners, who was also a member of the management committee has said, "I think a possible mistake that was made had to do with Steve's belief, and I think it was a true belief, that people had to earn what he told them they were going to earn. We were bringing in a lot of new people every year, and that first year is the toughest because you don't start billing for ninety days. And Steve really believed that if people did not get their numbers, they would have no loyalty, and they would leave."

I was sure most of the people who joined Finley, Kumble had left their old firms, at least in part, because of money considerations. Either those firms were not making enough money, or if they were, the individuals felt that they were not getting a big enough share of it. To attract them, we had to assure them that they would be compensated at a higher level. And then we had to see to it that we followed through on the assurances. We also knew that it was one of our most important recruiting tools because, unlike other firms, we could come up with a pretty damned accurate forecast of what a partner's profits would be. Keep in mind, these were partners in a law firm, not salaried employees.

While I was not concerned with making them all millionaires, I was concerned about trying to meet, within acceptable parameters, the expectations of these people.

If a lawyer thought he was going to earn $200,000 at Finley, Kumble, I was not worried that he make $300,000. But it was a matter of concern to me that he be making as close to $200,000 as possible. It would be very frustrating to someone who was making an enormous contribution to the firm if he did not realize his reasonable expectations for a given year. A partner was entitled to a percentage of the revenue. And that is what he got.

Over time, "making the numbers" got out of hand. Methods of computing compensation entitlement drifted more toward business origination. And as business origination grew to be the major determinant of compensation, other distortions crept in. Concurrently, greed took over and pushed senior people to demand increasingly outrageous amounts of money. In most firms, the ratio of compensation between the highest paid partner and the lowest would run between three to one and five to one. At Finley, Kumble, in the end, the ratio was a staggering seventeen to one. And a method of coming up with cash—borrowing against receivables, a method that was common in other businesses and one that Finley, Kumble used to its advantage—became uncontrollable. Not because it was a bad idea, but because the demands of the senior partners, who were the biggest rainmakers, became ruinous. A further complication was the explosive growth of the firm in the last three years of its existence. Greater numbers of lawyers, of offices, of staff, and overhead and capital expenditures constituted an expansion that skirted the edge of control. And in the final year or so, that growth had far more to do with the political advantage to be gained by the partner pushing for opening another office than it did with a rational vision of expansion.

Long before that happened, faced with the pressures of meeting the expectations of partners and constrained by an accounting method better suited to a mom-and-pop candy store than to an enterprise with revenues mounting into the many tens of millions of dollars, I consulted with our accountants at Peat, Marwick to begin a process of change.

Accounting gets a bad rap from people who don't understand it. It is an endeavor that requires a good bit of creativity and subtlety since what may appear to be simple decisions lead to highly complicated results. For as long as there had been law firms, the accounting system they used was known as cash-basis accounting. It is straightforward and it works well enough for a small, static practice.

In its simplest form, if you have a lemonade stand, for example, it is perfectly okay to figure out your performance on a cash basis. You make the lemonade and sell it. And that is the totality of your business. The money you lay out for the lemons and the sugar constitute expenses; the money you take in from the sale of lemonade is your revenue. At the end of the day, you count your money, and the difference between revenue and expense is profit (or loss).

What that does not take into account is a) what happens when you have lemonade left over at the end of the day? b) what if some of your customers owe you money for the lemonade that you sold them? c) what if you owe someone else money for the sugar or the lemons?

In a lemonade stand, those are not particularly compelling problems, so cash-basis accounting will do. But for a company that is complex, it is not a true reflection of the business. It is not sufficiently sophisticated. And that is particularly true for a rapidly growing business. Suppose, for example, you started a company tomorrow and each month you took on a new corporate account, the biggest corporate accounts in America. And to service each account, you took on the best available executive in the country. At the end of the year, using cash-basis accounting, it is quite possible it would look like you had gone bankrupt, when in fact, you could have had a fabulous year.

Why? Because you were paying out all kinds of money for all the people you had taken on, and for all the rent and all the overhead. At the same time, because people don't pay their bills the instant that the charge is clocked, you would have a mountain of money owed to you. Using cash-basis accounting, you would recognize (that's an accountant's term for booking or entering) expenses when you pay them, and recognize revenue when you collected it. You would have paid salaries and electric bills and telephone bills and rent and so forth. In a law firm, very few expenses can be deferred: not rent; not utility and phone bills; not payroll, which is the very biggest item of expense. When those expenditures are due, they must be paid.

Yet, on the revenue side, there would be a great overhang of money owed and highly likely to be paid. But none of that would show up as revenue since using cash-basis accounting you can't count revenue until you receive it. The revenue side is a disaster. As a general rule, at any given moment, work in process that has not been billed and accounts receivable together account for fifty percent of the annual revenues of a large law firm.

Because cash-basis accounting is highly distortive, no public company—save for a very few—may use the method. The Securities and Exchange Commission, among others, demands that accrual accounting be used. It is a system in which expenses are recognized when they are incurred, not paid, and revenues are recognized when goods are shipped or services rendered or billed, not when the money comes in.

As Finley, Kumble grew, we came to rely, as do most businesses, on bank lending for working capital and for capital improvements. We established lines of credit with Manufacturers Hanover Trust Co., Citibank, and Bankers Trust Co. And the bankers insisted that the firm, although its official books were kept on a cash-accounting basis, keep another set of books on the accrual basis since that would give them a better picture of what was going on.

What I saw was that the firm's success was much better measured by the accrual-basis method of accounting than by the cash-basis method. As we grew, we were doing better on an accrual basis than on a cash basis because, while we could not accrue many expenses, we could accrue a lot of revenue as accounts receivable and work in process continued to expand. If we had been manufacturing widgets, our revenues would have been out of sight because they would have been reflected in accounts receivable. But the internal and official books were on a cash basis, which created a problem of projecting income and fixing compensation.

Encouraged by Peat, Marwick, we began to make some changes. A significant drain on cash in any law firm is something called client disbursements, expenditures that a firm makes on behalf of a client and for which the client must reimburse the firm. For example, a company making a public offering has to pay a fee when it files a securities registration statement. Typically, Finley, Kumble would lay out the fee and then bill the client. Or, a client would call and say, "I want you to go to London tomorrow morning and meet with someone for me. Take the Concorde and stay at the Connaught." I buy the ticket. I go. I pay for meals and hotel and it's a $7,500 outlay.

Finley, Kumble would put that on its books as an expense. When the client reimbursed the firm for the outlay, it would put that payment on its books as revenue. On the firm's books, that looks like it has incurred an expense of $7,500 and later taken in $7,500 in revenues. There is no productivity, no profit. And it distorts the picture because there is a one hundred percent cost against that revenue.

Peat, Marwick told us that our system of accounting for client disbursements was terrible. They pointed out that we were simply advancing money to a client, making a loan to them. And they said it would make more sense to set up a separate account for client disbursements. When such a disbursement was made on behalf of a client, they said, show it as a client disbursement receivable. Debit cash and credit client disbursement receivables. When it's paid back, credit cash and debit the client disbursement receivable account. In that way, the money we advanced on behalf of clients would not adversely affect our reported annual profits.

Still, there was a problem. The client disbursement receivables account was always a big number. Toward the end, it amounted to over $10 million. We had laid out the money, but did not have the cash. And at the end of the year, we had to borrow the cash to pay the partners' profit distributions.

To put that in a broader context, keep in mind that we were growing like Topsy. At the beginning of each year, we would admit new partners and we would readjust compensation percentages to recognize the contribution people had made to the firm over the course of the prior year. Every firm does that and it can be traumatic because everyone wants to know what everyone else is getting. For many people, the most important thing was not the amount of their compensation, but the knowledge that they were getting more or less than someone else. Since at Finley, Kumble, the compensation schedules were part of the firm's financial statements, everyone knew what everyone else was making. It was the source of great friction.

We tried to predict at the beginning of the fiscal year how much a partner would make, based on his percentage of overall profits. That is hard enough, but it was made all the more difficult since we were using the cash-basis method of accounting. We knew the work was there, the business was there, and the clients would pay. But it was extremely difficult to forecast with unerring accuracy how much money we would actually receive in cash by January 31, the end of the fiscal year. It depended on the weather, the United States Postal Service, the whims of clients. Nevertheless, we would make a prediction, all the while knowing that in the course of the year we would probably grow, adding new people and new expenses.

Accounting procedures, particularly the cash versus accrual issue, remained largely academic until the merger with the Washington firm. They had substantial loans on their books, which we took over, and we also got their accounts receivable and work in process. We showed the loans on our books, but we could not, using cash-basis accounting, show the work in process or the receivables. So, our financial picture was distorted. In addition, a big chunk of the Washington firm's business was tied up in plaintiffs' multi-district, anti-trust litigation on which there were some big fees coming, but all those fees were subject to court approval before being disbursed.

Toward the end of 1981, Danzansky, Dickey, which had been by then a part of Finley, Kumble for nearly a year, was awarded a fee of several million dollars in a plaintiffs' anti-trust case. The first installment of that fee, about a million dollars was to be paid to us on January 31, 1982, the last day of our fiscal year. There was, in addition, another million due us at the same time in a bankruptcy matter. If those payments came on February 1, they would have to be booked in the next fiscal year and would not be available for payment as partners' distributions for fiscal 1982. I figured that the odds in favor of that money coming in on time were slim.

So, we went to Peat, Marwick and asked what we could do to recognize that income. We wanted to figure out a way to anticipate that income by a couple of days so we could meet everyone's expectations for the year. If the money came in even one day late, we could not count it for the fiscal year that had just closed. The people working on the cases had put in a ton of work, the fees had been earned well in advance of the payment. The accountants told us to switch to accrual accounting. We asked what we could do short of that, since if we had switched just then, we would have booked several million dollars in other additional revenues, and people would have been clamering for more in distributions.

The Peat, Marwick people said, "Look, the only ones you report to on a cash basis are the partners, and we can disclose to them any adjustments as modifications to cash-basis accounting. The banks already get financial statements from you that are prepared on an accrual basis." So, they said, "Why not do this? Form a new corporation. Sell to the corporation selected items of receivables and work in process. Borrow from the bank through the corporation using the receivables as collateral and use the proceeds of the loan to pay for the sale of the receivables. Then, you will reflect the cash received as income and you will have the cash available for partnership profit distributions."

I formed a corporation, called Accrual Corporation, and assigned the stock to the firm. Then, Accrual Corporation borrowed at the bank, with the firm guaranteeing the loan. The bank took a selected group of receivables as collateral and advanced us the cash. That enabled the firm to meet our projections. The loan was paid down over a period of time. At first, the loans were made in January and they'd be retired by June. Later, they were not repaid so quickly. By January 1987, Finley, Kumble's accounts receivable and work in process amounted to $110 million, and Accrual Corporation, and thus the firm, increased its borrowing to $27 million.

In the years following the formation of Accrual Corporation, the firm, which in early 1981 had 190 lawyers, continued to grow at a rapid pace. It was having a strong effect on our cash-basis accounting statements. We were doing mergers and taking people on in September, October, November, December, picking up the debts and the added expenses, but little or none of the cash. So, it was necessary to increase the amount of Accrual Corporation borrowings.

During those years, too, subtle and not so subtle changes were being felt. Finley, Kumble was never shy about hustling for business. It was a key element in the firm's ethos. Partners' compensation depended in part on drumming up business.

In the early years of growth, the development of new business was singularly important. No one knew us. No one had ever heard of us. No one had cause to come to see us. Later on, as we became more established and were doing different kinds of work and work of a different quality, with clients of a different character, teamwork became much more important. Salesmanship continued to be important to bringing in new business and I believe that any system has to provide incentives for that. But beyond a certain point, it makes no sense to have a system where a lawyer gets a straight commission for bringing in a piece of business.

But we had people who would kill to bring in business, and internally it became terribly competitive. It was a concept that was fostered, promoted, and advanced by several people in the firm, particularly Marshall Manley.

As Manley became a bigger producer, he pushed the idea that the key ingredient in determining compensation should be the amount of business a person originated. For him, it was not something to be considered along with other factors, it was all-important. And as Marshall gained in influence, the focus of attention became originating business. And not just getting the business, but receiving the credit for getting it.

If one lawyer introduced a client to the firm and someone else could help develop an opportunity for the client in a transaction that would generate significant legal fees, the original lawyer would still get the credit. The second lawyer's role was totally lost. So people demanded a share of the origination credit before they would agree to work on a matter. It created tensions and problems.

It became sick and crazy. For example, one of my clients introduced me to a shopping center developer. We took him on as a client and did a good deal of legal work for him. He needed some work done in Los Angeles, so I introduced the client to our Los Angeles office and told him to talk to Manley out there. At some point much later, I got a call from the client's inside counsel with a question on a bill. I thought the matter had been resolved long before, and, in fact, there was no more business on that item recorded in the New York office. What had happened was that in California, Manley had told him it would be better if he was to be Manley's client; that he'd do the work cheaper. So the California office opened the same matter under a different name and different number and continued the work. And Manley got the origination credit.

Another example, one that was more serious, had to do with opening a Chicago office. We all thought it would be a good idea for a national law firm like ours to have a full-service office there. In addition, we had been promised a lot of real estate business by the Chicago-based Gouletas family. (Hugh Cary's wife was Evangeline Gouletas.) There was a fellow I had known from Harvard Law who had been first in our class and was the senior partner in a small but well-respected firm in Chicago that represented the Gouletas's Chicago interests. We talked about a merger, and it would have been a good fit, but Manley was bitterly opposed to the idea. I think he saw it as a power base that would be loyal to me. That merger never went forward. We did open a Chicago office with a couple of people who were in the insurance business. The reason was that Alan Schwartz, a partner in the Beverly Hills office, had a piece of business from London that needed that kind of representation in Chicago. The crazy thing was that the business was listed as originating in California and the fees were recorded there.

There was far too much emphasis on who brought in the business. Toward the end, Harry and Leona Helmsley had spoken to us about the possibility of representing them on their tax problems. Paul Perito in the firm's Washington office was an outstanding criminal lawyer. But he was also motivated by the origination incentive. So, when I called him and asked him to come up to New York to sit in on a meeting on this matter—which might have resulted in millions of dollars in fees—Paul was too busy to come, too busy because I would get the origination credit.

This origination concept caused havoc. We were much too focused on it, and it was the major reason for the huge disparity in compensation. The firm was like a manufacturing company where only the salesmen got paid. Manley was always a huge rainmaker, and most of the business that he brought in could be traced to City Investing and later to the Home Group. Eventually, he was responsible for originating $15 million in business, most of it directly or indirectly from the Home Group. He was working full time as the president of the Home Group, so the only justification for the $1.75 million we paid him was the business he was originating.

For the firm to compensate Manley at seventeen times what the most junior partner was getting, when he did not do an hour's worth of legal work, was a system that was bound to run us into trouble.

Ultimately, that disparity was part of the reason people in the firm ran for the exits when they learned about our broader troubles. Behind the disparity lay greed and the desire for power. Partners were loyal, not to the firm as a whole, but to their own groups. Leaders of those groups, particularly Manley and Washington, dictated decisions on every issue. And then there were arrangements between groups. Manley and Washington and Myerson, but particularly Manley and Myerson, saw a potential of unbridled power and immense income. If only they could control the firm, they could line their own pockets.

I am not alone in my view of Manley and Myerson's caring more about money than anything else. Other former partners share the view. Heine, for example, who claims friendship with both men, says that Manley had been thrown out of Manatt, Phelps because, in part, of unreasonable demands for money. At Finley, Kumble, says Heine, Manley "was demanding more and more money. Marshall had a voracious appetite for money." Of Myerson, Heine said, "Harvey needed the money to live on."

Others, not so charitably inclined, say things like, "The only thing Myerson was interested in was Myerson. He lived high on the hog. We could never figure out how he could live the way he did, even on a million a year or whatever it was he was getting."

Even with his large compensation, Myerson still demanded more. Harvey complained constantly that he was underpaid. To make up the shortfall, Myerson borrowed huge amounts of money. And then, in at least two instances, he failed to pay it back. Banks and other lenders are loath to talk about who owes what. But in Myerson's case, the National Bank of Washington found it necessary to acknowledge he defaulted on two loans, one for $200,000, made in June 1986 and a second for $500,000, made in December 1986, after another of his lenders, Bankers Trust Co., insisted that he borrow no more money without informing its officers.

Answering a suit filed by the National Bank of Washington after the firm failed, Myerson proffered the excuse that the bank's chairman, Luther H. Hodges Jr., told him it would not be necessary to adhere to the letter of the notes he had signed. Hodges testified at the trial in late November 1988 in Federal District Court in New York that no such conversation ever took place. Judge Thomas P. Griesa found in favor of the bank and entered a judgment against Myerson for $932,560 to cover the principal and interest on the loans and the bank's court costs. (Myerson found the money to settle the judgment by getting his partners in his new firm, Myerson and Kuhn, to co-sign on a $900,000 loan from Marine Midland Bank.)

After delivering his own testimony, Myerson stepped from the witness stand so enraged his own attorney found it necessary to restrain him. He started shouting at Hodges, "I'm going to be a witness against you in Bob Washington's suit," referring to a fight between Hodges and Myerson's former partner Robert Washington for control of the bank, which had fallen on hard times, largely because of loans to Finley, Kumble and to its partners.

But while credit was still available and funds were flowing, the firm's chorus kept up the chant. "More. More." More money, certainly. Greed was a source of many of Finley, Kumble's problems. But at the root of things, along with greed, feeding on it and feeding back into it, was the lust for power, the pathological competitiveness. And the voices in the mismatched chorus, were, as often as not also raising the chant, "Me. Me."

THIRTEEN

On that cold Sunday afternoon in January 1987, when I met at my home with Harvey D. Myerson and Robert Washington, the issues we discussed were profit distributions for the fiscal year about to close and partners' compensation levels for the upcoming year.

At the long and nasty meeting, I argued, unsuccessfully, against their proposals for absurdly large increases in compensation for Finley, Kumble's top partners.

I told them that the symbolic effect of such increases would bring serious harm to the firm. The few hundred thousand dollars at the top was not the issue. The symbolic effect was. My prediction was directly on target. The management committee voted themselves average increases of more than twenty-five percent. And that percentage went right down the line, setting a standard that would prove impossible to achieve.

It was one more major piece that set the stage for the firm's ruin.

Less than a month later, when the management committee gathered at the Grand Bay Hotel in Miami for our quarterly meeting. The compensation schedules were on the meeting agenda. What happened was not.

When Joe Tydings led a delegation of partners to tell me they planned to strip the management of the firm from me and put Harvey Myerson in as head of the New York office, I told them it was crazy.

I said, "I helped build this firm from the beginning. Harvey has been here only a couple of years. He has all kinds of disastrous personal financial problems that the banks are aware of, and if he's placed in charge of the New York office and the firm's checkbook, it will cause serious trouble with the banks. And besides, it is not a decision that the management committee should make. It should be up to the New York partners."

And Joe said to me, "We believe that this action will strengthen the firm."

I said, "Strengthen the firm? What do you mean strengthen the firm? The firm will blow apart. It will be a catastrophe. Don't you understand?"

And Joe, my friend, said to me "We have the votes."

And they did.

As we began the management committee meeting, Tydings said he had a motion to propose. It was the motion to remove me. Neil Underberg, the chairman of the management committee and a long-time ally, told Tydings he was out of order. Neil said, "Wait a minute. This is not on the agenda."

Tydings's response was to say, "Look, I'm not going to screw around with penny-ante procedural stuff." Someone seconded the motion, and all sorts of people jumped up and started making speeches. I told the group the same thing I had told Tydings outside, that this was crazy, and it was going to cause irremediable damage. It became apparent right away that it was an explosive issue. The Florida people, who were always close to me, objected that there was no notice of this being an issue and since it hadn't been scheduled for discussion, it was wrong to bring it up.

Hugh Carey stood up and spoke coolly and forcefully about the impropriety of what was happening. He was a great advocate for order and fairness in the face of the putsch that was being engineered. He talked about precedent and rules of order, the procedural things he had mastered as a congressman. But they were not interested. They had the votes, and they were going to move ahead.

When Hugh finished, someone—I don't remember who—suggested that we caucus. So we broke up and spent the rest of the day in meetings; their group and our group; two enemy camps talking about this issue and a sweat-stained Myerson running back and forth between the two groups. At one point, he took me aside and said, "Look, Steve, I'm really your friend. I'm trying to save you from being thrown out of management entirely."

And Gelb, who had sold out to Myerson, was playing emissary, shuttling between the opposing groups, asking me on what basis I would step aside quietly.

Maybe they thought I would back away from a fight and quietly leave the firm. I told Myerson: "Harvey, this is insane. You just arrived here less than three years ago—and it took a lot of pushing and shoving to have you admitted to the firm over the strong objections of a number of partners, including your pal here, Alan. Half the partners in New York don't even know you, and the other half don't like you. Nobody in the firm except for a few people on the management committee has any idea this surprise takeover attempt is going on. If you think there is a ground swell of support for your becoming the maximum leader, you can forget it."

In the evening, as was usual when the management committee met, there was a cocktail party for the committee members and their wives, and for the local partners and associates and their wives or husbands. Peggy recalls talking with Nola Washington, Robert Washington's wife. "I like Nola very much. She's a super lady. We had become close over the years. And we both knew that what was going on in the firm meant that our own friendship would never be the same. When I saw her that evening, I told her that I thought that something was dying. We hugged each other, and we both cried."

We didn't resolve the issue that day, never went back from the caucuses to the meeting of the committee. Instead, we went from these gatherings of the two opposing camps to the cocktail party. My wife was there with tears in her eyes. Everyone was there. Tydings was there, all these people I had recruited, almost without exception, who had turned against me. I never felt so alone and ostracized in my life.

Tydings especially bothered me. He had been my close friend, but at the end he was a captive. He realized that his income and his future were at the mercy of Washington, Manley, Myerson, and Heine.

Subsequent to the coup, Joe would occasionally drop by my office, trying to make some gesture of friendship. And I would say to him, "Do you think the firm is stronger now?" I could not talk to him. And while it was not solely his fault, I was very disappointed in him personally. It was ironic that after the breakup of Finley, Kumble, Joe was pointedly not invited to join the new firm Washington and the other key people from the D.C. office put together.

I stayed up the whole night writing a speech I would give the next day. I was in a state of shock. It was impossible to believe that I had built this firm, and that now this was being done in a way that had no element of fairness or decency. But they had the tickets and they were determined to throw me out. I read the speech the next day to the reconvened meeting. It was impassioned, but it was straightforward, too.

I told them: "For twenty years, I have been working to build this law firm. Most of you sitting around this table, I helped recruit. I think that I have had a hand in improving and expanding the personal fortunes and professional horizons of each and every one of you. In all that time, I have had the responsibility of running the firm and the New York office of the firm, either alone or with others. That took twenty years of my life. Now, in twenty hours, you would like me to make a decision which could affect the rest of my professional life and the future of this firm.

"Well, I'm not that quick.

"The vote which you have been discussing—there is no precedent for it. The leaders of each office are selected by the lawyers in that office. When this firm was created, it was never contemplated that people from California or Washington would dictate who the leaders in Florida or New York would be—or how many there would be. There is no provision in our partnership agreement for this vote.

"A leader or manager is a person who is regarded as such by his peers. I can tell you that within the New York office and outside that office, I am looked to for leadership and so regarded. You can't legislate that away. This vote will have no binding legal or, more important, factual efficacy.

"Most of you have eaten at my table, and many of you have stayed in my home. Our families were close. Last night at the cocktail reception for the Florida partners, my wife was in tears.

"The way you went about this was very strange. No notice, no serious discussion, no item on the agenda. Just twenty minutes to think about my continuing relationship with a firm that bears my name. Meetings in the dark, behind closed doors. No discussion with the individuals involved. I guess some of the things they write about us are true. Shame on us.

"The consequences for me are difficult to assess. The consequences for the firm are clear. They will not be good. The firm could break apart. Banks hate turmoil, instability, and uncertainty. Orderliness, choosing the right representative to deal with the banks, a person whose sense of personal financial responsibility and integrity the banks respect, making a smooth transition. That's important.

"Recruiters and headhunters love instability. They thrive on it. Depending on how this situation is handled, I would expect our people to be harassed with phone calls. We have a tough enough time recruiting good people without this added problem.

"And the media. They will have a field day.

"What the fallout will be is hard to assess. But the effect will not be favorable.

"I urge you gentlemen not to proceed in this way. It will not be a proud day for the firm. I will take this vote as a statement that a majority of the people here wish me to remove myself from the management of the New York office. I would like the time to consider the implications of that for me and the firm. And I will be back to you with my response."

In the months to come, every grim prediction that I made would come to pass.

It took fifteen minutes for me to make this plea for reconsideration. Robert Washington then moved to adjourn the meeting so that the groups led by Manley, Myerson, Washington, and Heine could review my remarks. It took them only thirty minutes to reach a decision.

They either did not believe me or they did not care. They came back from their caucuses. Tydings called the matter to a vote and we lost, fourteen to nine. Six of the management committee members were not there. Wagner was not there. Laxalt and Long were not there. Peter Fass was not there. Four men, Manley, Myerson, Heine, and Washington, had stolen the law firm from its real owners, the partners, and none but a handful of partners even knew what was happening. It was a raw grab for power.

After it was over, there was another agreement: that everything that had happened be held in the strictest confidence. No one outside that small circle present in Miami was to know what had actually taken place.

I remained co-managing partner of the national firm, an empty title without a local power base. The firm prepared a press release and made the announcement that put a positive face on what had happened. But in fact, I had been effectively stripped of power. The news was kept under wraps for awhile.

In the months that followed, word would get out. Heine would once again talk to the press, revealing severely damaging information about what had happened. He could not contain his glee over my downfall.

What was unclear to all but a handful of people at the time was the web that held together the alliance that stripped me of my power. At the center of the web were money and the pursuit of the power needed to get the money.

Five months earlier, in September 1986, my enemies put in place the capstone that secured the accession to power of the Manley-Myerson-Washington-Heine cabal.

The management committee meetings were full of surprises. The September meeting in 1986 in California had nothing special on the agenda. Manley, by that time, had moved to the Home Group and had been its full-time president for one year.

He called my room at the Beverly Hills Hotel and asked me to come down to the Polo Lounge for a drink. I was sitting there sipping my margarita when he said he was going to resign the next morning as co-managing partner. Manley told me the reason was that his duties as president of the Home Group required so much of his attention. Manley was being paid for full-time work at both the law firm and the financial conglomerate.

Manley told me that in his place, he planned to appoint Harvey Myerson and Bob Washington as co-managing partners. I asked him what he meant, and he said, "Well, there will be three co-managing partners, you, Harvey, and Bob."

I told him that was a lousy idea. No business can be run by three people. It's hard enough with two, but three is ridiculous. Secondly, the arrangement completely cut out the Florida people. Third, Harvey Myerson owed so much money to the banks, and his reputation with them was such that it would be sure to cause trouble with our banks. Finally, Harvey had been at the firm only a short time, did not understand the administrative or financial mechanics of the firm, and did not deserve the job.

Manley said, "Well, that's what we are going to do. We have the votes, and it's all set. If I were you, I wouldn't oppose it."

I told him that it did not represent the wishes of the majority of the partners, it was bad for the firm, and I opposed it. I asked him why the hell he had not talked about it before then. His response was that it had just sort of come up.

I and others fought the idea in the meeting that began the next morning. At the meeting, there was a lot of yelling and screaming, but we lost. My partners from Florida said, "Look, we keep losing too many of these votes. You must see the handwriting on the wall. We need a contingency plan."

I said, "No. We'll keep fighting. We'll find a way."

At about the same time as that September meeting, *Fortune* magazine was preparing a major article on Finley, Kumble, and Manley was under some pressure from the Home Group to adopt a lower profile in the law firm. Their advice to him was to resign as a co-managing partner. He had to find someone who would be loyal to him, but who also had enough power to stand up to me. No single person in the firm had that much power. He couldn't completely trust Washington alone to do it, so he got Myerson as well.

Choosing Washington was a brilliant stroke. Manley had already split the New York office somewhat by getting Myerson and Heine into his corner along with a couple of other New York members of the management committee who feared Myerson and Heine. But until Bob Washington was named co-managing partner, the D.C. people had not been consistently in one camp. It was a way for Manley to seal the alliance. With California, Washington, and part of New York behind him, Manley could do as he pleased. In resigning his post as co-managing partner, Marshall Manley had found a way to get everything he wanted.

Perhaps losing that battle was inevitable. For by that time, I was fighting a war whose tactics and goals I did not fully understand. My wife, my friends, my allies on the management committee had cautioned me.

They're not just being accurate in hindsight. They did warn me. "Steve was done in by people whom he had brought into the firm," said one partner. "It was clear, long before the final blow, that it was coming. From the early part of 1986, or maybe a little before, the handwriting was on the wall. The feud with Heine was going full throttle. Myerson was on board and causing all kinds of trouble by his disruptiveness. And you could see in the way management committee meetings were going that there had been a shift."

But I was stubborn, blind really, and I stuck to my view that people would act for the good of the firm and to my conviction that I could control the forces unleashed by my ambitious and politically astute enemies. I had been insensitive in some cases, as with Alan Gelb, when I shoved Myerson down Gelb's throat as his replacement and boss. I lost Gelb as a friend and ally and, in the bargain, picked up Myerson as a formidable adversary.

I was the hatchet man in some cases, as with Joe Tydings, whom I had dealt a double blow. First, I pushed the firm to get out of the plaintiffs' anti-trust business that had been Tydings's bread and butter. Without that business and unable to replace it with a different kind of practice, Tydings lost power and influence in the firm. His business origination and billable hours lagged substantially behind other key Washington partners. He no longer had a meaningful role in administering the office. The final blow was struck when I had to bring him the news that his compensation was going to be less than that of some others in the D.C. office. He was really hurt by that and took it personally.

People like Gelb and Tydings were important but peripheral. I had, in one way or another, let them down; perhaps they saw it as betrayal. They were no longer on my side, and as power shifted in 1986 to Manley, Myerson, Washington, and Heine, they became more and more beholden to that group.

At the same time, Manley stepped up his godfather role, lining up votes on the management committee, trading favors. Management committee meetings were full of surprise agenda items. Manley would dictate how to vote to his people and then line up the few additional votes necessary to carry out his schemes, and the rest of us would get blindsided. I had always viewed the management committee as an informational forum and a kind of institutional glue for the firm. But it had been transformed into something much different.

We established the management committee in the 1970s as a forum for airing issues and as means of making quick decisions on matters that required immediate attention. It was never intended to be a forum where there would be different factions. Quite the opposite. For many years, we operated by consensus. If there was strong disagreement on an issue, we would not act. But Marshall Manley worked hard to see to it that it became a factionalized political forum. When that happened, the whole concept of having strong offices in different parts of the country began to break down. Individual offices began to feel that they were on their own and had to look out for themselves, rather than seeing themselves as part of a much larger organization whose best interests came first. They began politicking for themselves.

Because each major office had a great deal of autonomy, a schism developed between the Manley-Myerson-Heine-Washington group on one side and my group, which included the old guard in New York and the Florida partners, on the other. As that happened, the question of who became a member of the management committee had less to do with their contribution to the firm and more with how they would vote on any given issue.

I woke up, suddenly and too late, to the realization that the committee had been politicized. Operating by consensus gave way to bitterly contested votes, with the California people, who were over-represented on the committee, and the Washington people, who were also over-represented, voting as a bloc. The Florida office was under-represented. All Manley needed to swing things was a small handful of New York votes.

With New Yorkers Myerson and Heine in Manley's camp, the people who worked for them in the corporate department and the litigation department and were dependent on them would vote with Manley on policy issues. When the policy issue became replacing Manley as co-managing partner with Myerson and Washington, they voted for it. And suddenly, not only did Manley control the policy committee of the firm, he controlled the day-to-day management of the firm as well. He had replicated himself by producing the unlikely clones Myerson and Washington. Instead of there being a stand-off between Manley and me, the majority of the co-managing partners, Washington and Myerson, could call the shots on a two to one vote.

And Manley owned them.

Heine's intense dislike for me was apparent. He acted as agent provocateur with Manley, Myerson, and Washington. He had stood up for Myerson against me. He had shamelessly flattered Robert Washington, telling Bob that he could be the first black president of the United States. Far more important than simply befriending Myerson, he had lent Myerson a significant sum of money. And although, according to Heine, Myerson ultimately betrayed him, their alliance was in full flower by the beginning of 1986. In Manley, Heine had found the man who could bring it all together. The machinations needed to displace me, and

thus to punish me for taking the public credit for building
the firm, had been started on their inexorable way. It was
only a matter of time before Heine would have his revenge.

And he owed it to Marshall Manley.

Washington had become a power in his own right. Not
only had he achieved wealth and status in the local Washington, D.C., community, but he had also become a power
in the larger world of big-time law. He was co-managing
partner of one of the largest law firms in the country, a
position unique for a black man. He sat on the board of the
Home Group's reinsurance company. The law firm whose
Washington office he headed had done the will of the President of the United States.

And he owed it to Marshall Manley.

Harvey Myerson was all over the papers with his work on
the United States Football League case. *Fortune* had fea-
tured him in a lengthy story on high-powered litigators. He
wore a fur coat, drove a Ferrari, had more homes than he
could live in. He owed a ton of money. His profligate
spending was closing the bank coffers that had previously
been open to him, but he was able to stay afloat.

And he owed that financial buoyancy to Marshall Manley.

The connections were a wonder of intrigue.

Since the early 1980s, Marshall Manley had controlled,
and for a time served as the chairman of a bank, a small
bank to be sure, but a bank nevertheless—the Merchant
Bank of California, domiciled in Beverly Hills. Like most
banks, the Merchant Bank of California, which Manley had
founded, was in the business of lending money. Unlike
most banks, Manley's bank was lending a good deal of
money to executives and board members and shareholders
and special friends of the bank at very favorable rates. Myerson, a stockholder in the bank, was one of the benefi-
ciaries of this largesse, as was Heine.

By the end of 1985, the Merchant Bank of California,
Manley's Bank as it came to be known among the partners
of Finley, Kumble, was in deep trouble. It was in danger of

failing. The Federal Deposit Insurance Corporation, the
body that insured the bank's deposits and therefore had a
supervisory interest in the bank's health, went after Manley
and company, charging the bank with a long list of violations of law and banking regulations.

Cease and desist, said the order from the FDIC dated
March 7, 1986, and the consent order dated May 28 of the
same year. No more engaging in "unsafe . . . unsound"
banking practices: "operating with inadequate capital; operating with a large volume of poor quality loans; operating
with inadequate loan valuation reserve; operating without
adequate lending and collection policies; operating with
inadequate provisions for funds management; operating
without separate books and records for subsidiaries; operating in such a manner as to produce low earnings; operating with an employment bonus agreement with prior management which has motivated prior management to allow
the accumulation on the books of a large volume of worthless assets in order to justify the payment of bonuses under
said agreement; and operating in violation of Section 22 (h)
of the Federal Reserve Act . . ." the laws and regulations
that govern insider lending.

In short, the FDIC charged that the bank was being pil-
laged and run into the ground by the people who controlled it. It was clear that if the bank failed, Manley could
be the target of a spate of law suits. He had been the
chairman and was active in the running of the bank itself. If
the bank could squeak out of the trouble caused by the
FDIC's charges of violations of regulations and law, Manley
could avoid the problems that would arise from litigation.
That was doubly important because a big public scandal
would surely jeopardize his position with the Home Group,
itself a heavily regulated enterprise.

Among the remedies the FDIC demanded was the bank's
recapitalization. That could have been accomplished in a
variety of ways, including a public offering of common and/
or preferred stock or doing a private placement of stock.

Manley and his associates decided that a private placement was the way to go. And where better to stuff the
private placement of the stock of this deeply troubled bank
than into the hands of the partners of the law firm whose
co-managing partner he was? It was only a couple of million
dollars. If it became widely known that the bank was on the
brink of insolvency because of gross mismanagement, it
would reflect badly on Manley and other board members,
including Andrew Heine, and, they reasoned, on their law
firm.

But expecting the partners to come up with that kind of
money for so questionable an investment was really reach-
ing. It was not so much a golden opportunity as it was a
charitable contribution. It would have been a hard sell at
best.

But what if the partners could borrow the money? After
all, banks had entire departments devoted to doing business with what are known in the jargon as "high net-worth
individuals." And among the high net-worth individuals
that banks' "private banking groups" like to serve are lawyers, indeed entire firms of lawyers.

As luck would have it, Robert Washington, a man who
owed to Marshall Manley his seat on the board of the
Home's reinsurance company, his access to Ronald Reagan, and in the not too distant future his position as co-
managing partner of Finley, Kumble, had some banking
connections.

He had, with Luther H. Hodges, Jr., helped take over the
Washington Bancorporation, the parent of the capital's
oldest bank, the National Bank of Washington, and he sat
on its board.

Robert Washington, by many accounts, was not, and still
is not, a whiz kid when it comes to banking and finance, but
he was an effective influence peddler in banking circles.
When Citicorp needed approval to expand into the District
of Columbia, the New York banking company hired lawyer
Washington. He did yeoman service on Citi's behalf with

his friends on the Washington District Council. And when Washington wanted to get his partners in Finley, Kumble into the stock of Washington Bancorporation, his friends at Citibank were more than happy to provide the loans to buy the stock.

Washington himself, via a pair of trusts involving shares owned by Finley, Kumble partners, including Manley and Heine, controlled more than five percent of the Washington bank's stock. That bought him not only a seat on the board of directors and its executive committee, but also significant clout in the bank's operations.

When Washington's friends, benefactors and boosters, Marshall Manley and Andrew Heine, found their California bank in trouble with the FDIC and on the verge of insolvency, there appeared a credit facility, or something that looked a great deal like a credit facility at the National Bank of Washington, of more than $2.5 million. It looked for all the world like it had been earmarked for Finley, Kumble partners to borrow, without collateral, for the sole purpose of purchasing a new issue of the rather dicey stock of the Merchant Bank of California. That purchase would improve the California bank's capital position sufficiently, or at least close enough to mollify the regulators and supervisors.

Although the loans to the Finley, Kumble partners later became a key issue in a fight that began in late 1988 between Washington and Hodges for control of the National Bank of Washington, NBW officials earlier defended the lending on the grounds that banks make loans to all kinds of "high net-worth individuals," and that the bank already had a relationship with the firm's partners. True enough. But those were Washington office partners. The bank was not in the habit of lending significant sums to folks in California, New York, and Florida. Yet on this issue, senior people in the firm were dictating to partners in all Finley, Kumble's disparate offices the size of the investment they were to make, telling them that exactly that amount had been set aside for them to borrow from the National Bank of Washington, and providing them with promissory notes to be signed and returned to NBW.

The loans and the stock were jammed down the throats of Finley, Kumble partners. Manley, Heine, Myerson, and Washington told partners that they had to sign up. Jerome Kowalski, a litigation partner who tended to be independent, recalls, "I did not sign. I was importuned by Alan Gelb to sign the note. He told me that if I didn't, Harvey Myerson was going to think that I was not a team player. They circulated a memo saying that Marshall was a leader in the bank, that it had a close relationship with the firm, and that we should all invest. It was a printed memo, a Xerox, but there was a blank space filled in, in handwriting, with the number you were supposed to sign up for. Mine was $15,000. I refused. I said that I wasn't going to put my family at risk."

When John Schulte refused to go along with the scheme, Manley went into a rage. Schulte told him to his face that not only was he not going to contribute, but that he would oppose this nutty plan among the Florida partners. Manley lost control and began shouting and threatening Schulte: didn't John know that when compensation time rolled around that it was something that Manley would not forget?

When Manley first proposed the idea to me, I told him, "This is your problem. You fix it. Don't lean on other people to fix it." His response was that the firm had benefited. I said, "You got the benefits from the Merchant Bank; you got the credit for the legal fees the bank paid the firm. There is no way that some young partner should be forced to make a capital contribution to that floundering bank."

He said there was no need to worry; that Bob Washington had already arranged for the National Bank of Washington to lend everybody the money they needed to put into the Merchant Bank. Manley sloughed off his responsibility onto everyone else and got his pals, Heine and Myerson and Washington, to do his bidding and beat up on the partners to get them to contribute. It was like a Marshall Manley fund-raiser.

As an added fillip, Finley, Kumble represented the Merchant Bank. The memorandum for the private placement to raise the money required a considerable amount of legal work. Of course, the bank had to pay for that work. And Manley got the origination credit for bringing that revenue into the firm. He had it both ways.

Among them, they controlled the firm. Manley had a lock on the six California votes. Washington controlled all the votes in D.C. At the beginning of 1987, after taking on Russell Long and Paul Laxalt, who had both retired from the Senate, we made room for them on the management committee, bringing to seven the number of votes in the Washington office. In New York, there were Myerson and Heine, and that was enough for a majority on the 29-man management committee. In addition, Gelb, who was working for Myerson, and Don Bezahler, who worked for Heine, would both vote with them. And that provided a cushion. Florida, which was close to me, had nearly as many lawyers as California, and yet had only three votes on the management committee. They felt they were getting screwed.

This very small group controlled the management committee. With Washington and Myerson as co-managing partners of the firm, it also controlled its day-to-day operations.

I was out of the loop.

After the February 1987 meeting where I was summarily bounced, I was at a loss, frankly, about what to do. I did not know whether I should leave the firm. I was embarrassed and humiliated and did not know how to deal with the problem; did not know what public posture I should take. I really did not want to hurt the firm I had built up over so many years. At the same time, I felt very uncomfortable working in that environment.

But I did not know where else I could find a home. I was

aware that I was controversial and was unsure whether any law firm would be interested in having me join them. I didn't know whether I wanted to continue with the practice of law, or what else I might do to establish a new career. I was paralyzed by uncertainty.

So, I did nothing. I did not tell anyone what happened. I did not tell the banks. I did not say anything to anybody because I was too ashamed, too embarrassed to say anything.

The embarrassment served as a sanction because of the agreement at the February meeting to keep quiet about what had happened. The people who voted to throw me out were afraid that my predictions would come true. So, for the outside world's consumption, I was still a co-managing partner of the firm. They asked me to make an announcement in a statement prepared for distribution in the firm that because of my heavy responsibilities in managing the firm nationally, I had asked Harvey Myerson to replace me as head of the New York office.

I went along with that fiction under the threat that otherwise they would reveal to everyone that I had been thrown out.

FOURTEEN

With the shift of control complete, changes already in the wind or in place accelerated. The people running the firm paid themselves pretty much what they wanted and spent the firm's resources as they pleased. The growth of the firm exploded, but it was growth that had more to do with internal politics than any coherent plan. I had been pushed from power and effectively rendered impotent as the enforcer of billing and collections. And as I predicted, the banks, when they found out what had happened to me and that Harvey D. Myerson was in charge in New York, got very nervous, indeed. They stopped lending to the firm.

Manley and Myerson were the two most highly compensated people in the firm. At the same time that Manley was receiving an expense account of $200,000–$250,000 from the firm, he also had an unlimited expense account from the Home Group, the use of the company plane, and a car and driver. So what the Finley, Kumble expense account covered, God only knows. But he spent the allowance.

Myerson had, in addition to his expense allowance, secured for himself a stretch limo and driver that was paid for by us. And in the year that the firm cratered, he managed to spend $150,000–$160,000 of his expense allowance. And it was a short year. What did he spend it on? Who knows? In addition, he had his hands on the firm checkbook.

Bob Washington, who by the end was not much of a business producer, was getting about $900,000. He also had access to the firm checkbook. He was the one who approved non-accountable funds for the Washington office. Those are expenditures that are attributable to the office as a whole, not to any individual. He made use of them. Bob, too, had a driver on the firm payroll.

In addition, all of them were receiving compensation from other organizations that they were involved in, the banks on whose boards they served, and other board positions.

Even if there were no other problems in the firm, the speed of growth would have created difficulties. Solution: slow the growth. The people at the top have to be careful about setting everyone's standards so high that you can't achieve those standards during a period of growth. To avoid problems, the answer is pretty simple. Your grandmother could have told you: Slow down and digest what you have eaten. But that homily fell on totally deaf ears at Finley, Kumble.

In the final months of the firm's existence, the following happened:

*Myerson was working on a merger between Finley, Kumble and a London firm of solicitors, Berwyn, Leighton. The merger ultimately did not come about, but he was spending a great deal of time on it, flying back and forth between New York and London. He was managing partner of the New York office, but between his litigation practice, the failed merger talks in London, and his trips to California and Washington for personal politicking, Myerson was not spending much time running the firm.

*Finley, Kumble opened an office in Chicago in order to service some business that Alan Schwartz had picked up from a London insurance firm that needed representation in Chicago. That was essentially the only business the Chicago office had. Originations were credited to California. The existence of the office could be traced to firm politics not to any rational growth plan.

*At the beginning of the year, the firm took on, in its Washington office, former U.S. Senators Russell B. Long and Paul Laxalt. It opened an additional D.C. office, refurbished, at a cost of $1 million, to accommodate the staff and other lawyers they brought with them. In addition, as an accommodation to Long, the firm opened an office in Baton Rouge, Louisiana. Each man was guaranteed $800,000 a year. That $1.6 million outlay was augmented by the cost of their coteries and the cost of the new offices. Almost immediately after joining Finley, Kumble, Laxalt began spending full time seeking the Republican nomination for the presidency. He remained on the firm payroll although he did no work for the law firm.

*The firm brought in Peter Fass, the tax-shelter syndications expert, and his group of sixteen lawyers from Carro, Spanbock, Fass, Geller and Cuiffo at an annual compensation cost of nearly $2.3 million. Office space and support costs were additional.

*The firm expanded to Dallas. A political expansion to accommodate Washington litigation partner Paul Perito, who was representing members of the Hunt family in the highly publicized case involving the Hunts' manipulation of the silver market.

*The complete refurbishing of the Miami office at a cost of $5 million.

*Refurbishing the Fort Lauderdale office at a cost of $1.5 million.

*Refurbishing the Palm Beach office at a cost of $600,000.

*Opening an office, with about fifteen lawyers, in Talla-
hassee, Florida.

*Opening an office in Sacramento.

Beginning early in 1987, adding yet another obstacle,
political turmoil in the firm eroded whatever spirit of unity
had existed. In fact, the opposite prevailed. People were
pulling in opposing directions and making plans to leave.

All these things were being done for reasons that made
no sense in the context of an overall development plan.
That is not to say that none of the projects or additions to
the firm had merit. Any one of them might have made sense
if one were to spend the time planning and focussing the
attention of the firm in order to make it succeed. We could
make almost anything work. But we could not open several
offices simultaneously and integrate them into the whole
because there was no one to manage the process. No one
was interested in making these things work, except those
people who had a political stake in them.

Yet, the firm was continuing to grow and expand and
spend the money to do it. Heine attributes it to "the egos
and the greed and the immaturity of a number of people at
the top—Harvey and Marshall and Bob. They had no good
reason to be getting what they were getting at the end, but
there was nobody to stop them. We had a firm where there
were certain allegiances, and everyone was afraid to block
the others. Then, within the groups, when they had gotten
into their positions, they had to cater, pander really, to
their followers. I would think it very hard, if you are a
dictator, not to give the generals under you most anything
they want. It was that kind of situation."

The Miami people said they wanted to complete the con-
struction and furnishing of their offices, and that they were
going to do the work, spend every last nickel they needed to
do the work first class, on the chance that they would be
leaving Finley, Kumble. They intended to keep the offices
for the new firm.

Probably the dumbest thing the firm did was to expand to

Dallas. It made no sense at all. Paul Perito, a Washington litigation partner with a lot of experience in the criminal field, had merged his own firm with Finley, Kumble. He wanted to be involved in the administration of the firm, although he spent half his time on airplanes and the other half in court. One of Paul's big cases was representing a group of Hunt family members in an aspect of the big silver case. A Dallas lawyer named Roger Goldburg was representing the Hunt brothers' interests.

Perito had gotten to know Goldburg well and figured that if we would open an office in Dallas, headed by Goldburg, it would do two things. First, it would enhance Paul's position in the firm, give him a power base. And secondly, it would cement his relationship with the Hunts. Paul thought that if Goldburg were then able to bring over the balance of the Hunt business, it would be great for the firm and for Perito personally.

At the meeting where it was first brought up, I objected. First of all, Dallas and all of Texas were reeling under the blows of a very rough economy. The real estate industry there was dead and there were huge office towers in downtown Dallas that you could literally see through because they had so few tenants. Secondly, we had no client base in Dallas, and I did not think that Roger Goldburg would be able to bring in that much business. Moreover, as a firm we were not in a good position to add to the business he had down there, even with the business he had with the Hunts. More important, I personally did not have the time to devote to it and neither did anyone else have the management time it was going to take to establish the practice and the office there.

"No problem," they said. "Goldburg is going to make great inroads. Not only that, but Bob Washington has agreed to act as liaison with the Dallas office."

I stood up again and said, "Look, fellows, I am married to a woman who spent a big part of her life in the Dallas-Fort Worth area. She is a close friend of Bunker Hunt, and I know him as well. There is no way that Roger Goldburg and Bob Washington are going to steal away the business of the ultra-conservative Hunts' from Shank, Irwin. In addition, if you think Finley, Kumble can open a Dallas office in this lousy economy and capture the hearts and minds of the Dallas establishment with Roger Goldburg and Bob Washington spearheading the effort, guess again. This is the wrong time, Dallas is the wrong place, and we are doing this for the wrong reasons. Forget it. It is a big mistake and it will cost us a lot of money."

The firm opened a Dallas office.

Even Heine, who normally aligned himself with Washington was against it. He recalls: "Steve and I were together in opposing the opening of an office in Dallas. It was the worst business deal imaginable, unbelievably bad. The Dallas lawyer representing the Hunts in the silver case thought if he left his firm he could take the Hunts with him. It was the whole basis of his practice. Paul Perito, who was involved in that case, too, wanted to solidify himself with the Hunts.

"Bob Washington needed Paul politically, so he could not say no to him. That was probably the best example of the leaders catering to the followers. We opened more Florida offices because we were pandering to Steve's people. Another example was the London office. Marshall wanted it for his own ego, but it was also pandering to Alan Schwartz who was representing some English people and wanted a presence over there. It was a terrible deal, but Marshall could not say no to Alan. He didn't need the office. He already had the clients and had set up the Chicago office just for them."

All these things were going on at once. All of it was being approved by the management committee. People were saying to each other, "I'll vote for your office if you'll vote for mine." And it had nothing to do with economics or sound business practice. It was out of control. The firm was not being managed. If decisions are made on the basis of staying off someone's hit list, you're not going to get good decisions. But that is what was happening.

In a corporate structure, the board of directors is composed of corporate executives and outside directors. The outside directors can act as a check on the insiders. At Finley, Kumble we had no board. We had a management committee that was composed solely of partners in the firm. And the committee had lost sight of the greater good.

Meanwhile, with Harvey Myerson in charge of the New York office and me shunted aside and trying to figure out what I might do next, revenues began to fall off.

When my own authority was challenged and ultimately eliminated, things got out of hand. I did not have the support I needed to enforce discipline. Billing and collecting became very difficult to police. As long as people in the firm were afraid that their failure to comply with the system would bring down upon them my indignation and wrath, things were alright. But the minute they were insulated from that, protected by Manley or Washington or Myerson, the system began to falter.

Just how much less well it worked is staggering. The numbers may be on the high side, but in the first quarter of fiscal 1988, the year that began February 1, 1987, the firm's revenues were short of projections by a whopping $22 million, according to an estimate by one of the firm's bankers. High or not, even if the number were half that, it meant big trouble. Because at the same time that money was not being collected, expenditures were going through the roof.

Money was flooding out the door. The increased compensation schedule the management committee voted early in the year meant that partners' draws were up about twenty-five percent over the previous year. That alone meant an additional outflow of a half million dollars a month. The capital expenditures, increased overhead and staffing expenses, and the cost of bringing on new partners added to the cash drain.

The great Finley, Kumble cash machine was breaking

down. The firm had been a solid credit for the banks. It had
—certainly through clever accounting, but far more important because of its ability to turn legal work into cash—been
able to grow dramatically and to do so by paying the people
it sought better than anyone else.

At or before the beginning of the firm's 1988 fiscal year,
February 1, 1987, Finley, Kumble had entered into agreements for credit facilities totalling $80 million with its three
major banks—$25 million each from Citibank and Bankers
Trust Co., and $30 million, a $5 million increase over the
previous year, from Manufacturers Hanover Trust Co. In
addition, the firm received assurances from the National
Bank of Washington that the bank was "pleased to advise"
that it "is prepared to establish a new ten million dollar
($10,000,000) unsecured credit facility in favor of Finley,
Kumble, et al., to meet the firm's ongoing working capital
requirements."

By late April 1987, the New York banks were beginning
to get twitchy. Citibank rejected a request from the firm
that it be relieved of its guarantee of partner loans. A
"highly confidential" memo from Finley, Kumble's administrator, William Lang, highlighted conversations and
meetings with Citibank officers. Citi's C.J. Hamilton called
on the morning of April 28 to inform Lang that the bank's
credit committee had rejected the request. "He advised me
that the decision had nothing to do with the creditworthiness of the firm. Having received year-end financial statements, the bank had reviewed them and was more than
satisfied.

"The bank," the memo continues, "was concerned
about:
   a. stability of management in the national firm;
   b. disposition of management in the New York office;
   c. the perceived change in senior management;
   d. rumors in the street (unidentified);
   e. recent publicity which has left the bank with a feeling
of insecurity.

"Hamilton advised me that the bank could not act further on our request until such time as their concerns could be addressed with the co-managing partners of the firm."

Later the same day, Lang met with Citibank's John Cook. Cook, Lang informed his bosses, told him, "We are concerned with things on the periphery," not with the firm's creditworthiness. Lang's memo went further to describe the conversation with Cook about "things on the periphery."

"a. No other law firm customer of the bank is as large and geographically diversified as Finley, Kumble. Concern was expressed regarding the manageability of such a firm.

"b. Concern regarding the cohesiveness of interest in light of the number of strong personalities within the firm."

The bank was monitoring its activities with Myerson.

"c. Concerns regarding the impression of divisiveness created by recent publicity . . .

"e. While Manley and Kumble were viewed as adversaries, the departure of Manley as a co-managing partner from the 'active' day-to-day management of the firm was viewed as a sign of instability."

Inklings of what had happened in February had begun to surface in the press. Word was getting around. But many people did not know what really occurred, and as far as they could see, I was still functioning. I smiled. I walked around the halls. But by mid-spring, as the truth of what had taken place began to seep out, it became too humiliating for me. I began to prepare to leave the firm and took several steps in that direction. I changed my status from being an individual member of the firm to being a professional corporation. I started signing bank documents, "Steven J. Kumble, P.C." The banks noticed right away.

I started looking for a job. I felt that since my defrocking was now becoming public knowledge, anything I could do for the firm, any possibility of making a contribution, was destroyed. Quite apart from that, I was very unhappy.

I went to see my old Yale classmate, Russell Reynolds,

the head of the executive search firm. The day after I met privately with him, a story about it appeared in the *New York Post.* Russ sent a memo around telling his people not to talk to the press about who comes into the office. The next day, the *Post* ran a story about the memo. He called to apologize.

Meanwhile, within the firm itself, confusion and contention grew. The vow of secrecy the management committee had extracted with respect to my loss of position was crumbling quickly.

It was not enough for Heine that I had been bounced. Andy could not control himself. He was so happy about this turn of events—that he had succeeded in breaking me— that he wanted it generally known I had been emasculated. So, he leaked a story to the *American Lawyer.* That story was ultimately picked up by *Forbes.* There was no longer any reason to conceal what had happened from the public and from the banks.

When the June 1, 1987, issue of *Forbes* magazine hit the newsstands in New York on May 20, the story was there for all to read. "Fall of a Rainmaker" was the headline on an article that detailed my downfall following the management committee's actions at the February meeting. Partners were enraged and began to suggest that Heine be thrown out of the firm.

The banks' free-floating anxiety had taken form. The bankers were downright frightened. In prior years, Finley, Kumble's borrowings had trended lower as the year progressed. In 1987, instead of paying down the loans, the firm borrowed at an increasing rate. The bankers had heard rumors about trouble in the firm, but the combination of escalating borrowings, my own switch to professional corporation status, and then the *Forbes* article outlining the real change in power and authority in the firm confirmed their fears.

The banks had called me asking who the hell was running the show. I told them that I was no longer in charge. I told them that I would have a continuing relationship with the banks, but would be doing it in conjunction with Myerson. They were very distressed to hear that because they had all dealt with Harvey on his personal finances.

By the beginning of June, Finley, Kumble had drawn $18 million of its $25 million credit facility at Bankers Trust Co. On June 5, the bank told the firm it was freezing the facility at that level. In another "highly confidential" memorandum hand delivered to me, Myerson, and Washington, Bill Lang, the firm's administrator, wrote that the bank officers had told him that while they did not wish to "trigger" the loan, "they will not process any additional requests against our credit line until their concerns have been allayed."

Lang continued through the three-page, single-spaced typewritten memo delineating the bank's worries about the firm's creditworthiness and "management instability."

Among the sources of uneasiness about the firm's credit status were: "continuing apparent need by the firm for additional borrowing; use of borrowing to meet partner draws and distributions; lack of confidence exhibited by Kumble in the financial security of the firm by becoming a P.C. partner." Under the rubric "management instability," Lang detailed that the bank had "previously felt that firm was being directed by Kumble; current concern as to divergences of opinion among three co-managing partners (including negative inference from rumors in the street); concern resulting from removal of Kumble as New York co-managing partner and related publicity—*Forbes* article."

In addition, Lang wrote, it was apparent from the comments of the people he had met with, that Bankers Trust had directed its own in-house counsel to go over Finley, Kumble's partnership agreement and credit documents and would be requesting a new credit authorization "as a result of changes of members in the firm's management committee."

The bank wanted a meeting with Lang and the three co-managing partners, Myerson, Washington, and me. On the bank side would be not only the officers the firm dealt with regularly, but also the senior vice-president they reported to and the chief credit officer of the bank's private banking sector. The bank was playing hardball. If anyone hadn't gotten that message, Lang added, "They do not wish that such a meeting include lunch since it is not intended to be a 'getting-to-know-you' meeting."

Lang speculated that the bank would request a special multi-bank workout and restructuring of the firm's short-term debt; a commitment from the firm that it would not use borrowing to meet partner compensation; and a "show of confidence by the co-managing partners in the credit-worthiness of the firm by either reversing their P.C. status or issuing their personal guarantee as to outstanding loan balances."

As an aside, Lang wrote that prior to the requested meeting, the bankers "expect to voice their concerns to Myerson during a meeting initially scheduled to discuss Myerson's personal finances."

I started getting calls from our other bankers. Bob Hunt and John Cook at Citi and Peter Phelan at Manny Hanny phoned to ask me what the hell was going on. They insisted that we meet with them, and Myerson asked me if I would sit in on the meetings. He said we could tell the banks that I was going to be involved. I told him I'd be happy to sit in on the meetings, but the banks sensed that the relationship was tenuous at best.

Myerson was well known to all the banks. Washington had done some business with Citi. And the two of them would sit in these meetings telling the bankers how they were going to run the firm. But the banks were very concerned about our stability. The combination of the change in control, the conflicts and disputes at the top, the adverse publicity, and having a man like Harvey in administrative and financial control eroded our credibility.

Myerson did not really get what was going on. We would go to these meetings, and Harvey would walk out of them afterwards and say, "Well, that's all settled." He could not understand that bankers sitting around smiling did not mean a thing.

In the midst of all this financial turmoil, the firm made a deal with National Bank of Washington, taking advantage of the $10 million credit facility that NBW said it would be willing to provide. Papers were signed June 3, and the loan was approved later in the month by the bank's board. (Robert Washington's dual role, as co-managing partner in the firm and as a member of the board of the bank, would, a year-and-a-half later, become a matter of great contention between him and bank chairman Luther Hodges. Washington had by then moved to oust Hodges from his position at the bank. In the court fight that followed, Hodges would maintain that Washington had miscarried his responsibility to the bank by not informing the board of the upheaval at Finley, Kumble.)

At about the same time, the firm's malpractice insurance policy was due for its annual review, and Myerson called me and asked me join him and Washington in a meeting with our insurance broker. I told him that I would not attend the meeting. Myerson asked why not and I told him that I did not think it appropriate to make decisions of that nature if I was not going to continue with the firm. I had not yet made any announcement because I had not found a place to go. Myerson seemed taken aback and told me that it would be bad for the firm if I were to leave.

Harvey said Heine was the one who caused this and asked whether it would be helpful if we threw him out of the firm. I said, "Look, it is impossible for me to stay in a firm where we condone, or do nothing about, someone who is constantly pissing on the firm. I may leave anyway, but I won't stay in a firm with a fellow who is as crazy as I think Heine is."

Things were popping elsewhere as well. The people from Florida were calling me about the *Forbes* article, telling me that they were distressed and wanted to know whether I was going to stay or going to go. They talked about seceding from the firm. I told them that my staying would do nothing dramatic for the firm. I couldn't recruit since everyone knew I had no muscle anymore, no say. I couldn't make deals, couldn't really do anything about billing and collections. I couldn't act effectively with the banks because I did not have the authority.

But I told them I thought they should stay. They had a very good thing going down there, 140 lawyers in four offices, a successful and growing practice. I told them that it would be foolish to go.

The Florida partners felt left out. They had been recruited by me. They thought Myerson was a joke. They were not happy about working in a firm run by Robert Washington. They were deeply offended by Manley's shenanigans with the management committee and the affair with the Merchant Bank. And they were deeply angry about the compensation schedules. Thomas Tew, James Jorden, and John Schulte were running a very successful operation. In the fiscal year ended January 31, 1987, Tew and Jorden each originated over $3 million in business. Schulte originated over $2.5 million. The compensation for each was set at $550,000. When they looked at the compensation going to Robert Washington for the next year, $865,000, they wondered why he was getting half again as much as they for producing $2.7 million in business. And they wondered why Washington's pal, Paul Perito, with $1.8 million in originations, was getting $525,000. And why Manley's California pal, Richard Osborne, whose originations were about equal to those of Jorden and Tew, was getting $750,000.

They had a point. They were losing out because Manley, Myerson, Heine, and Washington were running the firm. The Florida people were doing work for every major insurer, doing important securities work. We had just finished handling the ESM case. Schulte was representing Citibank in a major case. They were representing Sun

Banks, Barnett Banks, NCNB, and a whole raft of other banks doing business in Florida.

They were doing great and the people in D.C. were not doing so well. They could not understand why Washington, who was doing less business than Tew and Jorden and only a bit more than Schulte, had been made co-managing partner. The people in Washington were getting large increases and they were not. They were on the outside looking in. And they asked why they should support all this.

The complexion of Finley, Kumble had changed. Manley, Myerson, Heine, and Washington were running the firm, and the Florida people found them distasteful. It was not the firm that they had joined, and, because of their friendship with me, they found themselves on the losing side.

The D.C. partners were not bringing in the money they thought they would bring in, and they had, particularly with the advent of Laxalt and Long, taken on significant new expenses. So they were just hemorrhaging money. And the Florida people felt they were paying for that. They said, "We're breaking our necks, bringing in all this money and business. We we don't even have a say in how the money is spent and these guys in Washington are spending like crazy."

What they forgot was that they were supported throughout their growth period until they got to the point where the cash machine kicked in. Also, they had just finished spending a fortune of money on capital improvements. Capital improvements didn't run through the financial statements in year one, but still they had to be paid for.

Finally, the idea of taking on Long and Laxalt was generally applauded in the firm. And if Finley, Kumble had been pulling together, it might have been a good thing. But the Florida partners chose to look on it as a D.C. problem. So, they were saying that the Washington office should get its house in order.

What bothered them most was the tremendous variation

in compensation between them and the D.C. partners. They knew that it was based solely on politics, not on the merits.

They told me that they were going to wait until the new offices were finished and then they were leaving. They said, "We did not come to this firm to work for Manley and Myerson and Bob Washington." I told them I didn't blame them for that, but it would be better to cool it.

FIFTEEN

Secession was in the Florida air, and any headhunter who could read, was on the phone. It was as though the firm were spewing pheromones into the atmosphere. The headhunters were calling everyone, telling people that the firm was about to sink. It was terribly destabilizing. People were becoming a lot more concerned about what would become of them than about doing their work.

Even before that, the tension was palpable. One of the younger New York partners was close to several of the partners in the California offices, and they would talk and try to piece together what was going on.

It was not until the *Forbes* magazine article that Myerson found out they were talking and he told this particular lawyer not to talk to the California partners. On a trip to the West Coast, Myerson had a meeting with the partners during which he bellowed uncontrollably at them and forbade them to talk to this fellow. He had little sensitivity, little sense of what it meant to be in a partnership, and even less skill as a manager.

With a few exceptions, the 2,000 people who worked at Finley, Kumble did not know it, but by May 1987, a handful of men had set forces in motion that would irrevocably change their lives and fortunes, as well as those of the law firm's creditors and many of its clients.

Before May wound down, the fighting was so intense that no one was running the firm. Meanwhile, the debt was rising and rising. And most of the members of the firm were in the dark about what was going on. Former partners even now complain that when someone would ask questions about the debt and the financial position of the firm, they would be met by a screaming, red-faced Myerson telling them, "It's none of your fucking business," or, alternatively, lying through his teeth and assuring them that everything was alright. They were partners. It was literally their business.

It was widely acknowledged that I was the one who was good at seeing that the bills got out and got paid. I was not doing it, and as a result, the firm was drawing down huge amounts of cash from its bank credit facilities. Myerson had taken over, and the only thing he was interested in was Myerson.

The rumors had circulated through the firm for weeks. Then, the *Forbes* article hit the street, confirming them. The effect was devastating, particularly among the younger partners. The scramble began. If greed ruled at the top, if it was indeed the force that drove those in the game of "Capture the Flag" that Myerson, Washington, and Manley had recently won, money was no less a major motive down through the ranks. One senior partner, a member of the management committee who argued for restraint both in growth and compensation levels, says, "What brought most people in was money. And I think that as soon as they got scared or nervous that the money would not be there, the lack of foundation and lack of loyalty led them to do what people who have no sense of loyalty always do: think about themselves."

The leaders of the firm had long been waging a war among themselves. The news that power had shifted and the hint that financial difficulties could be in the offing put anxiety on a trajectory approaching the vertical. People were running around, getting their resumes in order, looking to leave, calling headhunters, and taking calls from them. Money concerns exist at almost every law firm. But at Finley, Kumble they were paramount. The firm lacked the social fabric and the institutional glue that might hold another firm together in times of financial stress.

The headhunters, calling with predictions of disaster, were not far off in their assessment, even though their calls added to the difficulties the firm was facing. Finley, Kumble was running into trouble over its malpractice coverage, in part because of a large number of cases brought against California partners. The banks' actions had focused attention on the firm's liquidity problems. And the final showdown between Heine and me was about to be played out, although neither of us would be present to witness the battle.

A special Sunday management committee was called in Washington, D.C., for June 14 to discuss the impact of the articles that had come out and to discuss Andy's continued role in the management of the law firm. Andy had, over the years, repeatedly and consistently badmouthed the firm and me in the press. The articles in *Forbes* and the *American Lawyer* were the final insults. Any other business organization would have thrown out a person like that a long time before.

People knew that if he continued in the management of the firm, I would not stay. I was pointedly told that I should not be present at that meeting, nor should Heine be present. Myerson told me that what Andy had done was unconscionable and that he would take steps to have Heine removed.

Myerson's assurances to me proved to be so much blather. At the meeting, a rather raucous affair, Manley and

266 Steven J. Kumble and Kevin J. Lahart

Myerson vowed that Heine would be removed only over their dead bodies. They had not counted on the depth of feeling against Heine and found themselves with few allies in their support of their comrade. One partner, so enraged by Heine's constant dumping on the firm, proposed throwing Andy out the window. In the end, Heine's champions went down to defeat. The majority voted to strip Heine of his management roles in the firm. There was a reservoir of good will toward me, and faced with a choice of having me with them or continuing to deal with Heine, they cast their vote against Heine.

The management committee reached a consensus that Myerson and Washington should tell Heine about what had happened at the meeting and to obtain his resignation from every position of management responsibility he held in the firm, although not his resignation as a partner. He was told that he had to resign from membership on the management committee and as its co-chairman and from his post as head of the corporate department. He was given time to find a home for himself. The management committee was resolute in its action, but stopped well short of publicly humiliating their partner. To force him out of the firm would have taken an affirmative vote of sixty percent of all partnership shares and would have meant circulating a petition. Heine broke down and wept when Myerson and Washington gave him the bad news.

The following week at a June 23 meeting of the management committee, the partners formally implemented Heine's demotion. At the same meeting, the firm established an executive committee that included me, Myerson, Washington, Alan Schwartz from California, and a rotating member from Florida.

The firm issued a press release that made no mention of the Heine affair. But it did issue a strong expression of confidence, via an unanimous vote, in the three co-managing partners, the unlikely triumvirate of Myerson, Washington, and me.

At this late stage, Myerson was still totally absorbed with controlling the management committee. He demanded that the departing Heine be replaced on that committee with his ally, Richard DeScherer, a man Myerson had brought with him from Webster and Sheffield. Gelb and Myerson expressed open concern that nothing be done that would "allow Kumble to climb back to his former position of authority." Myerson and his allies saw to it that the newly-formed executive committee was structured to insure that a majority of the committee's members would be slavishly loyal to Myerson, Washington, and Manley.

Their obsession about what might happen to their personal gravy train if I were to return to a position of real authority far outweighed every other consideration, including any passing concern about what might happen to the law firm if it continued on its self-destructive course.

At the urging of the Florida partners and of Hugh Carey, with Heine beheaded and with an inkling that Myerson was looking to leave Finley, Kumble and that Manley was anxious to distance himself, I decided to stand firm.

The executive committee had a series of meetings over the course of the summer. They were very unpleasant. At the meetings, the Florida people demanded that the D.C. office cut costs by throwing out partners and associates and by cutting expenses in every way it could, including the partners taking sharp cuts in compensation.

As much as anything else, the Florida people wanted revenge for being dealt with unfairly earlier in the year. They wanted to jam it down the throat of the man who was running things. Bob Washington, for his part, was willing to cut in every area except compensation. He was adamant. The meetings went nowhere.

Myerson and Manley and Washington had gained control of the firm in a coup but did not realize they commanded little broad support. They discovered that their position was much less secure than they had thought.

As early as late June or early July 1987, a time when

Myerson was leading the meetings with the banks, he was also beginning his search for a new home for himself. He referred to one headhunter who acknowledged that Myerson was on the market as "a goddamned liar." But for Harvey Myerson, life was just filled with one "goddamned liar" after another. His major clients were beginning to express dismay that Myerson was trotting around town promising other firms that he could bring those clients with him from Finley, Kumble.

Myerson and Heine were not the only ones looking for a way out. Marshall Manley had decided that he didn't want to be a partner anymore and moved to change his status with the firm from partner to counsel. That was in July and August. He also wanted the status made retroactive to the beginning of the fiscal year. Myerson, still in Manley's debt, went along with the scheme. He was still in Heine's debt as well and when, in August, Heine withdrew from the firm, he was able, with Myerson's approval, to take his capital out in a lump sum.

Not long after Heine was removed as the head of the corporate department and as a member of the management committee, we heard that Brill was calling many of the partners of the firm and that he had a considerable amount of detail on the firm's finances. Some of us suspected that Heine had given it to him. We also heard that Brill was telling people that he was planning a lengthy article on Finley, Kumble that he described as a "devastating" look at what was going on. It was not good news. We had enough trouble without having to deal with one of Brill's hatchet jobs. I refused to talk to the writer.

We cast about for some means of counteracting what was sure to be the damaging fallout from such a story. We thought about hiring a lawyer to bring suit against him, but did not. I finally hit on the idea of talking with Jimmy Finkelstein of the *New York Law Journal* and the *National Law Journal.* Jimmy had been a friend of mine and his publications had, over the years, given the firm fair treatment. It

had by no means always been complimentary, but on balance it was fair.

I met with Jimmy and begged him to run a story about
the firm and how we were trying to solve our problems. I
said, "Look, Finley, Kumble is a great firm. We have problems, but a lot of firms have problems. Can you do a story
that would cast us in a favorable light?" He said he could
not do that, but he said he would be happy to have someone
do an in-depth look at the firm and write an article. It
would, however, have to be something new and interesting,
and he could not guarantee its content or interfere in the
article's preparation. He asked whether I would supply financial information about the firm. I decided to take the
chance. He hired Donna Dubeth, a Pulitzer Prize winning
free-lance writer, to do an article. The chance paid off. The
piece that the *New York Law Journal* published was fair. It
came out a day before the Brill piece in the *American Lawyer.*
But it contained a list of the compensation of the top one
hundred partners in the firm. Some of the partners were
furious.

The next day, Brill published his story. On the cover of
the September 1987 issue of the *American Lawyer,* in full
color, was the smiling countenance of Andrew Heine and
the headline: "Bye, Bye, Finley, Kumble. The firm everyone loves to hate is falling apart." Brill was right. It was
devastating. The young people started running out the
doors.

Although he had been repeatedly criticized for damning
the law firm in his public comments and had been removed
from its management because of his disparaging remarks,
Heine could not resist a parting shot at destroying the firm
that bore his name.

Virtually no one in the firm was quoted by name and it
was assumed that it was Heine who gave Finley, Kumble's
internal financial statements to Brill. Brill asserted that the
firm was accounting for revenue on an accrual basis and for
expenses on a cash basis. That was not true. Books were

kept on both bases and not mixed. The firm, moreover, had made the switch to accrual accounting for all purposes as of February 1, 1987.

Heine says that he went to Myerson before talking to Brill: "I got blamed for the Brill article, but before I spoke to Steve Brill, he told me that he had spoken to a lot of partners in the firm. I had not been talking to the newspapers at all. I went in to Harvey and said to him, 'Unless you as managing partner tell me that I should not meet with him, I will. I am not going to tell him anything, but I'm also not going to be taking these gratuitous slaps from Hugh Carey and John Schulte without defending myself. And I promise you that I will not give him any information about the firm except to correct mistakes.' (The two, particularly Carey, had been leading the publicity campaign to put the firm in a better light.)

"I met with Brill for breakfast. He knew when I met with him exactly what our debt was and what our balance sheet looked like. He knew everything.

"I did not know until a year later, when he [Brill] told me, that the weekend before, Harvey had given him all the figures. Harvey never told me this. I took the complete rap on that."

From September on, running the firm became a holding action. Myerson was looking to leave. Underberg was looking to leave. The Florida partners were moving closer to secession. Tew, Schulte, and Jorden demanded a meeting with the old guard: me, Carey, Underberg, Wagner, Blum. We met at the Yale Club, and Schulte announced that Florida would leave. I begged them not to. I told them that it would sink the firm. But they'd already given the story to the *Times.* The piece appeared and got picked up everywhere.

In the midst of all this, several of us—including Hugh Carey, Neil Underberg, Gary Blum, Bob Wagner, and I met to see whether we could not put together a new Finley, Kumble firm. We met at Neil's home, and it was Neil who said no, publicly. He said that his people would not go to work for a firm named Finley, Kumble. I told him, "Forget the name. I don't care what the firm is called, as long as we stay together."

He said, "No, I don't think it is in the cards."

I was deeply disappointed. I thought to myself, "When I met Neil he was making eighteen grand. Now, he's making close to a million bucks a year, owns a huge yacht, and we're meeting in his lovely apartment on Park Avenue." I thought he was being short-sighted, but I suppose at the end, he had concluded that I was not a winner, and he was not going to tie his future to a loser. That pretty much torpedoed the idea of continuing with the group assembled.

He was obviously looking for a new home for his real estate group. A great chunk of the business he was working on came from clients I had introduced him to. He did not ask me along; did not even ask me if I was interested in joining him when he moved. On the contrary, when I asked him to keep me in mind, he said, "No. I've got to do what I've got to do."

Still, he was a loyal friend for a very long time. I wished him well.

All during the final months of the firm's life, the bills for expenses kept coming in. Bank borrowings increased. Partners continued their draws at the high levels they had voted themselves at the beginning of the year. Revenues did not keep pace. No one had taken my place as the enforcer, and few partners were bothering much with collections. They were either far too busy looking for a way out, or they were stockpiling their accounts receivable against the day they left.

The situation with our clients was surprisingly orderly even after news about the turmoil at the firm became widely known. People would call wondering what the hell was going on, but it was hard to measure the impact on business. There were two aspects to the problem. On the one hand, you could not know what was on their minds. And so it is unclear what business we did not get, or what cases we were not called on to handle. But it was certain that when they saw instability, they weren't much inclined to hire us to work on a piece of business that was likely to take a long time to complete.

But for the most part, the clients remained loyal to individual partners of the firm and for the most part left with individual lawyers as those partners went to whatever firm they were going to. You can be sure that from a lawyer's point of view, the first people he called when he started thinking about leaving were the people he represented. He would tell each client that he was thinking about leaving and ask whether he could count on them to come with him to his new firm. That happened with individual lawyers and it happened with the offices that stayed intact. They kept the clients and the matters that they were working on.

There were exceptions to that, of course. Manufacturers Hanover was an important client. So was Citibank. So was National Bank of Washington. And you can bet that as they saw what was going on, and saw the possibility that they would be involved in litigation with us, they didn't send us a lot of new business. But there is no way to quantify the potential business we did not get.

The banks demanded meetings with the firm's management. Plans were drawn up and scrapped. Many of the partners saw cutting expenses as the way to solve the problem. But even whacking back severely would save only a few million dollars. I thought the effort was misdirected. Instead of cutting costs and expenses, we needed to get collections up. In a law firm, you cannot cut fast enough to make a difference. The real issue was to focus on revenues. The problem at Finley, Kumble was that there was no one to do that. Neither Bob Washington nor Harvey Myerson moved to oversee billing and collection. There was no support for me to do it. So, the focus shifted to cutting costs.

With a truly heroic effort to cut down in every possible

area, we might have been able to save $4 million or $5
million. That makes no difference. But to collect $100 mil-
lion; that was where the money was, and that was where we
should have made our effort. Instead, people were making
plans to leave. And if a lawyer were going to leave a law firm
and take clients with him, he would also want to take along
their receivables and unbilled work in process. So, why
collect what they owe? Revenues fell dramatically.

The money was important to the banks, obviously, but it
was not so much the money itself as the deep divisions
within the firm that prevented us from putting in place a
workable plan. It was not so much the amount of money as
it was the absence of effective management.

Myerson went to Washington, D.C., for the putative purpose of trying to work out something with the office there
so the D.C. partners could take steps that would allow
Florida to reverse itself and stay in the firm and everyone
could save face.

Myerson came back up to New York, and the next day
called a meeting of the New York management committee.
He told his partners, "I am here to announce the end of
Finley, Kumble. There will be a new firm. It will probably
be called Myerson, Laxalt and Washington and maybe
Schwartz. It will be smaller, maybe 250 or 300 lawyers. But
it won't involve any of you."

I thought to myself: That's the good news. But I also
thought: My God, what is going to happen when this gets
around the office? We had gone through so much already
with the problems and the articles and the rest. And at that
point, I lost heart, lost faith, lost whatever I had. It was like
watching a drama from the inside, but being removed from
it. And I said to myself: These people have no idea what is
going to happen; no idea of the disaster that is going to take
place.

Then, to compound things, Myerson suggested that the
debt problem could be solved by forming several different
practice groups that would operate as independent firms

simply by dividing up the firm's assets and dividing the $80 million in bank debt among four groups—New York, D.C., California, and Florida. About $20 million for each group. No problem. Remarkably, the banks bought the idea. Bank representatives began to meet with senior people in the firm, parceling out the firm's assets and making agreements about how the practice groups would buy their way out of the debt. That further induced partners to sit on accounts receivable. Cash flow slowed to a trickle. Partners' resignations came in torrents.

To a great degree, the banks were exacerbating the problems that already existed by encouraging and facilitating people going off in several directions instead of staying and working out the problems. There was no legal justification for the bank to participate in and encourage that wholesale distribution of all the assets of the law firm. If the banks had said to everyone involved that they would hold all the partners jointly and severally liable, instead of sitting in meetings divvying up assets, it could have quieted things down.

The *New York Times,* planning a big Sunday business section takeout in November on the firm's problems, was told that everything would be worked out. The paper did not bite. Even before the article was finished, one of the paper's photography editors was dispatched to our Park Avenue offices to help set up the shots. "It was kind of delicate," says the editor. "We knew it was going to be a very negative piece, and the original plan for the layout involved a group photograph of major partners that would then be torn apart. The concept did not work."

The concept may not have worked visually, but it was precisely what was happening at the firm. The *Times* ran the story on Sunday, November 15.

It was the end. There was no holding back the surge of leave-taking. Stiff upper lips were displayed in public posturing, but the scramble among name partners, founding partners, all partners, was on. Underberg announced he would leave. Carey sent in his resignation and announced that he would join W.R. Grace and Co. Myerson was whirling around with a different plan every other day. Finally, he teamed up with Bowie Kuhn, the former baseball commissioner. Manley was already gone as a partner. Heine had left in September. Finley, who was approaching his eightieth birthday and had for years played only a minor role in the firm, resigned.

Finley, Kumble, Wagner, Heine, Underberg, Manley, Myerson and Casey had run out of money, out of spirit, and out of control. It was quickly running out of name partners as well. Staff were not being paid. What partners were left met and decided officially to kill off the law firm as of January 4, 1988.

On December 15, I withdrew from the firm. My secretary was not being paid. I packed up my bag and walked out the door.

I tried to put together a group of the old guard to form a new Finley, Kumble firm, but they were too tired and did not think that the Finley, Kumble name was a great asset.

The firm was dead. What was left was a mess. On January 25, 1988, the firm's four creditor banks—Manufacturers Hanover Trust Co., Citibank, Bankers Trust Co. and National Bank of Washington—sued those of the firm's former partners who had not entered into side deals with the banks. A month later, on February 24, the banks moved to force the firm into involuntary Chapter 7 bankruptcy. The firm's own four-man liquidation committee filed for voluntary Chapter 11 reorganization. Their request was granted by U.S. Bankruptcy Judge Prudence Abram. Suits were stayed. Abram appointed Francis H. Musselman as bankruptcy trustee. The final dissolution began.

Looking back on it now, it is still painful. It was as though a bomb had exploded in the middle of a business organization and all the leaders had died. Rumors were rampant. No one was communicating with anyone. There was no control, no head, no one person or group who knew what was going on and could explain it to our clients, our trade creditors, our banks and, most importantly, to the younger lawyers and the staff. Careers were up in the air. Here was a business with 2,000 people on the payroll and their lives and careers were suddenly in shambles. They had mortgages to pay, bills to meet, kids to send to school. And nobody was talking to them. Nobody knew what was going on. It was confusion. It was hysteria.

I was sickened and saddened by what was happening.

I have personally witnessed businesses going through difficult financial times, going into bankruptcy. And I have seen the leadership of those organizations effectively take control, doing what was needed to be done in some orderly fashion.

But this was like a fire in a theater with people trampling each other to get to the exits, like an army in rout. And not only mass confusion. People had become like animals. Draw checks had been sent out to California, but because we did not have the funds to make the distribution to the partners, the administrative people in California were told to hold the checks. Using threats of physical harm, several of the partners in California forced the administrative staff to open the safe where the checks were kept and hand them over.

I had to drag myself to the office each day to see a whole stack of notices of withdrawal on my desk. Partners became aware that this was a dangerous situation for them personally, dangerous from the standpoint of their financial responsibility. Several people sent me resignation letters that read, "I am not a partner of this firm. I was never a partner of this firm, but if I was a partner of this firm, I resign. But my resignation should not in any way be construed as an indication that I was a partner. And besides, I have not received my draw in a long time."

Leon Finley's resignation said something about having retired. He claimed that he was not a partner but only a partner emeritus. Well, he was a member emeritus of the management committee, but he was sure as hell a partner in the law firm. Hugh Carey resigned saying that he was never really a member of the management committee, and if he was, he never had a say in those meetings, anyway.

I lived through it as though I was drifting through a fog. I felt like a well-used punching bag. All day long, partners and young lawyers would come into my office, and I was getting calls from all over the United States, always with the same questions: "What's happening? What's going on? Is there going to be a payroll this week?"

I had saved enough money that I did not have the immediate worry about how to pay the mortgage, but I knew there were people there who did have that worry. The uncertainty that prevailed was just horrible.

It was a matter of personal humiliation and deep, deep sadness for me as I saw what I had built up over all those years disintegrating before my eyes.

One day, late in the afternoon, Nora de la Serna, who ran our accounting department, came in to see me. She was a loyal, hardworking woman. I asked her to sit down and we talked for a while. She told me she had enjoyed the opportunity of working for the law firm; that it had been a good experience for her; and that she had particularly enjoyed working with me and that despite what was happening, she wanted to thank me personally for all the good years she'd had at the firm. And she wished me well. It was more than I could take, and I broke down. It was the only time I lost my grip.

I said to myself, even during this difficult period, I have really given my whole effort through the entire twenty years, given the very best that I have. I never regretted making the effort. I was sorry it turned out the way it did, but I never regretted making the effort.

But when Nora de la Serna came into my office, and the full impact of what had happened became clear to me, I regretted making the effort.

Today, I think to myself that the partners in the firm,

many of whom had opportunities they never would have had otherwise, and who grew professionally in ways they might not otherwise have done, and who were able to earn more money than they would otherwise have been able to earn or may ever earn again; I think: they resent the experience and blame me for the failure. And that is a tough indictment for twenty years of your life.

In a personal sense, it is worse than that. I always thought that the firm should operate on merit and that I could not play favorites, no matter how close a personal relationship I might have had with someone.

And as that attitude became clear to others, there was no point in being loyal to me.

It was particularly the case with Alan Gelb. On a personal level, I would have done anything for Alan. But when it came to business, to making decisions about what was good or bad for the firm, I called the shots the way I saw them.

I have since decided that the only thing that really counts is loyalty, even if it means that some people in a business organization are not carrying their weight. Loyalty is what is important, even in a business environment, because when you can't do anything about the economy or about the way things sometimes work, the only thing that binds you together are loyalty and friendship.

At Finley, Kumble, if I had to choose between two fellows —one, a good, loyal, hard-working, decent man, who had been with the firm a long time, but who for whatever reason was not terribly productive; and the other, an offensive, abrasive, disloyal man who had arrived last week, but who was a major rainmaker—I would have chosen the second fellow because he would bring in more money.

No more. If I have to go down for the count, I'd rather go down with a band of friends than with a bunch of disloyal pricks, because you go down just the same. And after it is over, you still have the friends.

It was the biggest mistake I made. I consistently announced to everyone, "It's all on the merits." Unfortunately, no one else believed it.

People have asked . . . why did Finley, Kumble fall apart? It was not because of any absence of professional capability or a lack of financial success. By any standards, the partners were uniformly top flight professionals, expert in their craft, amply rewarded and enjoying enviable lifestyles.

It was not the debt. To be sure, the bank debt was large when compared to the debt carried by other law firms. But Finley, Kumble was one of the biggest law firms in the country. It was, in fact, a bigger organization than many companies listed on the New York Stock Exchange. The bank debt was a reflection of our rapid growth, and was supported by $110,000,000 of accounts receivable and work in progress. Our client roster read like a Who's Who of corporate and financial America.

Finley, Kumble fell apart because it was never really together. At the top, there were too many strong egos, too many "maximum leader" types, and too little institutional glue. In the structure of the firm there was too much autonomy in the 18 separate offices. We encouraged that autonomy. That was great for promoting rapid growth and establishing a local identity; but it was disastrous when crisis time came.

EPILOGUE

Two and a half years after the firm collapsed, its bankruptcy still had not been settled. The barrage of lawsuits that had been filed by our former bankers and other creditors, along with a spate of suits between and among partners, remained on hold pending the resolution of attempts at a coherent settlement process that would cost each of the handful of senior partners a seven-figure sum.

Francis Musselman, the bankruptcy trustee appointed by the court, came up with a proposed plan whereby, to cover the shortfall, partners must come up with approximately $40 million. The plan allocates the debt based on the amount of money partners took out of the firm in the last four years of its existence and then weighs the allocation based on factors that include management roles, responsibility for the affairs of the firm and personal net worth.

In the last four years of its existence, Finley, Kumble had about 270 partners, some of whom had left the firm long

before it blew apart. The plan was tentatively accepted by
the court and the creditors' committee approved the contribution levels of about 220–230 partners. About 45 of the
partners' contributions remain a matter of dispute, but
those 45 represent more than half of the $40 million. To
the best of my knowledge, the creditors were seeking $5
million from Manley, $2.7 million from Heine, $1.8 million
from Myerson, $1.1 million each from Underberg and
Washington, and $5 million from me. In addition, they are
asking Finley, who really had no major management role in
the last several years, for $2.25 million, largely, I think,
because he is an old guy with no family and a lot of money.

Members of the firm have scattered. I dropped the full-
time practice of law, became counsel at Summit, Rovins &
Feldesman and devoted myself to helping run Lincolnshire
Management, Inc., a New York leveraged buyout firm that
Frank Wright and I had founded in 1986.

The change has been refreshing. For the last three or
four years of Finley, Kumble's existence, I dreaded going
to work. I hated what I was doing. I felt that I was on
quicksand. From the time I came into the office in the
morning, throughout the day, and late into the evening, I
was faced with solid unpleasantness: conspiracies, closed-
door meetings, closeted partners hatching schemes. I'm
not certain that I'm going to make a lot of money in my
current venture. I hope I will. But more to the point, I enjoy
coming to work. I like the people. Nobody here is looking
to kill me. It is a very pleasant place to be. Things are going
well.

That is more than can be said for many of my former
partners.

As of the spring of 1990, Marshall Manley was out of a
job. Under his leadership and vision the Home Group,
which changed its name to AmBase in May 1989, had em-
barked on an ill-timed expansion from insurance into
broad financial services including banking and the securities business. Manley had saddled the company with debt,

and bewildered and angry stockholders watched as their shares lost eighty percent of their value during his tenure. By March 1990, a matter of weeks after AmBase announced that it was putting the Home Insurance Company on the auction block, the AmBase board, under pressure from institutional investors, engineered Manley's removal from his post as president and chief executive officer of the company.

In the time since Andy Heine was thrown out of Finley, Kumble in August 1987, he has come and gone as counsel at another New York firm. He took on, and was removed from, the chairmanship of Kinney Systems. Finally, he engaged in a couple of ludicrously fouled-up attempts to take over two of Victor Posner's companies.

Upon Finley, Kumble's failure, Bob Washington formed a new firm, Laxalt, Washington, Perito and DuBuc. He continued his well-publicized and bitter fight to wrest control of the National Bank of Washington and its parent company, Washington Bancorporation, from Luther Hodges, Jr. On the glitter front, the Washington firm suffered a setback when Paul Laxalt, the former conservative Republican senator and "first friend" in the Reagan administration, left the partnership in early January 1990 after Bob registered the firm as foreign agent of the Marxist People's Republic of Angola.

Myerson's troubles continued. He drove his new firm, Myerson & Kuhn, into the ground in less than two years amid rumblings of mismanagement and highly questionable billing practices and accounting for expenses.

Other important or well-known partners present a mixed bag. Former New York Governor Hugh Carey went to work for W.R. Grace and became affiliated as counsel at Whitman and Ransom. After the firm finally dissolved, I lost touch with Hugh. I tried to maintain contact, but apparently he was not interested. I do not know what happened, though on several occasions I have attempted to reach out, to invite him to our home. He has not responded.

Manley brought former New York Mayor Robert Wagner into the Home Group. Joe Tydings, the former Democratic Senator from Maryland, was excluded from the new D.C. firm of Laxalt, Washington. Neil Underberg took his real estate group to Whitman and Ransom.

Alan U. Schwartz continued a path that has become a source of mirth among lawyers. When Schwartz's friend and client Mel Brooks immortalized the lawyer in his *Spaceballs,* the phrase "May the Schwartz be with you," was a blessing. Among law firms, if Schwartz is with you, watch out. His first firm, Greenbaum, Wolff and Ernst, tore itself apart. His next firm, after merging to form Fulop and Hardee went bankrupt. Then he joined the L.A. office of Finley, Kumble, and served as the de facto man in charge after Manley left for New York. After Finley, Kumble vaporized, Schwartz joined Shea & Gould as head of that New York firm's Los Angeles office.

After a relatively brief stint at Shea & Gould, Schwartz led seventeen other lawyers out of and into the chubby arms of Harvey Myerson as they all signed on as Myerson & Kuhn's western outpost. They were barely out the door when Shea and Gould gave up on Los Angeles and closed its office.

Schwartz should have known better than to join Myerson & Kuhn, but he reportedly claims that Kuhn's presence in the firm gave him hope. After Myerson & Kuhn went belly up, Alan stayed on for a while as a partner of the L.A. successor firm to Myerson & Kuhn, Cooper and Dempsey. Brooks apparently still believed in the efficacy of the mantra he had created for *Spaceballs.* In 1989, changing it slightly, he said, "May the Schwartz be with me," and invited Schwartz to become president of Brooksfilms if a pending deal to take the company public succeeded. Alas, the $15 million initial public offering came up $9 million short and the idea was scrapped in early 1990.

In April of that year, Schwartz joined Cooper, Epstein &

Hurewitz. When I heard about it, I considered sending them a sympathy card.

Alan Gelb, after spending two years with Myerson & Kuhn, did not go with Myerson as Harvey set out on a new course of disaster. Gelb ended up at Summit, Rovins & Feldesman, working on a contractual basis whereby he would get a set proportion of the business that he could generate.

The main partners in Finley, Kumble's Florida group, after practicing together in Tew, Jorden & Schulte for more than two years, parted company in the early spring of 1990. Tew, along with nine other lawyers from the firm, left Schulte and Jorden to form Tew, Garcia-Pedrosa & Borgognoni. There had been rumors that Tew was planning to leave for more than a year. I think that what finally got to him was the management style and the financial arrangements at Tew, Jorden & Schulte. Tom is a very egalitarian guy.

Tew said that he moved because of a "fundamental difference in philosophy" about the way the firm he formed with Jim Jorden and John Schulte was managed and that the attorneys who left with him wanted a greater say in managing firm affairs. At first, Tew, Jorden & Schulte had a standard kind of partnership arrangement, but at the time Tom left, they had switched to a structure where the three name partners were the sole owners. That is not a business arrangement that many lawyers will put up with over the long term. Lawyers like to have a say in what goes on in their firms and they want to have a piece of the action as well.

The Florida firm, both before and after the demise of Finley, Kumble, paid very well and attracted some of South Florida's most talented lawyers. But it was plagued with defections, falling from 130 lawyers in early 1988 to 57 by the spring of 1990. Tew summed it up: "Money is a great magnet, but it's not glue. It can bring people in, but it can't keep them."

Greed is not enough.

It's a lesson that seems not to have sunk in with Washington, Heine, Manley, and Myerson. They had hitched themselves to each other for the common cause of getting me out of the way and of nourishing their greed and power lust. The destruction of that partnership did little to moderate their tendencies toward self-aggrandizement or sharpen their judgments about its pursuit.

Until shortly before this writing, Robert Washington remained embroiled in his attempts to take over Washington Bancorporation, the holding company for the National Bank of Washington. At times, Bob seemed to think the bank was named after him. What was at stake for the attorney is control of an institution that might otherwise cause him considerable trouble because of the past relationship between the bank and Finley, Kumble. Beginning in the autumn of 1988, Washington attempted to dislodge Washington Bancorp's chairman, Luther H. Hodges, Jr. Washington, a member of the board, through a pair of limited partnerships of which he is the general partner, controlled five percent of the holding company's stock. At the time, the bank was facing the potential of significant losses arising from Finley, Kumble's bankruptcy. But Washington, in a grand display of chutzpah, laid the blame for the bank's woes at Hodges's feet. Hodges should go, Washington argued, because the bank was doing poorly and had suffered a loss in 1987.

For his part, Hodges had been trying to get rid of Washington, pointing to Bob as a major culprit in that very loss. Washington was, after all, co-managing partner of Finley, Kumble in June 1987 when the bank approved a $10 million loan to the firm, and after the law firm went under, the bank had to take the loss as a charge against earnings. Hodges and his allies were highly critical of Washington for not alerting the bank to the firm's troubles, which, they alleged, he surely must have been aware of. At the time the fight between Hodges and Washington was heating up, the

bank also had a suit going against Myerson—which the
bank won—to recover $700,000 in loans made to the ever-
strapped Harvey while he was a co-managing partner of the
firm along with Washington.

Through the fall of 1988, a special committee of the
holding company's board had overseen an investigation of
Washington's behavior vis-a-vis the loan to Finley, Kumble.
The committee concluded that Robert Washington should
have known, and arguably did know, that Finley, Kumble
was not creditworthy.

In January 1989, that committee asked Washington to
resign from the boards of directors of both the holding
company and the bank. Bob refused. In March 1989, the
directors of the bank voted to throw Washington off the
bank's board.

But Washington remained on the board of the holding
company. Removing him from that position would have
required a good deal more than simple board action. It
would have required a vote of a majority of the company's
common stock. More than a quarter of Washington
Bancorp's stock is held by a Washington ally, Wafic Said, a
Saudi Arabian investor. Along with the five percent of the
stock that Washington himself controlled, the anti-Hodges
forces commanded very close to one-third of the voting
shares of the holding company. For the anti-Washington
group to have staged a proxy fight against those kinds of
numbers would have been foolhardy.

For his part, Washington launched a series of attempts to
buy the bank that looked like a Dutch auction where each
succeeding offer is lower than the last. In July 1989, a group
headed by Washington bid $23 a share in cash and securi-
ties. The board, expressing skepticism about the real value
of the offer, rejected it.

So, in November of that same year, with more than a
score of equity partners and the promise from Drexel Burnham Lambert that it could raise the debt part of the financing, Washington, through his WBC Acquisition, made an-

other offer. This time it was for $19 a share, $4 less than the July bid, although Washington eventually raised the ante to $20.15 as other prospective bidders for the company emerged. As the year turned, the other bidders had dropped out of the running and the offer from Washington's WBC Acquisition was the only one on the table. The deal disintegrated in February of 1990 when Drexel Burnham Lambert filed for bankruptcy.

In the late spring of 1990, yet another deal was on the table. After the bid that was to have been financed by Drexel collapsed, several partners in WBC Acquisition pulled out of the group, leaving Washington to come up with replacements. He apparently succeeded, and in March 1990, WBC Acquisition Corp. offered $19.20 a share for the bank, reportedly with the backing of Manley and AmBase.

Hodges has repeatedly said that Washington's attempts to take over the banking company and the bank are no more than a maneuver to deflect attention from the issue of the Finley, Kumble loan. Whether that is true or not, I have no way of knowing. But if Washington were able to control the bank, he would have a shot at short-circuiting the serious problems he could face over not objecting, as a board member, to the June 1987 loan of $10 million to Finley, Kumble and over his role in the bank's 1986 loans of millions of dollars to Finley, Kumble partners for stock purchases in Manley's badly mismanaged Merchant Bank of California. Manley saw to it that Washington was appointed to the board of the Home's reinsurance subsidiary, U.S. International Reinsurance Co., to AmBase's advisory board and to that company's corporate responsibility committee. Washington was counting on Manley to come through with a large part of the financing of his third attempt to take over Washington Bancorp. With Manley no longer in control of AmBase's billions in investment funds, the chances of Washington succeeding seemed slim.

The entire situation was thrown into further confusion in

early May 1990 when the holding company, Washington Bancorporation, defaulted on about $26 million in short-term borrowings. Under federal banking regulations, subsidiary banks of bank holding companies are prohibited from making loans to the parent company. Further, because of an agreement between the holding company and federal regulators, the subsidiaries are prohibited from transferring funds to the parent.

The news sent Washington Bancorporation's stock plummeting to $3.50 a share. And the possibility loomed that the institution would be forced to file for protection under Chapter 11 of the Bankruptcy Code. That possibility was realized when, on August 1, 1990, Washington Bancorp announced that it had in fact made a bankruptcy filing. A spokesman for the company said that it expected its stockholders "will be unable to realize value for their interest in the company. . . ." and that the company's creditors "will likely receive less than the face value" of their securities. Bob Washington and his followers have personally lost a bundle on their investments.

Nor has life been kind to Heine. After he left Finley, Kumble he took careful aim at his foot and shot true. He signed on, and then left a position as counsel at Curtis, Mallet-Prevost, Colt & Mosle. In April 1989, Prudential Insurance Co. removed Andy from his post as chairman of Kinney System, Inc. Heine had engineered a 1986 buyout of the parking garage chain with financial backing from Prudential, and he became chairman several months later following the suicide of his predecessor. It is unclear just what happened between Heine and Prudential, but for the better part of the year previous, Andy had involved himself deeply in a series of laughable efforts to take over companies controlled by Victor Posner.

In 1988, Andy went after the nation's biggest electrical contractor, the Fischbach Corporation, a company in which Posner had a 56 percent stake. The company's shares had figured in charges of stock parking filed by the Securities and Exchange Commission against Ivan Boesky, Posner, and Posner's son, Steven. The Posners denied the charges.

In late September 1988, Heine, through F.A.C., Inc., his investment group, made an initial bid of $97.5 million, $25 a share for Fischbach. Then, less than two months later, he raised the ante by $10 to $35 a share. At a meeting with Fischbach directors in mid-January 1989, Heine is reported to have told the directors that First Boston Corp. had backed away from helping him finance the deal, and he lowered the bid back to $25 a share. A major ally in the group up until a short time before the September bid, according to Heine, was Leonard Pelullo, a Miami hotel developer and a man who the New Jersey State Commission on Investigation had termed "a key organized crime associate from Philadelphia" in 1985. Pelullo, who has vigorously denied the appellation, had been a client and friend of Heine's for many years and headed a company that had a consulting relationship with another of Posner's companies, D.W.G. Corp. Pelullo's role in F.A.C. after the initial bid is muddy, but in February of 1989, International Assets Advisory Corp., a Florida brokerage firm, filed a suit against Global Financial Corp., a company controlled by Pelullo, claiming that a $50,000 check issued the previous November to cover a margin order for 23,600 shares of Fischbach bounced.

On March 8, 1989, according to court documents and testimony filed in a suit related to Heine's next adventure in the takeover business, Heine's F.A.C., Inc., sold its interest in Fischbach at a profit of $850,000, one day before publicly withdrawing the offer for the company. D.W.G., in a suit filed in April 1990, said that amounted to manipulating the stock of Fischbach for their own profit.

Virtually coincidental with abandoning the Fischbach offer, another Heine group, Granada Investments, Inc., announced a $22-a-share, $572 million proposal for D.W.G. Corp., a company in which Posner held a 43 percent interest. Almost immediately, Heine's group became embroiled in a dispute with a brokerage firm over the ownership of the majority of the 562,000 shares that supposedly belonged to a member of the Heine group, Fairview Financial Corp., a company owned by Pelullo family trusts. A few days later, on March 14 and 15 of 1989, according to an SEC filing made public in mid-April of that year, the Heine group sold 384,492 of the more than 1.4 million shares that it said it held at the time of the takeover offer. Heine said at the time of the April filing that his group had lowered its stake because of the stock ownership dispute and had paid $350,000 to settle the disagreement. Nevertheless, he said, he planned to go "full speed ahead" with the takeover attempt and that he was seriously considering a proxy fight.

By mid-June, things were getting worse. Granada had severed its relationship with its investment banker, Trafalgar Holdings Ltd., the Los Angeles firm headed by Charles Knapp, the former head of one of California's more famous thrift institution disasters, Financial Corp. of America.

Then, on June 23, 1989, a federal grand jury indicted Pelullo on charges of defrauding a defunct Ohio savings institution. Heine said at the time that he was "flabbergasted" but undeterred in his resolve to go ahead with the D.W.G. deal.

Less than five weeks later, with charges flying between Heine's Granada and its unwilling target, D.W.G., both sides agreed to suspend the battle.

More than a year after the initial announcement of his takeover bid, Heine is still embroiled in claims and counter-claims with D.W.G. The smart money, now as then, says that Andy doesn't have a prayer.

Andy's financial situation is unclear, but in September 1989, several months after his divorce from his second wife, Joni Heine, became final, Heine submitted a sworn affidavit to a New York court saying that he was not able to pay an $800,000 judgment because he "had no current assets available . . . and no steady source of income. . . ." He owes his ex-wife an additional $2 million and is on the hook in the proposed Finley, Kumble bankruptcy settlement for another $2.7 million.

Manley, on the other hand, despite the loss of his job, still had a steady source of income. After he was forced to relinquish his post as president and CEO of AmBase, his termination payment was a matter of dispute. Nevertheless, he continued to receive his current annual salary, an office, secretarial help and a car and driver. Exactly how much he was to be paid was not clear, but the company's 1990 proxy statement pegged his annual base salary at "not less than $900,000." His 1989 cash compensation of $1,944,438 made him one of the most highly paid insurance executives in the world. The 1989 amount was $140,000 greater than the $1,803,444 Manley was paid in 1988. Why he got such a raise is not clear, and it is hard to imagine what he might have been paid if he had been doing a great job.

Clearly, he was not. During the years that Manley ran the Home Group/AmBase, the company loaded itself with debt, made highly questionable acquisitions in pursuit of becoming a major diversified financial services company, and saw the value of its stock reduced to a fraction of what it was when he took over. In addition, under Manley's aegis, the company loaded up on junk bonds and became one of Drexel Burnham Lambert's biggest creditors.

Debt was all the rage in the 1980s and Manley was in the swim. He so leveraged Home/AmBase that its debt rose twenty-five fold from a total of $94 million to $2.36 billion between 1985 and 1989.

In 1987, Manley, who had become chief executive officer of the Home Group in December 1986, made a deal to buy Gruntal & Co., a securities dealer whose main business is retail brokerage, for $148 million. A lot of people say he overpaid. Whether that is true or not, the October 1987 stock market crash and its disastrous impact on the retail end of the securities business have taken their toll. The next year, just in time for the collapse of the Northeast's real estate market and the crisis in the S & L industry,

Home bought Carteret Savings & Loan, a New Jersey thrift institution, for $261 million.

In addition, Home/AmBase put $400 million in junk bonds into its portfolio. As the high-yield market, already on the skids, was hit with news of Drexel Burnham Lambert's collapse in February 1990, the market value of such bonds fell even lower.

But Drexel's collapse affected more than AmBase's junk bond portfolio. Home Capital, an AmBase subsidiary, was number two on the bankrupt securities firm's list of creditors with a $42.7 million loan. Questions abounded about why the loan had been made in the first place and about why it had been priced at .25 percent above the federal funds rate (the benchmark rate at which banks lend overnight to each other) when it could have been put out to a better credit at a higher rate.

For such managerial brilliance, Manley was being paid as much as, if not more than, any insurance executive in the country. But the $1,944,438 he was paid in 1989 was only part of his compensation. Home had given Marshall a $2,987,000 interest-free loan when he moved to New York. Even a no-brainer investment of such an amount could return him another $300,000 a year. The loan is repayable on demand, but under Manley's contract, if the company demands repayment before August 14, 2000, the company is required to pay him the estimated cost of financing the outstanding balance of the loan for the remainder of the period and to reimburse him for incremental income taxes on such payments and reimbursement. There were, in addition, stock options, deferred compensation, vast retirement benefits, and some convoluted feats of financial legerdemain that put his real reward up in the neighborhood of $3 million a year.

All the while, the price of the company's stock continued its downward slide. Share prices, which had hit a high of $31.50 in 1986, had slumped to just over $7 by early 1990 and continued to deteriorate.

The decline in share values had a negative effect on Manley's personal fortunes as well. In February 1987, Home issued Manley options, good until early 1996, on 2,000,000 shares of its common stock at an exercise price of $27 a share. At that point, the stock was trading at $19.75, and because the price continued to head south he was not able to exercise the options. Manley's solution was typical: He got the board to change the rules. Effective July 1989, with the stock trading in the low teens, Manley's option, according to the 1990 proxy statement "was amended to reduce the option exercise price to $13.324 per share. . . ." Because the stock price continued to decline, he was still unable to make a killing.

The motivation is uncertain, but one interpretation of what happened next is that Manley saw a way to enrich himself in much the same way that Scharffenberger did after Manley took over as president of City Investing in 1985. At the time, City Investing was liquidating itself, spinning off the Home Insurance Company and other properties. By ceding control of the soon-to-disappear company to Manley, Scharffenberger was transformed from a highly compensated executive to a man who had lost his job and was thus able to activate a severance package that was worth nearly $18 million. Once City Investing was defunct, Manley became president of the Home and Scharffenberger came on as chairman.

Early in 1990, with AmBase in trouble, the holding company put up for sale its most important company, the Home Insurance Co. AmBase expected that it could get about $1 billion for its crown jewel. The reason, said Manley, was that AmBase's shares were undervalued. (In August 1990, with Manley ousted, when AmBase said it would sell Home and Gruntal for $620 million, its stock was trading at about $2.00.)

If the price could be pushed above the strike price of his options, Manley would stand to gain. And if AmBase were to be successful at selling off its insurance business, and then continue along a time-proven path of self-liquidation, Manley would stand to gain even more as his substantial golden parachute opened as he ditched the corporate plane he was piloting.

Whatever his plan was, it came a cropper. Under intense pressure from institutional holders of AmBase common shares, the board asked for Manley's resignation on March 15, 1990. The terms of his severance package called for him to receive three times his annual compensation if he were let go, in addition to a five-year consulting contract. AmBase's 1990 proxy statement says, however, that "a settlement is expected to be reached with Mr. Manley after the sale of the Home."

Another company spun off from City Investing, General Development Corporation, a company on whose board Manley sat, was having trouble as well. At a GDC board meeting on March 9, 1990, two of Manley's friends, GDC chairman, David F. Brown, and its president, Robert F. Ehrling, were asked to relinquish their posts at the Miami-based development company in the face of a grand jury investigation and pending indictments. At the same meeting, Manley and Scharffenberger also resigned from the board.

A week later, GDC pled guilty to one count of conspiracy to violate federal mail fraud statutes and on March 22, 1990, Brown and Ehrling pled guilty to fraud and conspiracy charges. Manley has not been charged.

He was, however, named in a $55 million RICO suit, filed by former Gruntal & Co. vice chairman Marshall Geller, a former Bear Stearns & Co. senior managing director whom Manley had recruited to run Gruntal in February 1989, and who was subsequently fired. Geller claimed that Manley had overstated the Home Group's capital and in an attempt to fatten Home/AmBase's share price "pressed Geller to issue inflated earnings projections to boost Home's fortunes." Geller claims that when he refused, he was fired.

Finally, there is Myerson.

Two years after Finley, Kumble filed for protection under Chapter 11 of the Bankruptcy Code, stories of another firm's demise were in the papers. Providing comic relief to the tale of that firm's problems were related stories that speculated on the whereabouts of former baseball commissioner Bowie Kuhn. "Where's Bowie?" the headlines asked.

Bowie, it was reported, was in Florida, buying a house. But no one could find him, and the secrecy of his whereabouts made subpoena service impossible. Under Florida law, a man's home is more than his castle; it's his protection against bankruptcy claims as well, an inviolate asset.

And why was Bowie Kuhn sinking roots in Florida while at the same time avoiding detection of his exact whereabouts? Simple. He had gone into partnership with Harvey Myerson, and barely two years after the firm of Myerson & Kuhn had been established, with overblown fanfare, the firm was in shambles and had filed for protection from its creditors under Chapter 11.

Harvey had been at it again. The *American Lawyer* was joined by the *Wall Street Journal* and the *New York Times* in the latter weeks of 1989 and early 1990 in profiling Myerson as he explored new depths. What was apparent to me about Harvey while we were partners at Finley, Kumble is now apparent to the world. By the end of 1989, almost exactly two years after Finley, Kumble's collapse, Myerson & Kuhn was seeking protection from its creditors and Myerson was under investigation by federal prosecutors, postal inspectors, and the New York State Appellate Division's Disciplinary Committee.

The press carried articles about the new firm from its beginning. And at first, they were uniformly uncritical. Even if the press did not understand Harvey, a lot of other people had a rather negative take on him. When Myerson & Kuhn retained a headhunting firm to find a senior man to whom Harvey said his firm would guarantee an annual compensation of $1 million, the headhunter found it necessary to call 1,500 lawyers before finding one with the proper credentials—if not a great deal of good sense—who was willing to take the job.

Similarly, Donald Trump—whom Harvey had helped to a Pyrrhic victory in the USFL case that resulted in a damage award of three dollars and legal bills that mounted into the millions—refused to use the new firm because, Trump was quoted in the *Wall Street Journal,* as Finley, Kumble was failing in late 1987, "Harvey started billing me four times more than he should have. The bills were too high and I wasn't satisfied."

Nor was it very long before Myerson's outrageous—and possibly illegal—behavior began capturing headlines. Myerson & Kuhn's biggest client, Shearson Lehman Hutton went after the firm for overbilling, suing them to the tune of $2 million and barring them from further legal work. Myerson & Kuhn settled the matter for $1 million. As the firm sank further and further into economic chaos, one partner after another, one group of partners after another left in disgust.

Harvey's personal greed was a major cause.

In the spring of 1988, Myerson called his firm's chief financial officer and ordered him to get over to Cartier's Fifth Avenue shop with a firm check for an $89,000 bauble that Harvey had just picked out.

Why didn't he pay for it himself? Who knows? Why did he borrow the American Express card of one of his young partners and use it to charge $23,000 in expenses for a European trip.

Following the blow dealt by Shearson's claim and withdrawal of business, Myerson's partners tightened their belts. At the end of 1988, they received only part of their end-of-year partnership distributions. In January and February of 1989, they saw payless paydays as several draws were missed. The firm's trade creditors had to wait longer and longer for their bills to be settled. By March, payments for medical insurance premiums and in-house reimbursements for business expenses were months behind.

Curious partners received their first financial statement in four months in April 1989. When they inquired about a $473,000 item that was listed as "advances to partners and staff," they discovered that Harvey had withdrawn the money between December 1988 and March 1989. Myerson offered the explanation that he was owed the money. More recently, investigators came up with information that an additional $600,000 in firm funds were withdrawn but not accounted for.

The firm owed a lot of people money. They did not get paid. But Harvey, who controlled the firm's checkbook, did. It was yet another sign of his warped view of his own importance.

As 1989 wore on, lawyers fled Myerson & Kuhn singly, in pairs, in droves. Rumors of the firm's imminent dissolution were rampant. In early October, Bowie Kuhn told a partners' meeting at which Myerson was not present that the firm should either get rid of Harvey or liquidate. By mid-October, with partners missing draws and associates missing their paychecks for more than a month, two dozen partners and forty-five associates had left the firm.

Harvey was boasting that he was representing Revlon and Sir James Goldsmith, the British corporate raider. Both denied that Myerson was working for them.

By early November, the last of their Washington office partners, including Samuel Sterret, the former chief judge of the U.S. Tax Court had resigned from Myerson & Kuhn and the managing partner of the firm's Philadelphia office, Stephen Cabot, had left.

As the year wound down, the firm collapsed. On December 26, 1989, Shearson Lehman Hutton filed a suit against Myerson & Kuhn for $488,000, the amount of unpaid installments the law firm had agreed to return as restitution for the overcharge against the securities firm. The next day, Myerson & Kuhn filed for bankruptcy.

Harvey's troubles are far from over. He's liable for millions of dollars in the bankruptcies of Finley, Kumble and of Myerson & Kuhn. In addition, as of this writing, the U.S. Attorney's investigation continues along with a federal grand jury inquiry. In March 1990, the prosecutors had subpoenaed the expense records of Myerson & Kuhn in an effort to determine whether Harvey had defrauded his partners when the firm paid for up to $1 million in alleged personal expenses including his $450-a-week chauffeur, an $8,000-a-month apartment in the Olympic Towers on Fifth Avenue, and the $89,000 Cartier necklace.

By late spring of 1990, the investigation had broadened. A federal grand jury investigating Myerson had called well over one hundred witnesses in its examination of Harvey's activities. The grand jury was reported to have granted immunity from prosecution to at least one of Myerson & Kuhn's key partners in return for testimony. The grant of immunity to a key witness is telling since it is often a signal that someone is singing and that an indictment is not far off.

It looked as though overbilling was involved in the criminal investigation as well. In addition to Shearson, the United Food and Commercial Workers Union had also complained that it was overcharged by about $550,000 for work done on its behalf by Myerson & Kuhn. The usual way the government nails lawyers on overbilling is through charges of mail fraud.

There were also press reports that Myerson said he was planning to sell his home and move his residence to Florida. He was going to do what Kuhn had done, and for the same reason. Florida is a great state to live in if you are planning to file for personal bankruptcy since the law there treats a man's home as his castle and digs a statutory moat around it to protect it from creditors. The minute the creditors committee for the Myerson & Kuhn Chapter 11 bankruptcy read about what Harvey said, they went to Bankruptcy Court Judge Prudence Abram and asked that she lift

the stay against lawsuits against the firm and its members—
specifically Myerson—so they could sue him and get a lien
on his assets.

In New York, one of the grounds for attachment is that a
debtor is planning to flee the jurisdiction with his assets. No
sooner had the creditors committee gone after Myerson,
but Harvey went to the bankruptcy court and said he would
offer sufficient collateral to cover his $900,000 share of the
Myerson & Kuhn bankruptcy. The judge agreed to maintain the stay against the firm's creditor's suing him.

The way he is collateralizing the $900,000 is intriguing.
He told Judge Abram that he planned to sell two homes
worth $9 million and on which there were already more
than $8 million in liens. His two homes consist of his apart-
ment on Central Park West, for which he paid $1 million,
and the place on the East End of Long Island, which he
bought from Don Marron for $2.2 million.

There are so many houses on the market in the Hamptons that you could shingle an airplane hangar with the
"For Sale" signs. And in Manhattan, things aren't much
better. The residential co-op and condo market is very soft.
My guess is that the two properties, which Myerson bought
near the top of the market for a total of $3.2 million, may
not now be worth $9 million.

But assume that they are. The liens against them are over
$8 million. If those represent mortgages, what must it cost
to service them? It has to be between $800,000 and $1
million a year. That plus taxes and maintenance. In addition, Harvey owes the $900,000 on the Myerson & Kuhn
bankruptcy, plus $1.8 million on the Finley, Kumble bank-
ruptcy, plus God knows what else.

Suppose he sells the homes and, unlikely as it might be in
a soft market, gets $9 million. Between the U.S. and New
York State he would have to pay 40 percent or more of his
profit in taxes on the capital gains on the properties. That
would leave him no more than $6.7 million to settle $9
million in debt just on the homes, before considering real

estate brokerage commissions, closing costs and the like. Harvey's creditors are not likely to see their money repaid any time soon.

It is not at all clear what will become of my old partners. Washington may get lucky and survive in the style to which he has become accustomed. For the Florida people, I think, things will settle down, and they will prosper over the long term. Most others, even with the Finley, Kumble bankruptcy still hanging over their heads, have carved new niches in other firms.

The ones I wouldn't put a lot of money on are Heine, Manley, and Myerson. J.P. Morgan said that at base, a man's character is his credit. Who is left to back Heine in his financial schemes? Who will believe Manley? Who would trust Myerson?

They have continued and will continue to leave wreckage and disruption in their wake. They have in themselves that kind of destructive quality. Everything they do can be summed up: "Me. Me. More. More."

As for the rest, Finley, Kumble was made up of hundreds of bright, well-educated, hardworking, resourceful lawyers, both young and old. For the most part, they have found new homes where they are making meaningful contributions to the practice of law and earning a good living for themselves and their families. They will probably not make the kind of money they made at Finley, Kumble. But neither, one hopes, will they work in an atmosphere that is as manic and disruptive. I wish them all well.

INDEX

Barovick, Konicky, Schwartz, Kay
  and Schiff, 114
Cohen and Abrams, 24
Cravath Swaine and Moore, 155
Danzansky, Dickey, Tydings, Quint
  and Gordon, 120, 122-123, 128-
  129
Davis, Polk, 101
Fine, Jacobson, 138
Finley, Kumble, 25, 39-49, 60-62,
  64-71, 94-107, 112-113, 128-
  129, 135-157, 181
Fulop & Hardee, 114-115
Goldstein, Judd and Gurfein, 23-
  24
Greenbaum, Wolff and Ernst, 114
Jones, Day, 155
Kidder Peabody, 130
McKenna and Fitting, 110-111
Manatt, Phelps, 177
Manatt, Phelps, Rothenberg,
  Manley and Tunney, 109-111
Morgan, Lewis and Bockius, 138
Mudge Rose, 129
Shea and Gould, 175
Skadden, Arps, Slate, Meagher and
  Flom, 31, 38, 108, 155, 165
Smathers and Thompson, 144
Stamer and Haft, 24
Sullivan and Cromwell, 101, 165
Tew, Critchlow, Sonberg, Traum
  and Friedbauer, 143-144
Webster and Sheffield, 90, 158
White and Case, 36-38
Lawsuits,
  between Finley, Kumble,
    Underberg, Persky, Roth and
    Weismans, 31-33
  Settlement
Laxalt, Paul, 13, 245
Leasco, running of, 48
Leist, Neil, client of Toboroff, 166
Levine, Leonard, working for real
  estate developer for Richard
  Cohen, 26
Liman, Arthur, 193
Lindner, Carl, buying out of Leist's
  stock position, 166
Lippmann, Walter, 48
Long, Russell, 245
  (former Senate Finance Committee

Chairman), capital gains tax and,
  62
partner of firm, 13

McCaghey, Charles, associate at
  Olwine, Connally, Chase,
  O'Donnell and Weyher, 32-33
McKenna and Fitting, Manley's job
  with, 110-111
Maher, Mike, 140
Mallow, Bob,
  firm's loss of, 144
  as leader of Florida office, 138
Manatt, Phelps, 177, 195-196
Manatt, Phelps, Rothenberg, Manley
  and Tunney, 109
Manatt, Phelps, Rothenberg, and
  Tunney, Manley's partnership
  with, 110-111
Mandelbaum, David, 62
Mandelbaum, Rosemary, 62
Manley, Marshall, 141, 156-157
  California negotiations with, 175-
    176
  client complaint regarding, 178-
    179
  conspiracy to break up/take over
    Finley, Kumble, 181-184
  divorce expenses of, 172-175
  investment banking and, 61-62
  joining of Finley, Kumble, 112
  Kumble's relationship with, 169-
    171
  personal/business background of,
    109-111
  recruiting ability of, 114
  relationship with Scharffenberger,
    179-180
  resignation as co-managing
    partner, 9-10
  shrewd business practices of, 116-
    117
Manny Hanny. See Manufacturers
  Hanover
Manufacturers Hanover, 62-63, 137
  credit line, 218
  Finley, Kumble failure and, 212
  Myerson cut off from, 12
  Wright's executive vice president
    at, 63